1295

THE FALL OF
CONSTANTINOPLE 1453

THE FALL OF CONSTANTINOPLE 1453

BY

STEVEN RUNCIMAN

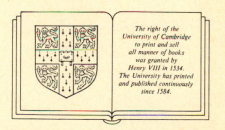

The right of the
University of Cambridge
to print and sell
all manner of books
was granted by
Henry VIII in 1534.
The University has printed
and published continuously
since 1584.

CAMBRIDGE UNIVERSITY PRESS

CAMBRIDGE

LONDON   NEW YORK   NEW ROCHELLE

MELBOURNE   SYDNEY

Published by the Press Syndicate of the University of Cambridge
The Pitt Building, Trumpington Street, Cambridge CB2 1RP
32 East 57th Street, New York, NY 10022, USA
10 Stamford Road, Oakleigh, Melbourne 3166, Australia

First published 1965
Reprinted 1965
First paperback edition 1969
Reprinted 1985

Printed in Great Britain by the University Press, Cambridge

ISBN 0 521 09573 5

UP

To

MY BROTHER

CONTENTS

CONTENTS

LIST OF PLATES

ix

LIST OF FIGURES

PREFACE

In the days when historians were simple folk the Fall of Constantinople, 1453, was held to mark the close of the Middle Ages. Nowadays we know too well that the stream of history flows on relentlessly and there is never a barrier across it. There is no point at which we can say that the medieval world changed itself into the modern world. Long before 1453 the movement that is called the Renaissance was under way in Italy and the Mediterranean world. Long after 1453 medieval ideas lasted on in the north. It was before 1453 that pioneers had begun to explore the ocean routes that were to alter the whole economy of the world; but it was several decades after 1453 before these routes were opened up and before their effect could be felt in Europe. The decline and fall of Byzantium and the triumph of the Ottoman Turks had their effect on these changes; but the effect was not due solely to the events of one year. Byzantine learning played its part in the Renaissance; but already for more than half a century before 1453 Byzantine scholars had left the poverty and uncertainty of their homeland to seek comfortable professorial Chairs in Italy, and the Greek scholars that followed them after 1453 came for the most part not as refugees from a new infidel rule but as students from islands where Venice still was in control. Already for many years the growth of Ottoman power had caused some embarrassment to the merchant cities of Italy, but it did not kill their trade, except in so far as it blocked the routes to the Black Sea. The Ottoman conquest of Egypt was more disastrous to Venice than the Ottoman conquest of Constantinople; and if Genoa was severely struck by the Sultan's control of the Straits, it was her precarious position in Italy rather than the loss of foreign commerce that was her downfall.

Even in the wide political field the fall of Constantinople altered very little. The Turks had already arrived on the banks of the

Danube and were threatening Central Europe; and anyone could
have seen that Constantinople was doomed, that an empire which
consisted of little more than one decaying city could not hold out
against an empire whose territory covered the greater part of the
Balkan peninsula and of Asia Minor, an empire vigorously
governed and provided with the best military machine of the age.
Christendom was, it is true, profoundly shocked by the fall of
Constantinople. Lacking our sage hindsight, the Western powers
failed to see how inevitable the Turkish conquest had become.
Yet the tragedy in no way changed their policy, or, rather, their
lack of policy, towards the Eastern Question. Only the Papacy
was genuinely upset and genuinely planned counter-action; and
it was soon to have more urgent problems nearer home.

It may seem, therefore, that the story of 1453 scarcely merits
another book. But, in fact, for two peoples the events of that
year were vitally important. For the Turks the capture of the old
imperial city not only gave them a new imperial capital; it also
guaranteed the permanence of their European empire. So long
as the city, situated as it was in the centre of their dominions, at
the crossing between Asia and Europe, was not in their hands,
they could not feel secure. They had no reason to fear the Greeks
alone; but a grand Christian alliance working from such a base
might still unseat them. With Constantinople in their hands they
were secure. Today, after all the vicissitudes of their history, the
Turks still possess Thrace; they still maintain their foothold in
Europe.

For the Greeks the fall of the city was even more momentous.
For them it was indeed the final ending of a chapter. The splendid
civilization of Byzantium had already played its part in civilizing
the world, and it was now dying with the dying city. But it was
not yet dead. The dwindling population of Constantinople on
the eve of its fall contained many of the finest intellects of the
time, belonging to men reared in a high cultured tradition that
stretched back to ancient Greece and Rome. And, so long as an

Emperor, Viceroy of God, lived on the Bosphorus, every Greek, enslaved though he might already be, could proudly feel that he still belonged to the true and orthodox Christian commonwealth. The Emperor might be able to do little to help him on earth, but he was still a focal point and a symbol of the rule of God. With the Emperor fallen with his fallen city the reign of anti-Christ began and Greece was driven underground, to survive as best she could. That Hellenism did not utterly perish is a tribute to the unquenchable vitality and courage of the Greek spirit.

In this story the Greek people is the tragic hero; and I have tried to tell it with that in mind. It has often been told before. It stirred Gibbon almost, but not quite, enough to make him forget his contempt of Byzantium. It was last fully told in English by Sir Edwin Pears, in a work which was published sixty years ago but which is still well worth reading. His account of the actual operations of the siege, based on a full study of the sources and intimate personal knowledge of the terrain, is still fully valid, though in other places modern research has made the book a little out-of-date. I am deeply indebted to his work, which remains the best account of the events of 1453 in any language. Since it was published many scholars have added to our knowledge. In particular the year 1953 saw the publication of many articles and essays in celebration of the quincentenary. But, apart from Gustave Schlumberger's book, published in 1914 and based almost entirely on Pears's, no full-length narrative of the siege has appeared during the last half-century in any Western language.

In this attempt to fill the gap I have made grateful use of the work of many recent scholars, living and dead. My indebtedness will be revealed in my notes. Amongst living Greek scholars I would like specially to mention Professor Zakythinos and Professor Zoras. For Ottoman history everyone must be indebted to Professor Babinger, even though his great book on the Conquering Sultan denies us the aid of references to his sources. For the understanding of earlier Turkish history Professor Wittek's books are invaluable; and amongst younger Turkish scholars mention must be made of Professor Inalcîk. Father Gill's important work on the Council of Florence and its aftermath has been of the greatest use to me.

I discuss briefly the principal sources for the story in an appendix. Not all of them are easily obtained. The Christian sources were collected together by the late Professor Dethier in two volumes, XXI and XXII, parts 1 and 2, of the *Monumenta Hungariae Historica*, some eighty years ago, but though the volumes were printed they were never published, apparently owing to the number of errors that they contained. Not many of the Moslem sources are readily accessible, particularly for anyone who can only read Ottoman Authors slowly and painfully. I hope that I have been able to extract the essence from them.

This book could never have been written but for the existence of the London Library; and I would like to express my gratitude to the Staff of the Reading Room of the British Museum for their patient help. I should like also to thank Mr S. J. Papastavrou for his help with the proofs, and the Syndics and staff of the Cambridge University Press for their unfailing forbearance and kindness.

Note on the transliteration of names

I cannot claim to any consistency in my transliteration of names from Greek or Turkish. For Greek names I have used whatever seems to me to be the familiar and natural form. For Turkish names I have used a simple phonetic spelling, except when I am citing words in modern Turkish, for which I use modern Turkish spelling. I have called the Conquering Sultan by his Turkish name of Mehmet, not Mahomet or Mohammed. I hope that my Turkish friends will forgive me for calling the city about which I write 'Constantinople' and not 'Istanbul'. It would have been pedantic to do otherwise.

STEVEN RUNCIMAN

LONDON
1964

CHAPTER I

THE DYING EMPIRE

On Christmas Day in the year 1400 King Henry IV of England gave a banquet in his palace of Eltham. His purpose was not only to celebrate the holy festival. He wished also to do honour to a distinguished guest. This was Manuel II Palaeologus, Emperor of the Greeks, as most Westerners called him, though some remembered that he was the true Emperor of the Romans. He had travelled through Italy and had paused at Paris, where King Charles VI of France had redecorated a wing of the Louvre to house him and where the professors at the Sorbonne had been delighted to meet a monarch who could argue with them with as much learning and subtlety as they themselves commanded. In England everyone was impressed by the dignity of his demeanour and by the spotless white robes that he and his courtiers wore. But, for all his high titles, his hosts were moved to pity for him; for he had come as a beggar, in a desperate search for help against the infidel who encompassed his empire. To the lawyer Adam of Usk, who was working at King Henry's court, it was tragic to see him there. 'I reflected', Adam wrote, 'how grievous it was that this great Christian prince should be driven by the Saracens from the furthest East to these furthest Western islands to seek aid against them. . . . O God', he added, 'what dost thou now, ancient glory of Rome?'[1]

Indeed, the ancient Roman Empire had shrunk to very little. Manuel was the lawful heir of Augustus and of Constantine; but many centuries had passed since the Emperors residing at Constantinople could command the allegiance of the Roman World. To the West they had become mere lords of the Greeks, or of Byzantium, unworthy rivals of the Emperors who had sprung up in the West. Till the eleventh century Byzantium had been a splendid and dominant power, the champion of Christendom against the onslaught of Islam. The Byzantines had done their duty vigorously and successfully, till in the mid-eleventh century a new Moslem challenge had come from the East with the invasion of the Turks; while Western Europe had developed so far as to attempt aggression of its own, in the persons of the Normans. Byzantium was entangled in a war on two fronts at a moment when it was passing through constitutional and dynastic difficulties. The Normans were driven back, though with the loss of Byzantine Italy; but the Byzantines had to abandon for ever to the Turks the lands that had supplied most of their soldiers and most of their food, the upland plains of Anatolia. Henceforward the Empire remained caught between two fires; and this middle position was complicated by the movement that we call the Crusades. As Christians the Byzantines sympathized with the Crusaders. But their long political experience had taught them to show some tolerance towards the infidel and to accept his existence. The Holy War as practised by the Westerners seemed to them dangerous and unrealistic.

They hoped, however, that advantages might be reaped from it. But a man in the middle can only be secure if he is strong. Byzantium continued to play the part of a great power when in fact its strength was already undermined. The loss of the Anatolian recruiting grounds in a period of constant warfare forced the Emperor to depend on foreign allies and foreign mercenaries; and both demanded payment, in money and in commercial concessions. The demands came at a time when the domestic economy of the Empire was upset by the loss of the Anatolian corn-fields. Throughout the twelfth century Constantinople seemed to be so rich and splendid a city, the Imperial court so magnificent and the wharves and bazaars so full of merchandise that the Emperor was still treated as a mighty potentate. But he was given no thanks by the Moslems for trying to restrain crusading ardour, while the Crusaders were offended by his lukewarm attitude towards their Holy War. Meanwhile, religious differences between Eastern and Western Christendom, deep-seated in origin and exacerbated by politics during the course of the eleventh century, steadily worsened, till by the end of the twelfth century the Churches of Rome and Constantinople were undeniably in schism.

The crisis came when a crusading army, lured by the ambition of its leaders, by the jealous greed of their Venetian allies, and by the resentment that every Westerner now felt against the Byzantine Church, turned against Constantinople and captured and sacked it, setting up a Latin Empire on its ruins. This Fourth Crusade of 1204 put an end to the old East Roman Empire as a supernational state. After half a century of exile at Nicaea, in north-western Asia Minor, the Imperial authorities re-entered Constantinople; and the Latin Empire collapsed. A new era of greatness seemed to be at hand. But the empire restored by Michael Palaeologus was no longer the dominant power in the Christian East. It retained something of its old mystical prestige. Constantinople was still New Rome, the hallowed historical capital of the Orthodox Christendom. The Emperor was still, at least in Eastern eyes, the Roman Emperor. But in reality he was only one prince among others equally or more powerful. There were other Greek rulers. To the East there was the Empire of Trebizond, the empire of the Grand Comnenus, enriched by its silver-mines and by the trade that came along the age-old route from Tabriz and Further Asia. In Epirus there was the Despotate of the princes of the House of Angelus, at one time rivals of the Nicaeans in the race to recapture the capital, but soon, now, to fade into impotence. In the Balkans were Bulgaria and Serbia, each in turn to dominate the peninsula. There were Frankish lordships and Italian colonies all over the Greek mainland and islands. To oust the Venetians from Constantinople the Byzantines had called in the Genoese, who had to be rewarded; and now the Genoese colony of Pera, or Galata, just across the Golden

Horn, had stolen most of the trade of the capital.¹ There were dangers all round. In Italy there were potentates eager to avenge the fall of the Latin Empire. Slav princes in the Balkans yearned for the Imperial title. In Asia the Turks for a while had been quiescent; indeed, without this quiescence Byzantium could hardly have survived. But they were soon now to revive under the leadership of a dynasty of brilliant chieftains, Osman and his Ottoman successors. The restored Byzantine Empire, with complicated commitments in Europe and a constant threat from the West, needed more money and men than it possessed. It economized on the eastern frontier until it was too late and the Ottoman Turks had broken through the defences.²

Disillusion set in. The fourteenth century was for Byzantium a period of political disaster. For some decades it seemed likely that the great Serbian kingdom would absorb the whole empire. The provinces were devastated by the revolt of a mercenary band, the Catalan Company. There was a long series of civil wars, begun by personal and dynastic quarrels at the Court and embittered when social and religious parties were embroiled. The Emperor John V Palaeologus, who reigned for fifty years, from 1341 to 1391, was dethroned no less than three times, once by his father-in-law, once by his son, and once by his grandson, though in the end he died on the throne.³ There were ruinous visitations of plague. The Black Death in 1347, striking at the height of the civil war, carried off at least a third of the Empire's population. The Turks took advantage of the troubles in Byzantium and the Balkans to cross into Europe and to penetrate further and further, till by the end of the century the Sultan's armies had reached the Danube, and Byzantium was entirely encircled by his dominions. All that was left of the Empire was Constantinople itself and a few towns strung along the Marmora coast of Thrace and the Black Sea coast, as far north as Mesembria, Thessalonica and its suburbs, a few small islands, and the Peloponnese, where the Despots of the Morea, cadets of the Imperial house, were enjoying some small successes in winning land back from the Franks. Some Latin lordships and colonies survived anxiously in Greece and in the Greek islands. Florentine Dukes still ruled in Athens and Veronese princes in the Aegean Archipelago. Elsewhere the Turks had taken everything.[1]

By a whim of history this period of political decline was accompanied by a cultural life more eager and more productive than had been known at any other time in Byzantine history. Artistically and intellectually the Palaeologan era was outstanding. The mosaics and frescoes of the early fourteenth century in the Church of the Chora at Constantinople show a vigour, a freshness and a beauty that make Italian work of the period look primitive and crude. Work of a similar quality was produced elsewhere in the capital and at Thessalonica.[2] But art of such splendour was costly to execute. Money began to run short. In 1347 it was noticed that the jewels in the diadems used for the coronation of John VI and his Empress were really made of glass.[3] By the end of the century, though minor works of art were still produced, it was only in the provinces, at Mistra in the Peloponnese or on Mount Athos, that new churches were built; and they were thriftily decorated. Intellectual life, however, which was less dependent on financial backing, lasted brilliantly on. The University of Constantinople had been refounded at the end of the thirteenth century by a great minister, Theodore Metochites, a man of fine taste and learning, to whose patronage the decoration of the Chora had been due.[4] He inspired the remarkable generation of scholars that followed. The chief intellectual figures of the fourteenth century, men like Nicephorus Gregoras the historian, Gregory Palamas the theologian, Nicholas Cabasilas the mystic, or the philosophers Demetrius Cydones and Akyndinus, all at some time studied at the University and came under the influence of Metochites. All, too, were helped and encouraged by his successor as chief minister, John Cantacuzenus, though some of them were to break with him after he usurped the Imperial crown. Each of these scholars was individual in his thought; their controversies were as lively as their friendships. They argued, as the Greeks had always argued for nearly two thousand years, on the rival merits of Plato and Aristotle. They argued over semantics and logic; and their arguments inevitably encroached upon theology. Orthodox tradition was nervous of philosophy. Good churchmen believed in a philosophical training. They used Platonic terms and Aristotelian methodology. But their theology was apophatic. They held that philosophy was incapable of solving divine problems, since God was essentially beyond human knowledge. Trouble arose in the middle of the fourteenth century, when certain of the philosophers, influenced by the scholasticism of the West, attacked the Church's traditional theory of mysticism; whose defenders had therefore to formulate their doctrine and to declare a belief in the uncreated Energies of God. This gave rise to a bitter controversy, dividing friends and parties. The doctrine of the Energies found its main support amongst the monks, who tended to be anti-intellectual. Its chief exponent, Palamas, whose name is often given to the doctrine, was a scholar with a powerful mind, but unsympathetic towards humanism. His allies, however, included such humanist intellectuals as John Cantacuzenus and Nicholas Cabasilas. Their victory was not, as has often been claimed, a victory for obscurantism.[1]

There was one dominant question which concerned not only the theologians and philosophers but also the politicians. This was the question of union with the Roman Church. The schism was now complete; and the triumph of Palamism deepened the chasm. But to many Byzantine statesmen it seemed clear that the Empire could not survive without help from the West. If such help could only be obtained at the price of submission to the Roman Church, then the Greeks must submit. Michael Palaeologus had tried to counter western plans for the re-establishment of the Latin Empire by committing his people to union with Rome at the Council of Lyons. His action was fiercely resented by most Byzantines; and when the danger was over his son, Andronicus II, repudiated the union. Now, with the Turks enveloping the Empire, the situation was far more alarming. Union was needed now not to buy off a Christian enemy but to win friends against a worse and infidel enemy. There were no powers in the Orthodox East who could bring aid. The princes of the Danubian lands and of the Caucasus were too feeble and themselves in grave peril; and the Russians were too far away, with problems of their own. But would any Catholic potentate come to the rescue of a people that he regarded as schismatic? Would he not consider the Turkish advance as a just punishment for the schism? With that in mind the Emperor John V had personally submitted to the Pope in Italy in 1369. But he prudently refused to involve his subjects, though he hoped, in vain, to persuade them to follow him.[1]

Neither Michael VIII nor John V was a theologian. To both the political advantages of union outweighed everything else. For theologians the problem was harder. From the earliest times Eastern and Western Christendom had been drifting apart in theology, in liturgical usage and in ecclesiastical theory and practice. They were now divided by one main theological issue, on the Procession of the Holy Ghost and the Latin addition of the word *Filioque* to the Creed. There were other lesser issues. The newly authorized doctrine of the Energies was unacceptable to the West. The Western dogma of Purgatory seemed to the East to be arrogantly cocksure. Over the liturgy the chief question was whether the bread at the Sacrament should be leavened or unleavened. To the East the Western use of unleavened bread seemed to be Judaistic and disrespectful to the Holy Spirit whom the leaven symbolized. A similar disrespect was shown by the Western refusal to admit the Epiklesis, the invocation to the Holy Spirit, without which, in Eastern eyes, the bread and wine were not fully sanctified. There were disputes over the giving of communion in both kinds to the laity and over the marriage of secular

7

priests. But the most fundamental disagreement was in the ecclesiastical sphere. Did the Bishop of Rome enjoy an honorary primacy or an absolute supremacy in the Church? Byzantine tradition clung to the old belief in the charismatic equality of bishops. None of them, not even the heir of Saint Peter, had the right to impose doctrine, however great the respect that his views might command. The definition of doctrine was for an Oecumenical Council alone, when, as at Pentecost, all the bishops of the Church were represented and the Holy Spirit would descend to inspire them. The Roman addition to the Creed shocked the East not only for theological reasons but because it was a unilateral alteration to a formula sanctified by an Oecumenical Council. Nor could Eastern tradition accept the administrative and disciplinary authority of Rome, believing that such powers lay with the Pentarchy of Patriarchs, of which Rome was the senior but not the supreme member. The Byzantines felt deeply about their traditions and their liturgy; but their doctrine of Economy, which recommended that minor differences should be overlooked in the interest of the smooth running of the House of God, allowed them some elasticity. The Roman Church, however, from its very nature, could not easily make concessions.[1]

The scholars in Byzantium were divided. Many of them were too loyal to their Church to contemplate union with Rome. But many others, especially among the philosophers, were ready to accept Roman supremacy so long as their own creed and usages were not utterly condemned. To them the unity of Christendom and of Christian civilization was now all-important. Some of them had been to Italy and had seen the liveliness of intellectual life there. They had seen, too, how highly nowadays Greek scholars were appreciated if they came as friends. In about 1340 Demetrius Cydones had translated the works of Thomas Aquinas into Greek. Aquinas's scholasticism attracted many Greek thinkers and showed them that Italian scholarship was not to be despised. They wished to strengthen intellectual links with Italy; and their desire was reciprocated. More and more of them were offered lucrative professorial chairs in the West. The idea of integrating Byzantine and Italian culture was increasingly attractive; and, so long as Greek traditions were safeguarded, need it matter if submission to Rome were involved, considering the honour paid to Rome in the past and the brilliance of Italian life as it now was displayed?[1]

It was only among politicians and intellectuals that supporters of the union were to be found. The monks and the lesser clergy were its bitter opponents. Few of them were moved by the cultural argument. They were proud of their faith and their traditions. They remembered the sufferings of their forefathers at the hands of Latin hierarchs under the Latin Emperors. It was they who influenced the minds of the people, telling them that union was morally wrong and that to accept it would be to risk eternal damnation. That would be a fate far worse than any disaster that might overcome them in this transient world. Against their opposition it would be hard for any Emperor to implement any promises of union; and they were supported by the scholars and theologians whose loyalty to tradition was intellectual as well as emotional, and by politicians who wondered if in fact the West would ever be capable of rescuing Byzantium.

These passionate debates took place in an atmosphere of material decay. Despite the brilliance of its scholars Constantinople by the close of the fourteenth century was a melancholy, dying city. The population which, with that of the suburbs had numbered about a million in the twelfth century, had shrunk now to no more than a hundred thousand and was still shrinking.[2] The suburbs across the Bosphorus were in Turkish hands. Pera, across the Golden Horn, was a Genoese colony. Of the suburbs along the Thracian shores of the Bosphorus and the Marmora, once studded with splendid villas and rich monasteries, only a few hamlets were left, clustering round some ancient church. The city itself, within its fourteen miles of encircling walls, had even in its greatest days been full of parks and gardens, dividing the various quarters. But now many quarters had disappeared, and fields and orchards separated those that remained. The traveller Ibn Battuta in the mid-fourteenth century counted thirteen distinct townlets within the walls. To Gonzalez de Clavijo, in the first years of the fifteenth century, it was astounding that so huge a city should be so full of ruins; and Bertrandon de la Broquière a few years later was aghast at its emptiness. Pero Tafur in 1437 remarked on its sparse and poverty-stricken population. In many districts you would have thought that you were in the open countryside, with wild roses blooming in the hedgerows in spring and nightingales singing in the copses.

At the south-east end of the city the buildings of the old Imperial Palace were no longer habitable. The last Latin Emperor in his extremity, after selling most of the city's holy relics to Saint Louis and before pawning his son and heir to the Venetians, had stripped the lead off all the roofs and disposed of them for cash. Neither Michael Palaeologus nor any of his successors had ever had money enough to spare to restore them. Only a few of the churches were maintained within its grounds, such as the Nea Basilica of Basil I and the Church of the Mother of God at the Pharos. Nearby the Hippodrome was crumbling; the young men of the nobility used the arena as a polo-ground. Across the square the Patriarchal Palace still contained the Patriarch's offices; but he no longer ventured to reside there. Only the great cathedral of the Holy Wisdom of God, Saint Sophia, was still splendid; its upkeep was a special charge on the state revenues.

The main street that ran along the central ridge of the city, from the Charisian Gate, the Adrianople Gate of today, to the old Palace, was dotted fitfully with shops and houses and was dominated by the Cathedral of the Holy Apostles. But that huge building was in poor repair. Along the Golden Horn the villages were closer together and more populous, especially at either end, at Blachernae, by the land walls, where the Emperor now had his palace, and towards the tip of the city, under the hill of the arsenal.

The Venetians had a prosperous quarter down by the harbour; and the streets allotted to other Western traders, the Anconitans and the Florentines, the Ragusans and the Catalans, and to the Jews were close by. There were warehouses and wharves along the foreshore, and bazaars in the area where the great Turkish bazaar still stands. But each district was separate, many of them surrounded by a wall or a palisade. On the southern slopes of the city, looking towards the Marmora, the villages were sparser and further from each other. At Studion, where the land walls came down to the Marmora, the buildings of the University and of the Patriarchal Academy were grouped round the ancient church of Saint John and its historic monastery with its fine library. To the east of it there were a few wharves at Psamathia. There were still a few fine mansions and monasteries and nunneries scattered through the city. You might still see richly clad lords and ladies riding or carried in litters through the city, though it grieved de la Brocquière to see how small was the escort that accompanied the lovely Empress Maria as she rode from the Church of the Holy Wisdom to the Palace. There was still merchandise in the bazaars and on the wharves, and Venetian or Slav or Moslem merchants, who preferred to do business in the old city rather than with the Genoese across the Horn. There was still a yearly inflow of pilgrims coming, mainly from Russia, to admire the churches and the relics that they contained. The state still maintained hostels to house them, together with such hospitals and orphanages as it could now afford.[1]

The only other important city left to the Empire was Thessalonica. It kept an air of greater prosperity. It was still the chief port of the Balkans. Its annual fair was still the meeting-place of merchants of all nations. Within its smaller area there was less emptiness and less decay. But it never fully recovered from troubles in the mid-fourteenth century, when it was held for some years by popular revolutionaries known as the Zealots, who destroyed many palaces, merchant-houses and monasteries before they were suppressed. Before the end of the century it had been occupied by the Turks: though it was later recovered for a time. Mistra in the Peloponnese, the capital of the Despot of the Morea, though it boasted of a palace and a castle, and several churches, monasteries and schools, was little more than a village.[1]

This tragic remnant of an Empire was the heritage that passed to the Emperor Manuel II in 1391. He himself was a tragic figure. His youth had been spent among family quarrels and wars, in which he alone had been loyal to his father, John V, whom on one occasion he had had to rescue from a debtors' prison in Venice. He had spent some years as a hostage at the Turkish court and had been forced to swear allegiance to the Sultan and even to lead a Byzantine regiment to aid his overlord to subdue the free Byzantine city of Philadelphia. He found consolation in scholarship, writing, amongst other works, a little book for his Turkish friends comparing Christianity with Islam which is a model of its kind. He was a worthy Emperor. Generously he co-opted as his colleague his nephew John VII, his elder brother's son, and was rewarded by the loyalty which that unstable youth showed to him for the rest of his short life. He tried to reform the monasteries and improve their standards; and he gave to the University all the money that he could spare. He saw the political need for help from the West. The Crusade of 1396 which set out, blessed by two rival popes, to perish owing to the folly of its leaders at Nicopolis on the Danube, was, it is true, a response to the supplications of the King of Hungary rather than to his own; but the French Marshal Boucicault came in answer to his appeals to Constantinople in 1399 with a few troops, though it was little that they achieved. He opposed the union of the Churches, partly from genuine religious convictions, which he was open enough to explain in a treatise written for the professors at the Sorbonne, and partly because he knew his subjects too well to believe that they would ever accept it. His advice to his son and successor, John VIII, was to keep up negotiations over union on a friendly basis

but to avoid commitments that might prove impossible to fulfil.
When he journeyed westward in search of aid he chose a moment
when the Papacy was discredited by the Great Schism, and he
made his appeal to lay potentates, hoping thus to escape ecclesiastical pressure. But, despite the pleasant impression that he made,
his travels brought him no material benefit beyond small sums of
money extracted by his hosts from their unenthusiastic subjects;
and he had to hurry home in 1402, on the news that the Sultan
was marching against Constantinople. His capital was saved
before he returned, when Timur the Tartar attacked the Turkish
dominions from the east. But the relief given to Byzantium by
Sultan Bayezit's defeat at Ankara could not restore the dying
Empire. The power of the Ottoman princes was crippled only
for a while. Dynastic quarrels kept them from aggression for two
decades; and when in 1423 Sultan Murad II marched against Constantinople he had to raise the siege almost at once because of
family intrigues and rumours of rebellion.[1]

The intervention of Timur postponed the fall of Constantinople
for half a century. But Manuel alone could take little advantage
of it. He won back a few towns in Thrace, and he secured the
accession of a friendly prince to the Sultanate. Had all the powers
of Europe been able at once to make a coalition against the Ottoman Turks the menace might have been ended. But coalitions
cannot be formed without time and good-will; and both were
lacking. The Genoese, fearful for their trade, hastened both to
send an embassy to Timur and to provide ships to transport the
defeated Turkish soldiers from Asia across to Europe. The Venetians, fearful of being outwitted by the Genoese, instructed their
colonial authorities to observe strict neutrality. The Papacy, in
the throes of the Great Schism, could not give a lead. The lay
powers of the West remembered the disaster at Nicopolis; and
each of them had distractions nearer at hand. The King of Hungary, believing that the Turks would no longer now threaten
him, was plunging into intrigues in Germany from which he

was to emerge as Western emperor. Constantinople was in no immediate danger. Why should anyone bother about it now?[1]

At Constantinople itself there was no such optimism. But, in spite of consciousness of danger, the brilliant intellectual life went on. The older generation of scholars was dead. Now, apart from the Emperor himself, the leading figure was Joseph Bryennius, headmaster of the Patriarchal Academy and professor at the University. He was the teacher who educated the last remarkable generation of Byzantine scholars. He was well versed in Western as well as in Greek literature and aided the Emperor in introducing Western studies into the University curriculum. He eagerly welcomed Western students. Indeed, Aeneas Sylvius Piccolomini, the future Pope Pius II, was to write later that in his youth any Italian with pretensions to scholarship always claimed to have studied at Constantinople. But Bryennius, like Manuel, opposed the union of the Churches. He could not accept Roman theology and he would not abandon Byzantine traditions.[2]

An even more remarkable scholar, George Gemistus Plethon, slightly younger than Bryennius, moved during these years from his native Constantinople to take up his residence at Mistra, under the patronage of the most erudite of the Emperor's sons, the Despot Theodore II of the Morea. There he founded a Platonic Academy and wrote a number of books pleading for a reorganization of the State along Platonic lines. Only this, he thought, would revive the Greek world. He offered suggestions on social, economic and military affairs, few of which were really practicable. In religion he advocated a Platonic cosmology, with a touch of Epicureanism and of Zoroastrianism added. Though nominally Orthodox he had little use for Christianity and liked to write of God as Zeus. His religious views were never openly published. The manuscript in which he aired them fell, after his death and after the fall of Constantinople, into the hands of his old friend and disputant, the Patriarch Gennadius, who read it with growing fascination and horror and at the end reluctantly ordered it to be burnt. Only a few fragments remain.[1]

Plethon eagerly supported a terminology which showed how greatly the Byzantine world had changed. Hitherto the word *Hellene* had been used by the Byzantines, except when they applied it to language, to describe a pagan Greek as opposed to a Christian. Now, with the Empire shrunken to be little more than a group of city-states, and with the Western world full of admiration for ancient Greece, the humanists began to call themselves Hellenes. The Empire was still officially the Roman Empire; but the word *Romaioi*, by which the Byzantines had always described themselves in the past, was abandoned by educated circles, till at last *Romaic* came to denote the language of the people, in contrast with the literary tongue. The fashion started at Thessalonica, where the intellectuals were very conscious of their Greek heritage. Nicholas Cabasilas, who was a Thessalonian, wrote of 'our community of Hellas'. Several of his contemporaries followed his example. By the end of the century Manuel was often addressed as Emperor of the Hellenes. A few centuries previously any Western embassy that arrived at Constantinople with letters addressed to the 'Emperor of the Greeks' was not received at Court. Now, though a few traditionalists disliked the new term and though no one intended it as an abdication of the Empire's oecumenical claims, it flourished, to remind the Byzantines of their Hellenic heritage. In its last decades Constantinople was consciously a Greek city.[2]

Manuel II retired from active life in 1423 and died two years later. His friend Sultan Mehmet I was already dead; and under the new Sultan, Murad II, the Ottoman power was stronger than ever. Many Greeks admired Murad, who, though devotedly Moslem, was kindly, honourable and just; but his temper was revealed when he marched against Constantinople in 1422. Though his attempt to besiege the city came to nothing, his pressure on other parts of the Empire was such that the governor of

Thessalonica, Manuel's third son, Andronicus, a sickly nervous man, despaired of holding his city and sold it to the Venetians. But they too could not maintain it. After a brief siege it fell to the Turks in 1430. During the following years Murad showed no great eagerness for aggression. But how long would the respite last?[1]

Manuel's eldest son, John VIII, was so certain that only Western aid could save the Empire that, neglecting his father's advice, he decided to press for union with Rome. Only the Western Church could rally the West to his rescue. The Papacy had recovered from the Schism; but it had been restored by means of a Conciliar movement. John knew that the only chance of inducing his people to accept union was for it to be decided by a council as oecumenical as circumstances would allow. The Papacy could not now reject the plan for a council. After long negotiations Pope Eugenius IV invited the Emperor to bring a delegation to a council to be held in Italy. John would have preferred to hold it at Constantinople, but he accepted the invitation. The Council opened at Ferrara in 1438 and was moved the next year to Florence, where the vital discussions took place.

The detailed story of the Council makes arid reading. There were disputes over precedence. Was the Emperor to preside, as emperors had presided over earlier councils? How was the Patriarch of Constantinople to be received by the Pope? It was decided that the debates should be conducted over the correct interpretation of the Canons of the Oecumenical Councils and over patristic texts. The Fathers of the Church, Latin as well as Greek, must be regarded as having been divinely inspired and their rulings followed. Unfortunately, inspiration did not seem to involve consistency. The Fathers had often disagreed with each other and sometimes even contradicted themselves. There were endless difficulties over language. It was seldom possible to find an exact equivalent in Latin for Greek theological terms; and the Greek and Latin versions of the Canons of the Councils often diverged. In the debates it must be admitted that the Latins had the better.

Their delegation was composed of highly trained controversialists who worked together as a team, with the Pope in the background to advise them. The Greek delegation was more diffuse. The bishops were a sorry lot, as many of the more reputable had refused to attend. To improve their standard the Emperor had raised three learned monks to metropolitan sees. These were Bessarion of Trebizond, Metropolitan of Nicaea, Isidore, Metropolitan of Kiev and All Russia, and Mark Eugenicus, Metropolitan of Ephesus. He added four lay philosophers, George Scholarius, George Amiroutzes, George of Trebizond and the aged Plethon. The Eastern Patriarchs were asked to nominate delegates from among the attending bishops; but they complied grudgingly, not allowing their representatives plenipotentiary powers. By Orthodox tradition every bishop, including the Patriarch, is equally inspired on doctrine while the laity are entitled to theological opinions. So each Greek disputant went his own way. The Patriarch, an amiable old man called Joseph, the bastard son of a Bulgarian prince and a Greek lady, was not very clever nor in good health and carried no weight. The Emperor himself would intervene to prevent the discussion of awkward points, such as the doctrine of the Energies. There was no coherence and no fixed policy among the Greeks; and all of them were kept short of money and were eager to go home.

In the end union was forced through. Of the philosophers George Scholarius, George Amiroutzes and George of Trebizond, all of them admirers of Aquinas, accepted it. Plethon apparently managed to withhold his signature. He considered the Latin Church to be even more hostile to free thought than the Greek. But he had a wonderful time in Florence. He was fêted as the leading Platonist scholar; and Cosimo de' Medici founded a Platonic Academy in his honour. So his opposition was muted. The Patriarch Joseph, after agreeing with the Latins that their formula of the Holy Ghost proceeding from the Son meant the same as the Greek formula of the Holy Ghost proceeding through the Son, fell ill and died. An unkind scholar remarked that after muddling his prepositions what else could he decently do? Bessarion and Isidore were won to the Latin view. They were impressed by the learning of the Italians and longed to integrate Greek and Italian culture. All the other Greek bishops, with one exception, signed the act of union, some of them under protest, complaining of pressure and threats from the Emperor. The exception was Mark of Ephesus, who would not subscribe, even though menaced with the loss of his see. The act itself, though it permitted certain Greek usages, was little more than a statement of Latin doctrine, though the clause on the Pope's relationship with the Councils was left slightly vague.[1]

It was easier to sign than to implement the union. When the delegation returned to Constantinople it was met with undisguised hostility. Soon Bessarion, greatly respected though he was, found it prudent to retire to Italy, where he was joined by Isidore, whom the Russians angrily repudiated. The Eastern Patriarchs refused to be bound by the signature of their delegates. The Emperor had difficulty in finding anyone to take over the Patriarchate of Constantinople. His first nominee died almost at once. The next, Gregory Mammas, appointed in 1445, grimly held on to the post for six years, boycotted by almost all of his clergy, then retired to the friendlier atmosphere of Rome. Mark of Ephesus was degraded, only to be treated by the people as the true head of the hierarchy. Of the philosophers, George of Trebizond moved to Italy. George Scholarius began to have doubts, more for political than for religious reasons. He remained an admirer of scholasticism but he decided that union was not in Greek interests. He retired into a monastery, under the monastic name of Gennadius. When Mark of Ephesus died he became the accepted leader of the anti-Unionist party. George Amiroutzes was to go further and to explore the possibilities of an understanding with Islam. The Emperor himself wondered whether he had done rightly. He would not repudiate the union, but, influenced by his mother, the Empress Helena, he ceased from pressing it. All that it had achieved was to bring division and bitterness to the dying city.[1]

Had it been promptly followed by a successful expedition against the Turks it might have won grudging acceptance. Pope Eugenius preached a Crusade in 1440 and at last organized an army, composed mainly of Hungarians which crossed the Danube in 1444. But the Papal legate, Cardinal Cesarini, after forcing the military leader, John Hunyadi, Voyevod of Transylvania, to break a solemn treaty with the Sultan on the ground that oaths sworn to infidels were invalid, then quarrelled with him over strategy. Sultan Murad had little difficulty in overwhelming the crusading force at Varna, on the shores of the Black Sea.[2]

To many Western historians it has seemed that the Byzantines in rejecting union were wantonly and obstinately committing suicide. The simple folk led by the monks were moved by a passionate loyalty to their creed, their liturgy and their traditions, which they believed to be divinely ordained; it would be sin to desert them. It was a religious age. The Byzantines knew that this earthly life was only a prelude to the everlasting life to come. To buy material safety here below at the price of eternal salvation was not to be considered. There was, too, a streak of fatalism in them. If disaster was to befall them it would be God's punishment for their sins. They were pessimists. In the damp, melancholy climate of the Bosphorus the natural gaiety of the Greeks was dimmed. Even in the great days of the Empire men had whispered of prophecies that it would not last for ever. It was well known that on stones throughout the city and in the books written by the sages of the past the list of emperors was written, and it was drawing to an end. The reign of anti-Christ could not be long delayed. Even those who trusted that the Mother of God would never allow a city dedicated to her to fall into infidel hands were now few in number. Union with the heretic West could not bring salvation nor could it alter fate.[3]

It may be that this pious view was ignorant and narrow. But there were thoughtful statesmen also who doubted the benefits of union. Many of them calculated, with reason, that the West would never be able or willing to send help effective enough to check the superbly organized military power of the Turks. Others, especially among the churchmen, feared that union would merely lead to further schism. Would not the Greeks who had been struggling so long to preserve their integrity against the per-secution of Frankish rulers feel that they had been betrayed? More and more Greeks had fallen under Turkish rule, and their connection with Constantinople could only be maintained through the Church. If the Patriarchate committed itself to the West would these congregations follow suit? Their overlords certainly would not approve. Would the Caucasian, the Danubian and the Russian Orthodox be ready to join? The sister-Patriarchates of the East made their disapproval clear. Was it to be hoped that the Orthodox dependent on the Byzantine Patriarchate but indepen-dent of the Empire would accept Western religious suzerainty merely to save the Empire? The Russians in particular were known to regard the Latin Church with hatred as the Church of their Polish and Scandinavian enemies. A memorandum dated in 1437 tells us that of the sixty-seven metropolitan sees dependent on the Patriarch of Constantinople only eight remained in the Emperor's own dominions and seven more in the Despotate of the Morea.[1] That is to say, union with Rome might well cost the Patriarch the loss of more than three-quarters of his dependent bishops. That was a formidable argument to add to the natural reluctance of the Byzantines to sacrifice their religious freedom. A few statesmen looked further ahead. Byzantium, as any cool observer could see, was doomed. The only chance of reuniting the Greek Church and with it the Greek people might well lie in accepting Turkish bondage, to which already the majority of the Greeks were subject. Only thus might it be possible to reconstitute the Orthodox Greek nation and so revive it that in time it might

regain enough strength to throw off the infidel yoke and recreate
Byzantium. With few exceptions, no Greek was so far lacking in
pride as to contemplate the voluntary submission of his body to
the infidel, any more than he would voluntarily submit his soul
to the Romans. But might not the former be the wiser course if
it excluded the latter? Greek integrity might well be better preserved by a united people under Moslem rule than by a fragment
attached to the rim of the Western world. The remark attributed
by his enemies to the last great minister of Byzantium, Lucas
Notaras: 'Better the Sultan's turban than the Cardinal's hat', was
not so outrageous as at first it sounds.[1]

To Bessarion and his fellow humanists, working eagerly and
devotedly in Italy to obtain help for their compatriots, the atmosphere at Constantinople seemed strange and foolish and narrow.
They were convinced that union with the West would bring such
new cultural and political vigour that Byzantium could yet rise
again. Who can say if they were wrong?[2]

The Emperor John VIII lived for nine unhappy years after his
return from Italy. He had come back to find his adored Empress,
Maria of Trebizond, dead of the plague. He had no children.
His brothers spent their time quarrelling with each other in the
Peloponnese or intriguing against him in Thrace. Of his family
he could only trust his aged mother, the Empress Helena; and she
disliked his policy. He tried as best he could to keep peace in his
divided capital by forbearance and tact. Prudently he spent all
the money that the State could spare on doing repairs to the great
land-walls of the city, that they might be ready for the inevitable
Turkish onslaught. Death came to him as a relief, on 31 October
1448.[3]

CHAPTER II

THE RISING SULTANATE

In the great days of the past the prosperity of Byzantium had been linked with the possession of Anatolia. The huge peninsula, known to the ancients as Asia Minor, had been in Roman times one of the most populous areas in the world. The decline of the Roman Empire, accompanied by plague and the spread of malaria and followed by the Persian and Arab invasions of the seventh and eighth centuries, had reduced the population. Security returned in the ninth century. A well planned system of defence lessened the risk of enemy raids. Agriculture could recover and find a market for its products in Constantinople and the prosperous cities of the coast. The rich valleys of the west teemed with olives and fruit-trees and cereals. Flocks of sheep and herds of cattle roamed on the uplands; and wherever irrigation could be maintained vast corn-fields were cultivated. The policy of the Emperors was to discourage large estates, preferring that the land should be held by village communes, many of which paid for their tenancy by providing soldiers for the Imperial army or for the local militia. The central government kept control by frequent inspection and by paying the salaries of provincial officials out of the Imperial treasury.

This prosperity depended upon well-guarded frontiers. There, on the marches, a different way of life prevailed. Their defence was entrusted to the border barons, the *akritai*, men whose lives were spent in raiding enemy lands or in countering enemy raids. They were lawless, independent men, resentful of any attempt by the government to control them, never willing to pay taxes, expecting, rather, to be rewarded for their services. They drew their followers from adventurers of all sorts; for there was little settled life or racial cohesion in those wild lands, except where the Armenians were settled and maintained their traditions. Warfare was continuous, whether or no the Byzantine and Arab governments were officially at peace; but the border barons were not unfriendly with their rivals over the frontier, who led similar lives. The Moslem frontier lords were perhaps a little more fanatical for their faith; but their fanaticism was not too great to prevent intercourse or even intermarriage. On neither side of the frontier was official religion very popular. Many of the *akritai* belonged to the Separated Armenian Church, and almost all of them willingly gave protection to heretics; while Moslem heretics could always find refuge with the Moslem frontier lords.[1]

The system broke down for a while owing to the decline of the Caliphate and a new aggressive spirit in Byzantium. From the mid-tenth century onwards Imperial armies won back great areas of frontier land, particularly in Syria. The new frontier no longer ran through wild mountains but across cultivated and well-populated lands. Its defence could be organized under officials from Constantinople stationed at Antioch or at some other re-captured city. The former border barons were unwanted. They compensated themselves by investing the riches gained on the recent campaigns in land all over Anatolia. But they remained proud and insubordinate, surrounding themselves with armies of retainers, largely drawn from former free villages over which they had, usually illegally, bought control. They formed the basis of the landed aristocracy whose power shook the Imperial government in the mid-eleventh century. Meanwhile the central administration tried to assume control of the Armenian frontier-lands, further to the north, and formally annexed large provinces, bringing them into the hated sphere of the Byzantine tax-collector and the Byzantine ecclesiastical authorities. The resentment that was caused weakened the defences.[2]

These were now to be challenged by a people with whom hitherto Byzantine contacts had usually been friendly. For some centuries past the great plains of Turkestan had been drying up and Turkish tribes were moving westward to seek new homes. Byzantium had been in touch with the Turks of central Asia in the sixth century and was well acquainted with the Turkish tribes that migrated into the Russian steppes, the sophisticated Judaizing Khazars, two of whose princesses married Byzantine Emperors, and the wilder Petchenegs and Cumans, who occasionally made raids into Imperial territory but who, more usefully, sent willing detachments to take service in the Imperial armies. Many of these mercenaries were given permanent homes within the Empire, especially in Anatolia, and became converts to Christianity. But the most active of the Turkish nations, the Oghuz, directed its migration through Persia towards the lands of the Arab Caliphate. There were Turkish regiments in the Caliph's armies as well as in the Emperor's; and these became Moslems. As the Caliph's power declined that of his Turkish vassals increased. The first great Moslem Turk, Mahmud the Ghazvanid, built up an empire in the east, stretching from Isfahan to Bokhara and Lahore. But after his death the hegemony among the Turks passed to the princes of an Oghuz tribe, the family of Seljuk. The descendants of that semi-mythical prince acquired an ascendancy over the Turks settled within the Caliphate; and immigrants from Turkestan readily accepted their leadership. By 1055 Tughril Bey, the head of the house, had not only established a personal kingdom comprising Persia and Khorasan, with his brothers and cousins in appanages on his northern borders, but he had also been invited by the Abbasid Caliph at Baghdad to take over the temporal government of his dominions.

The Caliph's invitation was due to fear of the rival Caliphate of the Fatimids of Egypt, which already controlled most of Syria. The Fatimids were on good terms with the Byzantine Empire; and the Seljuk princes were anxious to avoid any action by the Byzantines on the northern Abbasid frontier in support of a Fatimid attack. Already a number of Turkish princelings with their followers had settled on the Byzantine frontiers and were playing the part of border barons, raiding whenever an opportunity occurred. Tughril's successor, his nephew Alp Arslan, was determined to remove any danger of Byzantine aggression. He sacked and annexed the old Armenian capital of Ani and encouraged his border barons to increase their raids. Byzantium countered by taking over the last independent Armenian principality. But the Imperial garrisons were not strong enough to check the raids; and there were no *akritai* now to deal with them. In 1071 the Emperor Romanus Diogenes decided that a military expedition was needed to safeguard the frontier. Recent economies had reduced the Imperial army; and the Emperor was mainly dependent upon mercenaries, some from Western Europe and many more from the Cuman Turks. Alp Arslan was in Syria, campaigning against the Fatimids, when he heard of the expedition. He assumed it to be a move in the Fatimid-Byzantine alliance and hurried north to oppose it. It is curious that in this campaign, which was to be vital for world-history, each side believed itself to be taking defensive action.[1]

The decisive battle took place on Friday, 19 August 1071, near the town of Manzikert. Romanus was a gallant man but a poor tactician; and his hired troops were not to be trusted. His army was routed and destroyed and he himself was taken prisoner.[2]

Alp Arslan, satisfied that Byzantium would no longer threaten his flank, set his Imperial prisoner free on easy terms and returned to his main interests in Syria. But his border barons had other ideas. The Byzantine frontier defences were down; and political crises at Constantinople prevented any attempt to repair them. The few *akritai* that remained, most of them Armenians, were left without any means of communication with the capital. They moved to entrench themselves and their followers in isolated fortresses. The Turkish princelings intensified their raids; then, finding so little opposition, they settled in the districts to which they had penetrated, colonizing them with their followers and with other Turkish tribesmen who had heard of these rich lands that lay open for occupation.[1]

For some time past the Moslem frontier barons had been given the title of *ghazi*, warrior for the Faith. The *ghazi* was a rough equivalent to a Christian knight. He was apparently invested with some sort of insignia and took an oath of some sort to an overlord, ideally to the Caliph; and he obeyed the *futuwwa*, that mystical code of moral behaviour which developed in the tenth and eleventh centuries and was adopted by the guilds and corporations of the Islamic world. The Turkish *ghazis* were essentially fighters and conquerors. They were uninterested in organized government. As they advanced and took over territory they ruled it as they ruled their frontier domains, interfering very little with the local population, who indeed looked to them for protection against other raiders, and financing their rule by the booty obtained from their raids. In the border lands, used for centuries to such a way of life, their coming met with little resentment. Their followers might displace a few Christians, who fled to surer refuges. But the population was already mixed and fluid; the influx of Turks made little difference to the general pattern. But as they advanced further into Asia Minor the pattern changed. In some districts the Christians fled before them, leaving space for the Turkish tribesmen to occupy. In others the Christian towns and villages tried to maintain themselves but were soon isolated and forced to submit to the invaders' rule. The raids resulted in the swift decay of roads and bridges, wells and irrigation channels. The old economy could not survive.[2]

With no organized opposition the *ghazi* invaders were able to overrun the whole peninsula, leaving only a few coastal districts in Byzantine hands. It was not until the Emperor Alexius Comnenus reorganized the Empire, recreating the Imperial army and using diplomacy to play off each *ghazi* leader against his neighbour that ground was recovered. Meanwhile the Seljuk dynasty, alarmed by the chaos in Anatolia, sent one of its cadet members to organize the conquests into a settled Islamic kingdom. The task of the Seljuk ruler, Suleiman, and of his son, Kilij Arslan, was hampered by Alexius's wars and intrigues and by the help given to Byzantium by the soldiers of the First Crusade. Early in the twelfth century the boundary between Byzantine and Turkish lands was fixed along the rough line that separated the fertile valleys of western Anatolia and the coastal districts of the north and south from the central uplands. The Seljuk rulers were, however, less interested in their relations with Byzantium than in their attempts to impose themselves upon the *ghazi* princes, particularly upon the great Danishmend clan. They also kept careful watch on the countries to the east, where the centre of their family power lay.

The decline of Byzantium towards the end of the twelfth century and the disaster of the Fourth Crusade enabled the Seljuk kingdom to increase its territory. In the first half of the thirteenth century the Seljuk Sultans of Rum, as they were usually called after their possessions in the heart of old Roman and Byzantine lands, were respected and powerful figures in the Moslem world. They had established their authority over the *ghazi* princes. They were usually on good terms with their Byzantine neighbours, the Emperors of Nicaea. They had abandoned their eastern ambitions and were content to administer their orderly and tolerant state from their capital of Konya. They revived urban life and repaired communications; they encouraged the arts and learning. It is a tribute to their wise and able government that the transition of Anatolia from a mainly Christian to a mainly Moslem country was achieved so smoothly that no one troubled to record the details.[1]

The beneficent rule of the Seljuks was ended by the Mongol invasions. First, a number of Turkish tribes, fleeing before the Mongol armies, entered Asia Minor. They were settled on the western frontier, where they joined the *ghazis* who were fretting under Seljuk control. In 1243 the Mongols themselves appeared.

27

The Seljuk Sultan suffered an overwhelming defeat, from which his kingdom never recovered. Henceforward he and his successors were the tributaries and vassals of the Mongol Ilkhan of Persia, and their power and authority decayed. In less than a century the dynasty was extinct.[1]

The decline of the Seljuk Sultanate gradually freed the *ghazi* princes of the frontier from restraint. More and more refugees from Mongol rule joined them, officials from Seljuk cities, countryfolk from devastated or overtaxed areas, holy men, sheikhs and dervishes, many of whom were considered heretical in strict Moslem circles but whose fanaticism fitted in with the frontier spirit. Pressure and faith alike urged them on to attack the Christians. It was not easy at first. The Nicaean Emperors had taken great care of the frontier, reviving the *akritai* but keeping them under control.[2] But the recovery of Constantinople in 1261, glorious though it was, had its disadvantages. The Empire was henceforward deeply involved in Europe, facing threats not only from the Balkan powers but from Westerners eager to avenge the fall of the Latin Empire. Troops were withdrawn from the Asiatic garrisons. Economies in the navy weakened the coastal defences. Taxation rose all over the Empire, to pay for its new commitments. The *akritai* found themselves ill-supported and ill-paid. During the last three decades of the thirteenth century several *ghazis* penetrated across the frontier. Overcrowded on their side of the border, eager for booty and spurred on by their religious leaders, they and their followers poured into the remaining lands of Byzantine Asia. Fitful attempts by the Imperial army to drive them back were unsuccessful. Some of the more enterprising of them, such as the princes of Menteshe and Aydin, attacked by sea as well as by land; and the Byzantine navy was too feeble to prevent them from occupying several islands as well as the western Anatolian coast-lands. By 1300 all that remained to Byzantium in Asia, apart from one or two isolated cities, were the plains between Bithynian Olympus and the Sea of Marmora,

the peninsula that juts out to the Bosphorus, as far inland as the
river Sangarius, and the Black Sea coastline for a hundred miles
eastward.

In these movements the emirate of Menteshe, in the south-west
of Asia Minor, had first taken the lead. But its power was curtailed when the Knights Hospitaller captured and established themselves in Rhodes. The hegemony passed to the emirs of Aydin,
the first of the Asiatic Turks to raid the European coasts of the
Aegean. It took the combined might of Venice, Cyprus and the
Hospitallers to restrain them. Further north were the princes of
Sarakhan, with their headquarters at Manisa, or Magnesia, recently
the second capital of the Nicaean Emperors, and next to them the
Karasi princes, settled on the plain of Troy. On the Black Sea
coast there was Ghazi Chelebi's emirate at Sinope, famous for its
piratical exploits. There were several smaller emirates in the
interior; and there were the two great emirates of Karaman and
Germiyan, both seeing themselves as heirs of the Seljuks and both
determined to set up an orderly state with the *ghazi* elements
under control. The Karaman princes, who occupied Konya in
1327, were far enough from the frontier to be able to eliminate
the local *ghazis*. The Germiyan princes, whose capital was
Kutahya, refused to bear the title of *ghazi* but tried to establish
some authority over the neighbouring *ghazi* lords, many of whom
were in origin Germiyan military leaders. They were in the main
successful. With one exception, the emirates along the Aegean
coast and the Byzantine frontier treated them with deference and
respect, while never actually admitting their suzerainty.[1]

The one exception was a small state established during the
second half of the thirteenth century in the border lands stretching
eastward from Bithynian Olympus. Its founder was a certain
Ertughrul, who died in 1281 and was succeeded by his son Osman.
The origins of the Osmanli, or Ottoman, family, as Osman's
descendants were called, have been twisted and ornamented by
legends created after the family had become great. We are given

a list of twenty-one ancestors going back to Noah, though thirty-one more were later added, to make the chronology more convincing. The line passes through the eponymous hero Oghuz Khan, founder of the Oghuz Turks, and through his son Gök Alp and his grandson Chamundur, who is the same as Chavuldur, according to other legends one of the twenty-four grandsons of Oghuz, from whom the twenty-four principal Oghuz tribes were descended. But, though there was a Chaudar tribe which was absorbed into the Ottoman polity in the late thirteenth century, it was a distinct tribe, hostile at first to Osman's leadership. Another legend enhanced the family by giving it Oghuz's eldest grandson, Qayi, son of Gun Khan, as its ancestor, thus making the Ottomans a branch of the senior Oghuz tribe. But this tradition only appears in the fifteenth century, after the alternative tradition of the descent from Gök Alp had been generally accepted. Court flatterers in the fifteenth century complicated the issue by giving the dynasty Arab ancestors, though it never claimed descent from the Prophet himself; the pedigrees of his descendants were too well known.[1] The Conquering Sultan, Mehmet II, sought to impress both his Turkish and his Greek subjects by supporting a theory that his family was descended from a prince of the Imperial house of Comnenus, who migrated to Konya and there became a convert to Islam and the husband of a Seljuk princess.[2]

There is no sound evidence to support any of these theories. The prudent historian will conclude that Ertughrul was not a tribal leader but an able *ghazi* commander of unknown origin who somehow made his way to the frontier and there by his prowess gathered around him a sufficient number of followers to enable him to found an emirate. His main asset was the geographical position of the lands that he occupied. A *ghazi* community to justify its existence had to raid and to advance into infidel territory. But by the end of the thirteenth century nearly all the *ghazi* emirs had reached the limits of Asia Minor. The

Byzantines had gone; and the sea blocked further progress. Though enterprising pirates such as the emirs of Aydin and Sinope might profitably raid enemy coasts, none of them had enough sea-power to contemplate the transport of sufficient of their people to establish colonies overseas. Apart from the emirates that bordered on the Empire of Trebizond, away to the east, only the territory which Osman had inherited still faced an infidel frontier. It was into Osman's lands that the most enterprising elements among the Turks now poured, *ghazi* leaders eager to find rich lands that still could be raided, dervishes and scholars eager to escape further from the hated Mongols, and a solid mass of peasant tribesmen still looking for homes in which to settle with their flocks. Osman thus found himself with human resources quite out of proportion with his small emirate.

Had Osman not been a leader of genius he might have been swamped by the immigrants. We know little of how he dealt with them. It is significant that in the oldest surviving inscription in which an Ottoman ruler gives himself the title of Sultan, an inscription placed by Osman's son Orhan on a mosque in Brusa, the formula runs: 'Sultan, son of the Sultan of the Ghazis, Ghazi, son of Ghazis, Margrave of the horizons, hero of the world.'[1] It was as a supreme *ghazi* leader that Osman established his authority. While other *ghazi* emirs, unable to expand along the only lines that they knew, began to quarrel with each other, Osman offered a *ghazi* life to anyone who accepted his command.

The Byzantine Empire could not ignore the challenge. Perhaps its wisest course would have been quickly to evacuate its armies out of Anatolia and to abandon the country to Osman, concentrating its strength on naval forces strong enough to prevent any crossing of the Straits into Europe. Then, when Osman found his expansion blocked by the sea, his emirate too might have declined and his followers have dispersed in search of other fields. But such foresight and self-restraint were not to be expected. Osman's importance was not at first realized at Constantinople. It was against the Turks of Aydin and Manisa that Imperial armies were sent, with no success, during the last decades of the thirteenth century. It was only when Osman defeated a Byzantine force at Baphaeum, between Nicaea and Nicomedia, in 1301, and began to settle his people north of Mount Olympus that serious attention was paid to him. The Byzantines could not tamely permit Moslem occupation of their last Asiatic possessions, lands that were in sight of the capital itself. But their opposition was ill-organized and ineffectual. In 1305 the Catalan Company, which the Emperor Andronicus II had hired as mercenaries, defeated Osman near Leuke. But the Catalans soon revolted against the Emperor and involved the Empire in ten years of civil war. During those years not only did numbers of Turkish troops, hired either by the Emperor or by the Catalans, move to and fro across the Dardanelles, but Osman was able to consolidate his hold on the countryside as far as the Sea of Marmora. He also took the lead in expeditions that were not strictly his concern. In 1308 it was his troops that took the major part in capturing the last remaining Byzantine city on the Aegean coast, Ephesus, though it was given to the emir of Aydin. During the next few years he took possession of the Byzantine towns along the Black Sea coast, from Inebolu to the Sangarius.

The departure of the Catalans was followed in Byzantium by dynastic civil wars. Again Osman was left with little opposition to face. His armies consisted mainly of cavalry; and he had no siege engines. In order to capture fortified cities he would sweep through the surrounding countryside, driving out or enslaving the local peasants and settling his own followers there. The city would thus be cut off from its sources of supply and, unless a relieving army cut its way through, would be starved into surrender. He now concentrated on the city of Brusa, set on the northern slopes of the Olympus range, with strong natural defences and well placed to be a centre for operations along the Marmora coast. Its fortifications and the richness of the countryside below its walls enabled it to defy him for ten years. But the Emperor could send no relief. In the autumn of 1326 it was starved into capitulation. When the news reached Osman he was a dying man; he died a few days later, that November. By the brilliant use of his opportunities he had turned a small border emirate into the chief power among the Turks and the spearhead of the *ghazi* into Christendom.[1]

Osman was fortunate in his children. His elder son, Orhan, succeeded to the throne. It was said that as Turkish tradition demanded he offered to share the sovereignty with his brother, Ala ed-Din; but Ala ed-Din generously insisted that the monarchy should not be divided and remained a loyal subject. Orhan inherited also an able minister, whose name was likewise Ala ed-Din. It is not easy to know whether it was to the ruler or to the minister that the remarkable development of the Ottoman state was due. Like his father Orhan was a *ghazi* leader, pledged to conquer the infidel. In 1329 the historic city of Nicaea, which, like Brusa, had been isolated for many years, surrendered to him. The Emperor Andronicus III and his minister John Cantacuzenus had attempted to relieve it. But after an indecisive battle discontent among their troops and bad news from Europe forced them to retire. Orhan's next objective was the great sea-port of Nicomedia. It resisted him for nine years, receiving supplies and reinforcements by sea. But when he managed to blockade the narrow gulf on which it stood, it was forced to capitulate in 1337. With Nicomedia in his hands the Sultan, as he now called himself, was able to occupy all the country almost up to the Bosphorus.[2]

By now Byzantium was being harassed by the great Serbian empire of Stephen Dushan, while in 1341 civil war broke out between John Cantacuzenus and the regents governing in the name of the child-Emperor John V. For some time past Byzantine generals had hired the services of Turkish troops from various tribes, in spite of the Turks' incorrigible habit of pillaging the lands through which they passed. Orhan's men were the most

33

effective and the best disciplined. So, while John V's supporters engaged mercenaries from Manisa and Aydin, John Cantacuzenus won Orhan's support in 1344 by giving him his daughter Theodora in marriage. In return the Sultan sent six thousand men to fight in Thrace. After Cantacuzenus had won the throne he still called on Ottoman troops, to help him in his wars against the Serbs. When the campaigns were over many of these Turks seem to have settled in Thrace.[1]

John Cantacuzenus's fall from power in 1355 gave Orhan the excuse that he wanted for invading Europe on his own behalf. In 1356 an army under his son Suleiman was ferried across the Dardanelles. Within a year his troops had captured Chorlu and Didymoticum and had pressed inland to occupy Adrianople. As with his Asiatic conquests the Sultan encouraged Turkish tribesmen to follow the *ghazi* leaders and at once settle in the country that they conquered. When Orhan died, probably in 1362, the Turks were masters of western Thrace. The Sultan had also increased his territory in Asia, less by warfare than by the eagerness of other Turks to join so successful a *ghazi* state. He seems to have absorbed the Sarakhan and Karasi emirates in the north-west. The Germiyan power was declining; and he was able to establish his rule in Eskishehir and Ankara. His chief foe in Asia was the emirate of Aydin, which blocked him to the south-west.[2]

It was not only for his conquests that Orhan was a great ruler. With his vizier's help he gave a solid organization to his state without destroying the *ghazi* quality which provided its impetus. He encouraged urban developments, making use of the *akhis*, guilds of artisans and merchants who followed the *futuwwa*. He countered the somewhat disruptive influence of the dervishes by inviting the co-operation of the *ulema*, the official guardians of the Moslem faith and its traditions. Their teaching ensured proper treatment for his increasing number of Christian subjects. If a town or district had resisted him and was taken by force of arms, the Christians had no rights. One-fifth of the population might be enslaved, the men sent to work on the conquerors' lands, and the boys trained for the army. If they had capitulated they were allowed to retain their churches and their customs. Many Christians preferred his rule to that of the Emperor because his taxation was less exorbitant. Though some of them adopted Islam from a natural desire to join the ruling classes there was no forcible conversion. The *ulema* furthermore built *medreses*, or mosque-schools, in every city to which they came and were thus able to provide the Sultan with an educated élite to form his civil service.[1]

At the same time the army was reorganized. Hitherto it had consisted almost entirely of light cavalry drawn from tribes that were still basically nomadic. Now it was replanned in two main sections. There was a regular militia composed of men who were allotted land by the Sultan and paid for it with a small money rent and the obligation to do military service whenever required. Such a fief, which was hereditary, was known as a *timar*. Larger or more valuable fiefs, known as *ziamet*, involved a bigger rent, and the tenant held a higher position in the army, with greater obligations to provide his equipment. The richest of these *zaims* became a *pasha* or a *sanjakbey*, or even a *beylerbey*, with administrative duties and higher military powers and obligations. Side by side with this locally based militia there was an army paid for its services. The Janissaries, who served for life and were later to form the Sultan's guard, were as yet an infantry regiment composed of Christian or ex-Christian slaves. The main force in Orhan's day was known loosely as the *sipahis*. They provided the gunners, the armourers and smiths and the marines. Many of them had been allotted lands and were liable for military service at any time, but they were paid for it and were usually hired only for a single campaign. With the *sipahis* were the *piyade*, the infantry. The name was later reserved for those that held lands, the others being called the *azabs*, who came to be associated with the *bashi-bazouks*, irregulars who served for whatever loot and plunder they could obtain; as did the *akibi*, a light cavalry spear-head. Orhan insisted on a distinctive uniform for each section of his army. He also set up efficient means for mobilization, so that he could at any time gather together a large and well trained force at the shortest notice.[1]

His successor, Murad I, took full advantage of this fine fighting force. Murad's mother was a Greek, known to the Turks as Nilüfer, the Water-lily, the daughter of an akritic chieftain. His elder full-brother, Suleiman, had died a few months before Orhan. There was an older half-brother, Ibrahim, whom Murad promptly put to death, and a younger, Halil, the son of Theodora Cantacuzena, who died, perhaps naturally, soon afterwards. During the first years of his reign Murad was engaged on his Asiatic frontier where rival emirs were making trouble and had to be repressed. Some of the towns conquered in Thrace were reoccupied by the Byzantines, though the Turks could not be driven out of the countryside. When Murad returned to Europe in 1365 he had no difficulty in recovering them and in establishing his European capital at Adrianople. Constantinople and its surroundings were now isolated except by sea. Its Asiatic suburbs were already in Turkish hands.[2]

It was now that Europe began to realize the menace presented by the Turks. Venice and Genoa, both worried about their colonies and their trade, began to explore possibilities of a general alliance against the infidel; but nothing came of their attempts. The Emperor John V journeyed to Italy to tell of the dangers that threatened and to try to hire Western mercenaries, for whom he could not pay. On his return he was forced, in 1373, to recognize the Sultan as his overlord, promising him a yearly tribute and military aid whenever required; and his son Manuel went as a hostage to Murad's court. John was a loyal vassal. He was rewarded when in 1374 his eldest son Andronicus plotted with Murad's son Sauji against their two fathers. It was Murad whose troops repressed the rebellion. When Andronicus revolted again,

holding Constantinople from 1376 to 1379, Manuel was able to
obtain from the Sultan sufficient help to enable him to restore
his father. But the price that he then paid was the obligation to
join the Turkish army in its conquest of the loyal, gallant, isolated
Greek city of Philadelphia, the last Byzantine possession in Asia,
apart from the Empire of Trebizond.[1]

Though the West was now seriously worried, abortively plan-
ning crusades, the only government to keep up a constant attack
on the Turks was the Order of the Hospital at Rhodes. But its
chief enemy was the emir of Aydin; and any curtailment of his
power was to the advantage of his rival the Ottoman Sultan.
Murad was thus free to advance into the Balkans. Hordes of
Turks from all over Anatolia were now pouring into Thrace,
with their families and often with their flocks. The urge to expand
continued. Serbia was still the chief power in the peninsula,
though it had been divided into two after Dushan's death in 1355.
Bulgaria had never recovered from its defeat by the Serbs at
Velbuzhd in 1330; but the Serbian policy of humiliating Bulgaria
merely eliminated what could have been a useful buffer-state. The
Bulgars did little to oppose the Turkish advance, except to send
a contingent to the large army which Vukashin, King of Southern
Serbia, sent towards Thrace in 1371. Vukashin had hoped to con-
tain the Turks; but he was a poor general. He allowed himself
to be surprised and routed by a far smaller Turkish army at
Chirmen on the river Maritsa. The victory of the Maritsa put
the greater part of Bulgaria, as well as Serbian Macedonia, into
Murad's hands. The Bulgarian king, John Shishman, had to accept
Murad as his overlord and send his daughter Thamar to the
Sultan's harem. Lazar Hrebeljanovich, the north Serbian prince
who now took over the whole Serbian kingdom, found that he
too had to accept the status of a vassal.[2]

Murad spent the later years of his reign in consolidating his
conquests. He organized the immigration of Turks into Europe.
The occupation of his newer European provinces could not be as

solid as it was in Anatolia or even in Thrace; but soon Turkish military fiefs were scattered among the Greek, Slav or Vlach villages, and Turkish beys and pashas dominated the countryside. By 1386 Murad's empire stretched as far west as Monastir, close to the borders of Albania, and as far north as Nish. The following year Thessalonica, which had been blockaded for four years, surrendered to him. Its prosperity was based on trade from the hinterland; it could not exist in isolation. Murad treated it gently, installing a Turkish governor but not interfering with its internal life.[1]

In 1381 the Sultan, who had by now reduced the Germiyan emirate to vassaldom, found it necessary to send an expedition against the Karaman emir; and he ordered his Balkan vassals to provide contingents. The shame felt by the proud Serbs at the demand was so great that King Lazar renounced his vassaldom. A swift Turkish attack that deprived him of the city of Nish forced him to submit again. But meanwhile he planned a pan-Balkan alliance against the invaders; and in 1387 the Serbs won their first and only victory over the Sultan's army on the banks of the river Toplitsa. Murad was not slow to take vengeance. After marching quickly on Bulgaria, where he stripped the two local kings, John Shishman of Tirnovo and John Sracimir of Vidin, of most of their territory, he crossed into southern Serbia, where a client prince, Constantine of Kiustendil, entertained him and provided a regiment to join his army. He then turned northward, to meet King Lazar on the plain of Kossovo, the Plain of Blackbirds.

Early in the morning of 15 June 1389, as the Sultan was dressing, a Serbian deserter was introduced into his tent, promising him information about the Christian positions. He approached the Sultan and suddenly leaned forward and stabbed him in the heart. He himself was promptly slain; and his sacrifice was useless. The Sultan's two sons were with the army. The elder, Bayezit, at once took command, suppressing the news of his father's death till the battle should be over. The Turks fought with perfect discipline, unlike the Christians who, when their first forceful attack could not be sustained, began to waver, while whispers of treachery spread through their ranks. By nightfall the Turkish victory was complete. King Lazar was taken prisoner and was slaughtered in the tent where Murad had died. Bayezit now proclaimed himself Sultan, and gave orders that his brother should be immediately strangled. There was to be no question of dividing the sovereignty.[1]

In the thirty years of his reign Murad I, by making brilliant use of his army and organization bequeathed to him by his father, had transformed a *ghazi* emirate into the strongest military power in south-eastern Europe. His own character was symbolic of the changed nature of his state. Unlike his father and his grandfather, he was fond of pomp and ceremony; he saw himself as an emperor. He was stern, even cruel, with a touch of cynicism inherited, perhaps, from his Greek ancestors. But he could be generous, and he was always just, and a stickler for discipline.

Bayezit, his heir, was also, it seems, the son of a Greek woman; but, unlike Nilüfer, she was probably a slave, called Gülchichek, or Rose-flower. He shared his father's taste for pomp; but he was more self-indulgent and hotter tempered, ungenerous to others and less successful as a disciplinarian. His swift reactions earned him the nickname of Yilderim, the thunderbolt; but he was not a great commander. His reign began brilliantly. The victory at Kossovo gave him complete mastery of the Balkans. It seemed likely that in a few years he would absorb the whole peninsula, including those areas in Greece and Albania into which the Turks had not yet penetrated. Lazar's son Stephen succeeded to the Serbian throne, but with the modest title of Despot, and as a vassal of the Sultan, to whom he gave his sister Maria in marriage. The Bulgarian kingdom of Tirnovo was extinguished in 1393. A Turkish army invaded the Peloponnese in 1394, reducing the local princes to vassaldom. In 1396 Bayezit planned to capture Constantinople itself; but as he marched up to the city walls news reached him of the crusade organized by King Sigismund of Hungary and knights from all over the West. He turned and hurried north, justifying his name of Thunderbolt, and fell upon the Western army at Nicopolis. The folly of the Westerners helped him to win an overwhelming victory, which enabled him then to annex the remaining Bulgarian kingdom of Vidin and to reduce the prince of Wallachia, across the Danube, to vassaldom. Having established his authority along the Danube frontier, he returned towards Constantinople but did not venture again to attack it, apparently because he had heard rumours that an armada was being fitted out by the Italian maritime powers.[1] Instead, he tried vainly to turn the co-Emperor John VII against his uncle Manuel II, with whom, in contrast to the usual Byzantine practice, he was sharing the throne in perfect amity. The only Western help that actually arrived at Byzantium was the handful of troops brought by Marshal Boucicault. They remained for a year in Constantinople with no achievements to their credit.[2] When they were gone, Bayezit, seeing how feeble were the Western efforts to provide aid, was ready to make another attempt against the Imperial city. He had recently completed the castle now known as Anadolu Hisar, on the Asiatic side of the narrows of the Bosphorus. In the spring of 1402 he sent a haughty message to the Emperor bidding him to surrender his capital. Manuel II was still touring Western Europe; but John VII replied to the Sultan's envoys, with pious courage: 'Tell your master that we are weak, but that we trust in God, Who can make us strong and can put down the mightiest from their seats. Let your master do as he pleases.'[3]

John's trust in God was the more confident because of news that was coming through from the east. Timur the Tartar, known to English drama as Tamurlane, was in fact a Turk but descended in the female line from the great Mongol clan of Jenghiz Khan. He was born at Kesh in Turkestan in 1336. By the end of the fourteenth century he had built up an empire that stretched from the borders of China and the Bay of Bengal to the Mediterranean Sea. In the brilliance of his military exploits he resembled Jenghiz Khan himself; and he resembled him, too, in his ruthless savagery. But he lacked the ability to organize his conquests that the Mongol Khans had shown. His death was to cause the disruption of his realm; but while he lived he was a fierce and formidable enemy. Though he was a pious Moslem there was nothing of the *ghazi* about him. He fought for his own aggrandizement, not for the Faith; the chief victims of his massacres were Moslems. He had long resented the existence of the Ottoman Sultanate, partly from jealousy that there should be any other Turkish potentate, and partly because he feared that it might endanger his control of his western provinces. Already in 1386 he had advanced into eastern Anatolia and defeated an army sent by the Anatolian emirs at Erzinjan. He had then retired, but threatened to return. Eight years later Bayezit, who had married a Germiyan princess and taken over most of her family's lands as her dowry, himself went to Erzinjan, to see to the defences of the peninsula. But in 1395 Timur appeared again and broke through to Sivas, massacring the population, including a son of Bayezit's, who had been governing the province. To Bayezit's relief, the Tartar army moved eastward, to sack Aleppo, Damascus and Baghdad. But the Ottoman Sultan's troubles were not ended; Timur was in closer touch with his enemies than he realized. When the Ottoman forces were assembled before the walls of Constantinople envoys from Timur arrived at the camp with a stern command that Bayezit should return to the Christian Emperor all the land that he had filched from him. Bayezit replied in terms of gross insult. He then raised the siege of Constantinople and transported his army to Anatolia. Timur's had already reached Sivas. The decisive battle took place at Ankara, on 25 July 1402. By his arrogance Bayezit let himself be put at a tactical disadvantage, while his soldiers were undisciplined and resentful of his parsimony. When Timur's vast force, strengthened by an elephant corps from India, launched a fierce attack, the Ottoman forces broke and fled, leaving Bayezit and his second son, Musa, captive in Timur's hands. The only regiment to stand its ground was a Serbian contingent led by the Despot Stephen. He was able to rescue the Sultan's eldest son, Suleiman, and one of Suleiman's brothers. A fourth brother, Mustafa, disappeared during the battle. The survivors fled to the safety of Anadolu Hisar, while Timur marched triumphantly through western Anatolia, sacking its cities, including the old Ottoman capital of Brusa, where the ladies of the Sultan's harem fell into his hands. He carried the captive Sultan with him in a litter, which later legend transformed into a golden cage. Bayezit was in fact treated with courtesy; and when he died, probably by his own hand, in March 1403, his son Musa was freed and allowed to convey the corpse to the family mausoleum at Brusa. Timur himself left Anatolia later that year and returned to his chief capital, Samarkand, where he died in 1405, aged seventy-two, while making plans for the conquest of China.[1]

This was the moment when, had the powers of Europe been able and willing to come swiftly together in a great coalition, the Ottoman threat to Christendom might have been broken for ever. But, though the dynasty might have perished, a Turkish problem still would have remained. Historians who blame the Christians for missing a heaven-sent opportunity forget that there were already hundreds of thousands of Turks settled firmly in Europe. It would have been a formidable task to subdue them and almost impossible to expel them. Indeed, Timur's intervention had added to their strength; for families and even whole tribes fled before his armies to the safety of the European provinces, the Genoese making a handsome profit out of the ferrying services that they provided. In about 1410, so the historian Ducas believed, there were more Turks in Europe than in Anatolia. Moreover, Bayezit had left large armed forces there to guard the frontiers and police the provinces. The Ottoman dynasty had been humili-

ated at Ankara, and their military machine had been weakened.
It had not been destroyed.[1]

Manuel II made the best use that he could of the time-honoured
Byzantine weapon of diplomacy. Bayezit's sons began to fight
for the throne. Suleiman, the eldest, proclaimed himself Sultan,
but he was insecure. To obtain Manuel's help he retroceded to
him Thessalonica and several towns on the coast of Thrace, and
promised several towns in Asia which he did not in fact control.
He sent his youngest brother, Kasim, as a hostage to Constantinople and in return was given as a bride the Emperor's niece, the
illegitimate daughter of Theodore I, Despot of the Morea. He
defeated and killed his brother Isa in 1405; but he was a neurotic
man, given to long bouts of drunkenness and lethargy. His
soldiers lost their respect for him and transferred their allegiance
to his brother Musa, who came forward as the champion of Islam
against the pro-Byzantine policy of Suleiman. In 1409 Suleiman
was deserted by his troops and murdered as he tried to flee to
Constantinople. Musa succeeded as Sultan. He brutally ravaged
Serbia for having supported his brother. He recaptured and
sacked Thessalonica, which had been defended for the Christians
by Suleiman's son, Orhan, who was taken prisoner and blinded.
Though defeated in a sea-battle he brought his land-forces up against
the walls of Constantinople. But a younger brother, Mehmet, who
had been restoring Ottoman rule in Anatolia, now marched against
him, and, with the help of the Byzantines and the Serbs and of
Turkish regiments who were disgusted by Musa's brutality, he
defeated and slew his brother in 1413 and himself became Sultan.[2]

Mehmet, whom his contemporaries surnamed Chelebi, a word
best translated here as 'gentleman', had shown himself a fine
soldier but was by temperament a man of peace. He returned
Thessalonica and other towns annexed by Musa to Manuel, with
whom he remained all his life on terms of cordial friendship. He
was forced into an inconclusive war with Venice in 1416 and one
with Hungary in 1419; and he had to suppress the rebellion of a

man who claimed to be his brother Mustafa and to have survived the battle of Ankara. Most of his time was spent in building fortresses along his frontiers and in consolidating his administration, and in beautifying the cities of his empire. The exquisite Green Mosque at Brusa is a lasting memorial to this kindly and cultivated potentate. He died of apoplexy at Adrianople in December, 1421.[1]

Mehmet's eldest son, Murad, was acting as his father's viceroy in Anatolia. The news of the Sultan's death was suppressed till he could arrive at Adrianople and take over the government. Like Mehmet Murad was a man of peace by temperament. He was said to have belonged to a dervish order, and he longed to retire to lead a life of meditation.[2] But he was a conscientious ruler; and circumstances demanded of him that he should be a soldier and administrator. The pretender Mustafa was still at large; and Murad suspected that he was obtaining help from Constantinople. He sent to Manuel to complain of this and to ask that the friendship that had existed between the Emperor and his father should be continued. Manuel would gladly have agreed; but he was old and tired and let himself be overruled by his son, John VIII, who, with the support of the Byzantine Senate, believed that trouble could profitably be stirred up within the Ottoman dynasty. John therefore demanded that two of the Sultan's brothers be sent to Constantinople as hostages. Murad not unnaturally refused the suggestion, and, having disposed of Mustafa, he laid siege to Constantinople in June 1422. But the walls were too strong for an army without siege engines; and John's calculations had some justification. A revolt broke out in Anatolia, nominally under Murad's thirteen-year-old brother Mustafa but animated by the jealous Germiyan and Karaman emirs. Murad abandoned the siege to deal with the rebels, then contented himself with sending an army to ravage the Peloponnese.[3]

He was allowed little of the peace that he desired. In 1428 he had to beat off an invasion from across the Danube, led by the Kings of Hungary and Poland. In 1430 his troops entered Janina in Epirus. That same year he captured Thessalonica from the Venetians, who had held it for seven years. Serbia, where George Brankovich had succeeded his uncle Stephen Lazarovich as Despot in 1427, was reduced to a closer vassalage, and the Despot was forced to break off an alliance with the Hungarians, to whom he had ceded Belgrade. He was also told to give his daughter Mara as a bride to the Sultan; his delay in doing so provoked a Turkish expedition against him. Murad mistrusted the Despot. In 1440 he led another army against him and destroyed the fortress of Semendria on the Danube which he himself had given the Serbs permission to build. He went on to besiege Belgrade; but its defences were too strong for him. He was forced to retire.[1]

The check before Belgrade encouraged Murad's enemies. The Pope, delighted with the success of the Council of Florence, organized a crusade. King Ladislas of Hungary eagerly welcomed it. The Serbian Despot agreed to help the Hungarians. The leading Albanian chieftain, George Castriota, surnamed Scanderbeg, declared war on the Sultan; and the Karaman emir was persuaded to attack him in Asia.[2] While Murad was busy punishing the Karamanians, the Hungarian army with its allies, under the royal bastard John Corvinus Hunyadi, Voyevod of Transylvania, crossed the Danube and swept the Turks out of the Serbian despotate. Murad hurried back in full force to Europe and marched up to the Danube. But he was not eager to risk a battle; and he found King Ladislas in a similar mood. The Hungarians had been joined by troops that the Pope had recruited in the West, under the command of his legate, Cardinal Julian Cesarini; but Ladislas had hoped for more. He and Murad agreed to meet at Szegedin, in June 1444. There each of them swore, Murad on the Koran and Ladislas on the Gospels, to observe a truce for ten years, during which time neither of them would attempt to cross the Danube. Hunyadi, who disapproved of the truce, refused to be involved.

Murad now felt that he could retire to lead the life of contemplation that he had long desired. But no sooner had he withdrawn his army from the frontier and announced his plans for his abdication than news came that the King of Hungary had crossed the Danube and was marching through Bulgaria. Cardinal Cesarini had pronounced that an oath sworn to an infidel was invalid; and the opportunity seemed too good to miss. The perjury shocked the Orthodox Christians as well as the Turks. The Emperor John VIII refused to offer help. George Brankovich of Serbia withdrew his forces and prevented Scanderbeg from joining the allies. Hunyadi followed the expedition reluctantly; and his advice over strategy was ignored by the Cardinal. Murad, who had been setting things in order in Anatolia in preparation for his retirement, hurried back with his army northward. On 11 November 1444 he fell upon the Christians at Varna, with a force three times the size of theirs. They were routed. King Ladislas and the Cardinal were killed. Only Hunyadi and his regiments escaped from the slaughter. The victory restored the Sultan's control of the country up to the Danube.[1]

Soon afterwards Murad formally abdicated in favour of his twelve-year-old son Mehmet and retired to Manisa. But again he was allowed no peace. His ministers and the army were dissatisfied with their new ruler, who was precocious, opinionated and haughty; while there was still trouble along the European frontier. Public opinion and governmental necessity brought Murad back to the throne. Scanderbeg was undefeated in Albania and Turkish expeditions against him continued to fail. In 1446 Murad sent an army into Greece, which ravaged the Peloponnese. In 1448, Hunyadi, now Regent of Hungary, resumed the offensive with an army of Hungarians, Wallachians, Bohemians and German mercenaries. He arranged to meet Scanderbeg on the plain of Kossovo. But before the Albanians could reach him a huge Turkish army suddenly appeared and annihilated his forces. He himself only escaped with the help of his German and Bohemian troops. The disaster, following so soon upon the disaster at Varna, crippled the military power of Hungary for a generation. The Hungarian flag still flew over Belgrade; but there could be no more expeditions south of the Danube. When the crisis came Hunyadi could do nothing to help Constantinople. In all the Balkan peninsula only in the Albanian mountains was there any constant opposition to Turkish rule.[1]

Murad had been equally successful in Anatolia. In these latter years of his reign he absorbed the emirates of Aydin and Germiyan and the Karamanians were cowed. Other autonomous princes, such as the emirs of Sinope and Attalia, acknowledged Ottoman supremacy. The Emperor of Trebizond was as powerless and deferential as his brother-in-law at Constantinople.[2] Internally the Ottoman empire was orderly and prosperous. Murad's chief military reform was to reorganize the Janissary regiments, hitherto composed of captured slave-boys. He now set up a regular system by which any Christian family, Greek, Slav, Vlach or Armenian, was obliged if required to hand over a male child to the Sultan's officials. These boys were brought up at their own schools as strict Moslems. Some with special talents were used as technicians or civil servants; but most of them became highly trained soldiers, who formed the Sultan's crack regiment of Guards. They had their own barracks and were forbidden to marry, so that their whole lives should be dedicated to the Sultan's service.[3] In spite of this bitterly resented imposition and in spite of his occasional demands for mass conversion to Islam, Murad was not unpopular with his Christian subjects, who found him scrupulous and just. He had many Christian friends and was said to be greatly influenced by his beautiful Serbian wife, to whom he was devoted. Indeed, to many Greeks life under his well-ordered and usually tolerant rule seemed easier than in the anxious, tormented remnants of the old Christian Empire.[4]

Murad died at Adrianople on 13 February 1451, leaving a splendid heritage to his successor.

CHAPTER III

THE EMPEROR AND THE SULTAN

The late Emperor John VIII had been the eldest of six brothers, the sons of Manuel II and his Empress Helena, the daughter of a Serbian prince with lands in Macedonia and his Greek wife. Next to John in age was Theodore; then came Andronicus, Constantine, Demetrius and Thomas. Theodore and Andronicus predeceased him. The latter was sickly and insignificant. His only important action had been the sale of Thessalonica to the Venetians in 1423. He then retired to the monastery of the Pantocrator at Constantinople, under the monastic name of Acacius, and died there in March 1428.[1] Theodore was more remarkable. He inherited his father's intellectual tastes and was a brilliant mathematician. But he was moody and neurotic, energetic and ambitious at one moment and at the next eager to leave the world for the holy peace of a monastery. He had succeeded his uncle Theodore I as Despot of the Morea in 1407, while he was still a child; and for several years his father had spent much of his time in the Despotate trying to restore its order and building the great fortifications known as the Hexamilion which stretched across the Isthmus of Corinth, only to see them destroyed by the Turks in a raid in 1423.[2] Theodore was a good ruler in so far as his moods and jealousies allowed. In 1421 he married an Italian princess, Cleope Malatesta, a cousin of Pope Martin V. Her life was not easy, owing to her husband's temperament. She joined the Greek Church, to the fury of the Pope, who blamed her husband for it; but her conversion seems in fact to have been willing. She and Theodore maintained an austere but highly cultured court at Mistra, though its lustre diminished after her death in 1433. Its main star was Plethon, who was devoted to them both. As being next in age

48

II*a*   The Emperor John VIII Palaeologus

II*b*   Sultan Mehmet II as a young man

Overleaf: I   The Siege of Constantinople by the Turks

to John, Theodore considered himself to be heir to the Empire; and in 1443, when it was clear that John would have no children, he exchanged his Despotate for the lordship of the city of Selymbria, in Thrace, some forty miles from the capital, to be at hand when John should die. But fate cheated him. He fell ill of the plague in the summer of 1448 and died in July, three months before the Emperor.[1] His only child was a daughter, Helena, who had been married ten years previously to King John II of Cyprus.[2]

The two youngest brothers, Demetrius and Thomas, were unpraiseworthy characters. Demetrius was restless, ambitious and unscrupulous. He saw himself as the champion of the Greek faith against the Latinizing tendencies of his brother John, whom he had accompanied to the Council of Florence. He had married a lady of the illustrious Greco-Bulgarian family of the Asen, against the wishes of his family and hers. He had friends at the Turkish court and in 1442 had attempted to attack Constantinople with the help of Turkish soldiers; and the Emperor had only been saved by the hasty arrival of his brother Constantine with reinforcements. Demetrius was forgiven and was allowed to stay on in Constantinople. When his brother Theodore died he inherited Selymbria.[3]

Thomas was staider but weaker. As a young man he had been sent in 1430 to help his brothers in the Morea. There he had married Catherine Zaccaria, heiress of the last Frankish prince of Achaea, and had been given an appanage out of the former lands of her family. He followed with fairly constant loyalty the lead of his brother Constantine.[4]

Constantine was the ablest of the brothers. He had been born in 1404 and as a youth had been given Selymbria and the neighbouring Thracian towns as his appanage. In 1427 he went to the Peloponnese, to help John VIII conquer the last Frankish lands there. His presence had been all the more necessary as his brother Theodore was announcing his intention of retiring into a monastery. Theodore soon thought better of it; but meanwhile, in

March 1428, Constantine made a politic marriage with the niece of Carlo Tocco, lord of Epirus and much of western Greece. As a dowry he obtained the Tocco lands in the Peloponnese; and though the young princess Magdalena, rechristened Theodora on her marriage, died childless two years later, Constantine retained her lands and made of them a base from which he planned to conquer the rest of the peninsula. His relations with Theodore were often strained. Theodore was particularly hurt when John VIII summoned Constantine to govern Constantinople during his absence in Italy for the Councils, as that indicated that John intended to make Constantine his heir. Amity was not restored until Constantine exchanged his Thracian possessions and the claim of succession to the Empire for Mistra and the Despotate. Thenceforward Constantine was established as Despot at Mistra, with Thomas as Despot at Clarenza on the west coast to back him. The conquest of the Peloponnese, with the exception of the four Venetian cities of Argos, Nauplia, Croton and Modon, had been completed in 1433. Now Constantine planned to annex Attica and Boeotia. In 1444, encouraged by news of Hunyadi's success in Serbia, he marched northward from Corinth, while his ablest general, John Cantacuzenus, crossed from Patras into Phocis. Soon all Greece up to the Pindus range was in his power, except for the Acropolis of Athens, whose Duke, Nerio II, cowered there calling for help from the Turks. Unfortunately the Turks were soon able to provide help; for, while Constantine was sweeping through Boeotia, Sultan Murad won his great victory at Varna. In 1446 the Sultan himself led an army into Greece. Constantine retired to the Hexamilion, which he had refortified. But Murad had brought heavy artillery with him. After a fortnight of steady bombardment his soldiers broke through the wall. Constantine and Thomas had barely time to escape with their lives. Their troops, especially their Albanian mercenaries, behaved with a marked lack of loyalty and courage. The Sultan destroyed the wall once more and marched on Patras and Clarenza, slaughtering the population as he passed by. He then retired after extracting new promises of vassaldom and an annual tribute from the Despots.[1]

The damage done to the Despotate and the loss of life had been vast. Constantine could no longer embark upon imperialistic ventures. Instead, he sought to protect himself by a network of foreign alliances. He had been married for a second time in 1441. His bride was Catherine, daughter of Dorino Gattilusi, Prince of Lesbos, of a Genoese dynasty whose founder, Francesco, had married the sister of the Emperor John V and which had become thoroughly Graecized. But the bride died childless the following year. He now sought a new wife, with a dowry and useful connections. He made an offer for the hand of Isabella Orsini, sister of the lord of Taranto. His ambassadors at Naples made inquiries about an Infanta of Portugal. A Venetian ambassador suggested that a daughter of the Doge, Francesco Foscari, might be available. But no princess would come and share his precarious throne; nor was it possible to make a firm alliance with any Western power. Meanwhile his faithful secretary and friend, George Phrantzes, who was suspicious of Westerners, bustled off to Trebizond to secure for his master the hand of a daughter of the Grand Comnenus. Her father was politically weak, it was true, but he was still rich, with his silver-mines and the trade that passed through his capital. The girl would probably bring a good dowry; and the princesses of Trebizond were famed for their beauty. Her aunt, John VIII's Empress, was held to be the loveliest woman of her time, though de la Brocquière, who saw her, deplored her excessive and, he thought, unnecessary use of paint. But Phrantzes failed in his mission.[2] Constantine sent his niece Helena, Thomas's eldest daughter, to marry the son of George Brankovich, Despot of Serbia. But even George was too prudent to provoke the Turks by making a pact with the Despots of the Morea.[3]

When John VIII died Constantine was at Mistra, but Thomas

was on his way to visit Constantinople. His arrival there on 13 November 1448, exactly two weeks after the Emperor's death, was timely; for their brother Demetrius, hurrying from his appanage at Selymbria, had already claimed the throne. He hoped for the support of the enemies of church-union. But in the absence of a crowned Emperor constitutional practice lodged the sovereignty with the crowned Empress. The aged Empress-Mother Helena used her authority to insist on the proclamation of Constantine, her eldest surviving son; and public opinion supported her. Demetrius's hopes faded; and when Thomas appeared he admitted himself to be beaten and joined in acknowledging Constantine. Phrantzes, who was in Constantinople where one of his young sons had just died, was sent by the Empress to announce her son's accession to Sultan Murad, who graciously gave his approval. Two high officials, Alexius Lascaris Philanthropenus and Manuel Palaeologus Iagrus, went to Mistra with the Imperial crown. There, on 6 January 1449, Constantine was crowned in the cathedral by the local Metropolitan.[1] It was the first Imperial coronation for a thousand years, apart from the Nicaean period, not to take place in Constantinople and the first not to be performed by a Patriarch. Though no one was to challenge Constantine's rule, there was some doubt over the legality of the ceremony. But it was thought necessary that he should be given authority as quickly as possible; while a coronation at Constantinople might have been difficult to arrange, as the actual Patriarch, Gregory Mammas, was being boycotted by most of his clergy.[2]

Constantine arrived at the Imperial capital on 12 March, having travelled with his suite from the Morea in Catalan galleys. A few days later he invested his brothers Demetrius and Thomas as joint Despots of the Morea. Demetrius was to have Mistra and the south-eastern half of the peninsula, and Thomas the north-western half, with Clarenza and Patras. At a solemn ceremony attended by the Empress-Mother and the high officials of the

Empire the two brothers swore allegiance to the Emperor and eternal friendship with each other. Though they were frequently to break their vows of friendship their departure left Constantine master of Constantinople.[1]

The Emperor was now nearly forty-five years of age. We have no full description of his appearance. He seems to have been tallish and spare, with the strong, regular features of his family and its dark colouring. He had no particular interest in intellectual matters, in philosophy or theology, though he had been friendly with Plethon at Mistra, and his last action before he left for Constantinople had been to confirm Plethon's sons in the properties which their father had been given. He had shown himself to be a good soldier and a competent administrator. Above all, he had integrity. He never behaved dishonourably. He had shown generosity and patience in dealing with his difficult brothers. His friends and officials were devoted to him, even if they sometimes disagreed with him; and he had the gift of inspiring admiration and affection among all his subjects. His arrival at Constantinople had been welcomed with genuine rejoicing.[2]

He needed this affection, in the embittered and melancholy city to which he had come. The hatred against the official union of the Church with Rome was unabated. Constantine considered himself bound by his brother's commitments at Florence. But at first he took no drastic action. This was probably due to his mother's influence; for he greatly relied upon her. Her death, on 23 March 1450, was a cruel loss to him. He tried to surround himself with ministers of all parties. The senior minister, the Megadux, Grand Admiral of the Fleet, was Lucas Notaras, who was opposed to union but not fanatical. John Cantacuzenus, an intimate friend of his Peloponnesian days and a strenuous advocate of union, was made Stratopedarch. The Grand Logothete, Metochites, and the Protostrator, Demetrius Cantacuzenus, seem to have doubted the wisdom of union but were ready to accept whatever policy the Emperor might ordain. His secretary Phrantzes, who was probably his closest confidant, shared their view.[1] The Patriarch Gregory was disappointed at the lack of support given to him by the new Emperor. In August 1451, he retired to Rome where he was better appreciated and where he poured out complaints against the lukewarm Imperial regime.[2]

Constantine was still searching for a wife. Probably at his mother's suggestion, to placate the anti-Latin feelings of his people, he decided to find one in the Orthodox world. In 1450 the faithful Phrantzes was sent eastward again, to the courts of Georgia and Trebizond. He considered the Georgian princess very suitable. But he was taken aback when her father, King George, announced that in his country it was usual for husbands to give dowries to their wives, not wives to their husbands. However, His Majesty went on to say that there is no accounting for the habits of different races. After all, he pointed out, in Britain one woman often has several husbands and one man several wives. He promised to be generous on this occasion and even offered to adopt Phrantzes's own daughter.

While he was in Georgia Phrantzes heard of the death of Sultan Murad; and when he arrived at Trebizond and discussed the news with the Emperor John, he was told that the Sultan's Christian widow, Mara of Serbia, who was the niece of the Empress of Trebizond, had been sent home to her father, loaded with gifts and honours. Phrantzes had a brilliant idea. He wrote at once to Constantine to say that there was the right bride for him. The Sultana was still young; she was wealthy; and she had been very popular at the Turkish court and was said to have an influence over her step-son, the new Sultan. He pointed out that it would not be undignified for the Emperor to marry the widow of an infidel ruler; for Constantine's step grandmother, the Emperor John's second wife, had been the wife of a Turcoman lord and had even borne him children before she married the Emperor. Phrantzes hurried home to press his suggestion. The Emperor was interested, but he complained that all his ministers gave him different advice. His mother, who could have decided it for him, was dead; and his intimate friend John Cantacuzenus had just died. However, the Sultana herself ruined the scheme. She had vowed that if ever she escaped from the infidel harem she would devote the rest of her life to good works in celibacy. Constantine then chose the Georgian princess. An embassy was sent to Georgia to fix up the contract and to bring the bride to Constantinople. But there were delays. Before she could leave her home she learnt that it was too late.[1]

The Emperor of Trebizond had expected Phrantzes to rejoice with him over the news of Sultan Murad's death. Phrantzes took the opposite view. Murad, he pointed out, had been fundamentally a man of peace who no longer wanted the strain and effort of warfare. But the new Sultan was known to have been an enemy of the Christians from his early childhood; he would certainly seek to attack and destroy the Christian Empires, Trebizond as well as Constantinople. Phrantzes's fears were shared by his own Imperial master. Reports from the agents kept by the Byzantines at the Turkish Court gave ample warning of the danger.[2]

The warnings were justified. The new Sultan, Mehmet II, was now aged nineteen. He had been born at Adrianople on 30 March 1432. His childhood had been unhappy. His mother, Huma Hatun, had been a slave-girl, almost certainly Turkish, though later legend, not entirely discouraged by Mehmet himself, transformed her into a high-born Frankish lady. His father paid little attention to him, preferring his sons by his nobler wives. He spent his early boyhood quietly at Adrianople with his mother and his nurse, a formidable and pious Turkish lady known as Daye Hatun. But his eldest brother, Ahmet, died suddenly at Amasia in 1437; and the second, Ala ed-Din, was mysteriously murdered in that same city six years later. Mehmet was left at the age of eleven heir to the throne and the only living prince of the Ottoman dynasty apart from the Sultan and a distant cousin, Sultan Suleiman's grandson Orhan, who was in exile at Constantinople. Murad summoned the boy to the Court and was shocked to see how his education had been neglected. An army of tutors, headed by an illustrious Kurdish professor, Ahmet Kurani, was hired to instruct him. They did their work thoroughly. Mehmet was well trained in the sciences and in philosophy and well-read in Islamic and Greek literature. Besides his native Turkish he learnt to be fluent in Greek, Arabic, Latin, Persian and Hebrew. Soon his father began to initiate him in the arts of government.[1]

Mehmet was aged twelve when Murad, after signing his truce with King Ladislas, decided to retire from active life, leaving his son in charge of his empire. First it was necessary to suppress disorders in Anatolia; and Murad was still engaged there when news came of the Christian advance on Varna. The vizier, Halil Pasha, summoned him hastily back to Europe, all the more eagerly as he was alarmed by the young Mehmet's behaviour. Murad had intended that his son should be under the tutelage of Halil, who was an old and trusted friend. But the boy at once showed a determination to go his own way. Hardly had Murad left for Anatolia than there was a crisis over a heretical Persian dervish whom Mehmet befriended but whom Halil, the son and grandson of a vizier and a Moslem of the old school, strongly deplored. Mehmet was forced to surrender the heretic to the Chief Mufti, Fahreddin, who incited the populace to burn the wretch. So anxious was the Mufti to see that the fire was properly stoked that he came too close and singed his own beard.[2]

Nevertheless when Murad returned from his victory at Varna he would not be deflected from his determination to retire; and Mehmet was left as ruler of the empire, under Halil's tutelage. Once again the experiment was disastrous. There were wars on the Albanian and Greek frontiers. Mehmet was furious with his guardians when they rejected an impracticable scheme of his for attacking Constantinople. His arrogant manners and his unapproachability offended both the Court and the populace. But it was the army that showed the greatest discontent. In order to prevent an open military revolt Halil persuaded Murad to return to Adrianople and resume the government. His arrival there in the autumn of 1446 was greeted with general rejoicing. Mehmet was sent to Manisa, the scene of his father's interrupted retirement.[1]

It is possible that Murad thought of disinheriting Mehmet; for he had a high-born wife, the daughter of Ibrahim, the Chandaroghlu emir, of a family already connected to the Ottoman house, and she soon was to bear him a son.[2] But he thought better of it. After two years of exile Mehmet was summoned back to take part in the campaign against Hunyadi that resulted in the victory of Kossovo. Earlier that year a slave-girl, Gülbehar, daughter of Abdulla, probably an Albanian convert to Islam, bore him a son, Bayezit.[3] Murad disapproved of the liaison. In 1450 he ordered Mehmet to marry the daughter of a wealthy Turcoman prince, Suleiman Zulkadroghlu, lord of Malatia. The marriage was pompously celebrated. But Mehmet never cared for Sitt Hatun, this bride who had been imposed on him. She spent the rest of her days neglected and childless in the palace harem at Adrianople.[4]

For the remainder of his father's reign Mehmet was treated with greater friendliness. He appeared now and then at the Court and accompanied the Sultan on one or two campaigns. But he was often back in his palace at Manisa. He was there when his mother died in August 1450; and he saw that she was honourably buried at Brusa, with an inscription that barely mentions Murad. He was there again when Murad himself died of a fit of apoplexy at Adrianople on 2 February 1451.[5]

No one doubted that Mehmet was heir to the throne. A sealed letter sent to him by Halil Pasha brought him hurrying from Manisa. By the time that he had crossed the Dardanelles he knew that his succession was not to be disputed; so he paused for two days at Gallipoli while a fitting reception was arranged for him at Adrianople. He arrived there on 18 February. The Grand Vizier and all the high officials of the state rode out to meet him; at one league from the gates they dismounted, in order to walk back to the city in procession ahead of his horse. On reaching the palace he held a reception. His father's ministers stood nervously in the background until he told Shehab ed-Din, the Chief Eunuch, to bid them take their usual places. He then confirmed the Grand Vizier in his post. The Second Vizier, Ishak Pasha, who had been Murad's closest friend, was appointed Governor of Anatolia, a position of great dignity and importance but one that would remove him from his ally Halil. Saruja Pasha and Zaganos Pasha, both of them devoted to Murad but less friendly with Halil, were appointed assistant viziers, together with Shehab ed-Din. Soon afterwards his father's widow, the daughter of Ibrahim Bey, came to offer her condolences on Murad's death and her congratulations on Mehmet's succession. While he was giving her a gracious welcome his servants hastened to the harem to smother her young son Ahmet in his bath. The bereaved mother was eventually ordered to marry Ishak Pasha and retired with him to Anatolia. As Phrantzes was to be informed at Trebizond, Murad's Christian widow, Mara of Serbia, was sent back with every honour to her father.[1]

Having established his administration and tidied his palace, the young Sultan settled down to plan his policy. The outside world only knew of him as an inexperienced youth whose early career had been lamentable. But those who saw him now were impressed by him. He was handsome, of middle height but strongly built. His face was dominated by a pair of piercing eyes, under arched eyebrows, and a thin hooked nose that curved over a mouth with full red lips. In later life his features reminded men of a parrot about to eat ripe cherries. His manner was dignified and rather distant, except when he had drunk overmuch; for he shared his family's impious liking for alcohol. But he would always be gracious, even cordial, to anyone whose scholarship he respected, and he enjoyed the company of artists. He was notoriously secretive. The unhappy events of his childhood had taught him to trust no one. It was impossible to tell what he might be thinking. He would never make himself beloved; he had no desire for popularity. But his intelligence, his energy and his determination commanded respect. No one who knew him could venture to hope that this formidable young man would ever allow himself to be deflected from the tasks that he had set himself to perform; of which the first and the greatest was the conquest of Constantinople.[1]

CHAPTER IV

THE PRICE OF WESTERN AID

The Emperor of Trebizond was not alone in sighing with relief when he heard of Sultan Murad's death. In the West a similar happy optimism was felt. Ambassadors who had been recently to Murad's court had reported on the fiasco of Mehmet's earlier tenure of the throne. This incapable young man was unlikely, they thought, to prove a menace to Christendom. The illusion was confirmed by the amiable readiness of the Sultan to confirm treaties that his father had made. In the late summer of 1451, when the news of his accession had penetrated through Europe, a stream of embassies arrived at Adrianople. On 10 September Mehmet received a Venetian mission and formally renewed the peace-treaty which his father had signed with the Republic five years previously. Ten days later he signed a pact with John Hunyadi's representatives, arranging for a truce which should last for three years. The Ragusan embassy was received with special favour as it brought an offer to raise the tribute paid by the city annually to the Sultan by five hundred pieces of gold. Envoys from the Grand Master of the Knights at Rhodes, from the Prince of Wallachia and from the lord of Lesbos and the government of Chios, all of whom came laden with handsome presents, were given assurances of good-will. The Serbian Despot not only received his daughter back but was permitted to reoccupy some towns in the upper Struma valley. Even the Emperor Constantine's ambassadors, who had been the first to arrive and who came in some trepidation, being better informed of the Sultan's character, were cheered by their reception. The Sultan not only swore on the Koran before them that he would respect the integrity of Byzantine territory but he also promised to pay the Emperor the

annual sum of three thousand aspers from the revenues of some
Greek towns in the lower Struma valley. The towns legally belonged to the Ottoman prince Orhan; and the money was to be
used to maintain him so long as he was kept in honourable deten-
tion at Constantinople. Even the monastic community of Mount
Athos, which had prudently acknowledged Ottoman suzerainty
after Murad's capture of Thessalonica, was assured that there
would be no interference with its autonomy.[1]

It appeared that the new Sultan was under the influence of
Murad's old minister, Halil, who was known to have shared his
master's taste for peace. Byzantine diplomats had carefully cultivated Halil's friendship. It was gratifying to find their efforts
rewarded. But shrewder observers could have realized that Mehmet's pacific gestures were not genuine. It suited him to have
peace round his frontiers while he planned his great campaign.
Halil's influence was not as great as the Christians thought. He
had never really been forgiven by Mehmet for the part that he
had played in 1446. His ally, Ishak Pasha, was away in Anatolia.
Zaganos Pasha, now Second Vizier, had been on cold terms with
him for some years and was a close friend of Shehab ed-Din, the
eunuch who was Mehmet's intimate and an advocate of war.[2]

The inner politics of the Ottoman court were, however, unknown to the European world. Western Christendom was delighted to hear from Venice and from Budapest of the Sultan's
amiability. After the humiliations of Nicopolis and Varna no
Western potentate was anxious to have to go out again to fight
the Turks. It was far more agreeable to believe that there was no
need for it. Indeed, none of them was in a position to take action;
all had distractions at home. In central Europe Frederick III of
Habsburg was far too busily occupied in arranging for his
Imperial coronation at Rome, which was to take place in 1452
and for which he had sold the liberties of the German Church
fourteen years before. He had moreover to make good a claim
to the thrones of Bohemia and Hungary and so would never

dream of co-operating with John Hunyadi, Regent for his rival, the boy Ladislas V. King Charles VII of France had enough to do in trying to rehabilitate his country after the strain of the Hundred Years' War; and he had a dangerously powerful vassal in his cousin, Philip the Good, Duke of Burgundy, whose lands and whose wealth were far greater than his own. Philip fancied himself as a crusader; but, even if he could have risked absenting himself from his duchy, he remembered all too well the miserable story of the captivity of his father, John, taken prisoner by the Turks at Nicopolis. England, weakened by the disasters of the French wars and ruled by a saintly but half-imbecile king, was unlikely to spare soldiers for foreign adventures. No help nor even any interest could be expected from such distant monarchs as the Scandinavian kings or the king of Scotland; and the kings of Castile and Portugal had infidel enemies to fight nearer home. The only monarch to pay any attention to the Levant was Alfonso V of Aragon, who had taken over the throne of Naples in 1443. He professed himself eager to lead an expedition to the East. But as his openly expressed ambition was to make himself Emperor of Constantinople his offers of help were suspect and hardly practicable.[1]

Even at the Papal court there was a hopeful belief that the new Sultan was negligible. But there the Greek refugees pressed for action, before he should acquire experience in government. Their spokesman was an Italian, Francesco Filelfo of Tolentino, who had married the daughter of the Greek professor John Chrysoloras, and whose mother-in-law lived at Constantinople. He wrote a passionate appeal to King Charles of France, choosing him because France in the past had taken the lead in the Crusades. He urged the King to organize an army swiftly and to rush it to the East. The Turks would be unable to put up any resistance, he maintained. But King Charles made no response.[2] The Pope, Nicholas V, who had succeeded Eugenius IV in 1447, was a scholar and a man of peace, whose noblest achievement was the foundation of the Vatican Library. His friendship for Bessarion, whose learning he greatly admired, made him sympathetic with the Greek cause. But he did not know to what secular potentate he could turn for support; nor was he eager to send help to a city which still refused to implement the union signed by its Emperor on its behalf at Florence.[1]

The Emperor Constantine was well aware of this difficulty. In the summer of 1451 he sent an ambassador to the West, Andronicus Bryennius Leontaris, who went first to Venice to arrange permission for the Emperor to recruit archers in Crete for his army. He then went on to Rome with a friendly message from Constantine to the Pope and with a letter addressed to the Pope written by a committee of the anti-unionists. They called themselves a Synaxis, as the word *synod* could not be legally employed by a body acting without the Patriarch. The Emperor had put pressure on them to send this appeal, apparently on the advice of Lucas Notaras. The Synaxis proposed the holding of a new council, this time at Constantinople, which should be properly oecumenical, with the Eastern Patriarchates fully represented and the Roman delegation reduced in numbers. It was signed by many anti-unionists, though George Scholarius Gennadius refused to subscribe, believing that no good would come of it. He was right. The Pope was not prepared to set aside the Council of Florence nor to condone the dissidents' complaints. It was particularly unfortunate that at this moment, probably while Bryennius was still in Rome, that the Patriarch Gregory Mammas arrived from Constantinople in voluntary exile. His complaints did not incline Nicholas to be conciliatory. No answer was sent to the Synaxis; but the Emperor was informed that while the delicacies of his position were realized at Rome he clearly exaggerated the difficulty of enforcing union. Firm action was needed. The Patriarch must be recalled and reinstated. Greeks who refused to understand the decree of union should be sent to Rome for re-education. The Pope's crucial sentence read: 'If you, with your nobles and the people of Constantinople, accept the decree of union, you will find Us and Our venerable brothers, the Cardinals of the holy Roman Church, ever eager to support your honour and your empire. But if you and your people refuse to accept the decree, you will force Us to take such measures as are necessary for your salvation and Our honour.'[1]

Such an ultimatum was not likely to ease the Emperor's task. Instead, it strengthened Gennadius's hold over the opposition. A few months later an envoy reached Constantinople from the Hussite Church of Prague, a man called Constantine Platris and surnamed the Englishman, perhaps because he was the son of a Lollard refugee from England. He made a public declaration of faith amid popular enthusiasm; and he was sent back to Prague with a letter strongly attacking Papal pretensions, signed by the leading members of the Synaxis, including Gennadius. Bitterness in the city increased at the very time when happy illusions about Mehmet's incompetence had finally to be abandoned.[2]

The Emperor himself was to blame for a worsening of the relations between the Empire and the Turks. In the autumn of 1451 the Karamanian Emir, Ibrahim Bey, believing, like the princes of the West, in the new Sultan's incompetence, organized a concerted rising of the recently subdued emirates of Aydin and Germiyan and the emirate of Menteshe against him. Young princes of each dynasty were sent to claim their family thrones, while Ibrahim himself invaded Ottoman territory. The local Ottoman commander, Isa Bey, was lazy and ineffectual; and Ishak, as governor of Anatolia, begged the Sultan to come himself to crush the rebellion. His prompt arrival in Asia had its effect. Resistance crumbled. Ibrahim Bey soon sent to ask forgiveness, while Ishak led a regiment to take over the Menteshe territory. But while the Sultan was on his way back to Europe he was faced with unrest in his Janissary regiments, who demanded higher pay. Mehmet yielded to some of their demands, but he degraded their commander, and he attached to the regiments

III   Straits of the Bosphorus
Anadolu Hisar is on the left of the picture and Rumeli Hisar on the right

IV   Sultan Mehmet II

large numbers of kennelmen and falconers from the Chief Hunts-
man's department, on whose loyalty he could rely.[1]

Encouraged, apparently, by the Sultan's difficulties, Constantine
sent envoys to him to complain that the moneys promised for the
maintenance of Prince Orhan had not been paid, and to hint that
it was well to remember that there was an Ottoman pretender at
the Byzantine court. When the embassy reached the Sultan, probably at Brusa, Halil Pasha was embarrassed and angry. He knew
his master well enough now to realize what his reactions to such
impertinence would be. The whole peace policy that he had
advocated would be endangered and his own position made
impossible. He publicly lost his temper with the ambassadors.
Mehmet, however, contented himself with answering coldly that
he would look into the matter when he returned to Adrianople.[2]
He cannot have regretted the insolent and fruitless demand; it
would help to justify him in breaking his oath not to invade
Byzantine territory. He intended to return to Europe by the
usual route taken by the Turks, across the Dardanelles; but he
heard that an Italian squadron was cruising up and down the
strait. So he moved to the Bosphorus and shipped himself and
his army across from Bayezit's castle at Anadolu Hisar. The land
on the European shore was officially still Byzantine; but Mehmet
disdained to ask the Emperor's permission to disembark there.
Instead, his keen eye saw how useful it would be to build a fortress
at that spot, over the narrows opposite to Anadolu Hisar.

Once back at Adrianople, Mehmet ordered the expulsion of the
Greeks from the towns of the lower Struma and the confiscation
of all the revenues. Then in the winter of 1451 he sent orders all
over his dominions to collect a thousand skilled masons and a pro-
portionate number of unskilled workmen, who were to assemble
early next spring at the site that he had chosen, at the narrowest
part of the Bosphorus, just beyond the village then called Asoma-
ton and now called Bebek, where a ridge juts out into the strait.
The winter was hardly over before his surveyors were examining

the ground and labourers began to demolish the churches and monasteries nearby, collecting from them such pieces of masonry as could be used again.[1]

His orders caused consternation at Constantinople. It was clear that this was the first move towards the siege of the city. The Emperor hastened to send an embassy to the Sultan to point out that he was breaking a solemn treaty and to remind him that Sultan Bayezit had asked the Emperor Manuel's permission before building his castle at Anadolu Hisar. The ambassadors were dismissed without an audience. On Saturday, 15 April, work started on the construction of the new fortress. Constantine countered by imprisoning all the Turks that were then in Constantinople, then realized that the gesture was futile and released them. Instead, he sent envoys laden with gifts to ask that at least the Greek villages on the Bosphorus should not be harmed. The Sultan paid no attention. In June Constantine made his last effort to obtain from Mehmet an assurance that the building of the castle did not mean that an attack on Constantinople was to follow. His ambassadors were thrown into prison and decapitated. It was virtually a declaration of war.[2]

The castle, known then to the Turks as Boghaz-kesen, the cutter of the strait or, alternatively, the cutter of the throat, and now called Rumeli Hisar, was completed on Thursday, 31 August 1452. Mehmet had spent the previous days in its neighbourhood, then marched with his army right up to the walls of Constantinople. He remained there for three days, carefully examining the fortifications. There could be no doubt now of his intentions. Meanwhile he issued a proclamation that every ship passing up or down the Bosphorus must pause off the castle to be inspected. Any that disobeyed would be sunk. To make good his order he had three great cannons, the largest that had yet been seen, placed on one of the towers nearest to the water. It was not an idle threat. Early in November two Venetian ships sailing from the Black Sea refused to stop. The guns were turned on them; but they escaped without damage. A fortnight later a third tried to follow their example; but she was sunk by a cannon-ball and the captain, Antonio Rizzo, and the crew taken prisoner and brought to Didymoticum, where the Sultan was in residence. He ordered the immediate decapitation of the crew; but Rizzo was sentenced to be impaled and his body to be exposed by the roadside.[1]

The fate of the Venetian sailors ended any illusions that the West still held about the character and ambition of the Sultan. Venice found herself in a difficult position. She had her quarter in Constantinople; and her commercial privileges had been confirmed by Constantine in 1450. But she was also trading very profitably in Ottoman ports; and there were Venetians who believed that the Turkish conquest of Constantinople might bring greater stability and prosperity to the commerce of the Levant. On the other hand, once he had captured Constantinople the Sultan would certainly cast his eyes next on the Venetian colonies in Greece and the Aegean. In a debate in the Senate at the end of August only seven votes had been cast for a motion recommending that Constantinople should be left to its fate; seventy-four senators thought otherwise. But what could Venice do? She had a small but costly war in Lombardy on her hands. Her relations with the Pope were not cordial, especially as the Papacy had never paid for some galleys hired from the Republic in 1444. Co-operation with Genoa was impossible. The Venetian ambassador at Naples was told to beg for King Alfonso's help; but the King's response was vague. The Venetian fleet was busy enough protecting the colonies. It was expensive to convert merchant ships into effective men-of-war. The dignity of the Republic now demanded that relations with the Sultan be broken off. But Venetian commanders in the Levant were given equivocal orders. They were to help and protect the Christians; but they must not attack nor provoke the Turks. Meanwhile the Emperor was granted permission to recruit Cretan soldiers and sailors.[2]

Genoa was in a similar plight and reacted even more nervously.

She too had troubles in Europe; she needed ships to protect her home waters as well as her eastern colonies. The government published one or two exhortations to the peoples of Christendom to send help against the Turks; but it was not prepared to send any itself. Private Genoese citizens were given permission to do as they pleased. There was particular anxiety about Pera and the Black Sea colonies. The Podestà of Pera was instructed to make whatever arrangement he thought best with the Turks, in the hope that even if Constantinople fell the colony might be spared. Similar instructions were given to the Mahona, the committee that governed Chios. In any event the Turks must not be unnecessarily provoked.[1]

The Ragusans, like the Venetians, had recently had their privileges at Constantinople confirmed by the Emperor. But they too traded in Ottoman ports. They were not going to risk any of their small fleet against the Sultan's, except, perhaps, as part of a great coalition.[2]

For all his dissatisfaction with the Byzantines, Pope Nicholas was sincerely shocked by the proof of the Sultan's intentions. He had induced Frederick III, when he came to Rome to be crowned Emperor in March 1452, to send a stern ultimatum to the Sultan. But it was empty bombast; everyone knew that Frederick had neither the power nor the desire to follow it with action. Alfonso was more deeply involved. He was King of Naples with interests and claims in Greece; and the Catalans who traded in Constantinople were his subjects. He was full of promises, and fulfilled them so far as to send a flotilla of ten ships, for which the Pope paid most of the expenses, into Aegean waters; but he withdrew it a few months later when he allied himself with the Venetians against Francesco Sforza of Milan and was nervous of Genoese reactions. Nicholas, with Bessarion at his side, vainly sought for help elsewhere. Neither his ambassadors nor Constantine's received any response to their appeals. He was now eager to do what he could for the Emperor, as he had received a letter, written soon after the Sultan had completed the building of Rumeli Hisar, in which Constantine undertook to implement the union.[1]

Isidore, rejected Metropolitan of Kiev and All Russia and recently created a Cardinal of the Roman Church, had been appointed Papal Legate to the Emperor in May 1452. He now left for Constantinople. He paused on the way at Naples, where he recruited at the Pope's expense a force of two hundred archers, and at Mitylene, where he was joined by the Archbishop, Leonard of Chios, a Genoese by origin. He arrived at Constantinople on 26 October. His military escort, small though it was, was a token that the Pope would send practical assistance to a people that recognized his authority. The gesture was not wasted. Not only was Isidore welcomed with deference by the Emperor and his court, but there was even some enthusiasm among the populace. The Emperor was quick to follow this up. Committees representing the people of the city and the nobles were appointed, to give their adherence to the union. The people's committee agreed, as the opponents of union refused to sit on it. The nobles' committee, where the discussions were more serious, would have preferred a compromise by which the Pope's name would be commemorated in the liturgy but the actual promulgation of union would be deferred; but the Emperor, pushed by Isidore, overruled them. It was almost certainly Lucas Notaras who handled the negotiations, acting with great tact; but he received no thanks for it. To Gennadius and the intransigent opponents of union he seemed to be deserting the cause, while Isidore and the Latins doubted his sincerity. They were so far right in that he seems to have advocated the use of Economy, that doctrine dear to Orthodox theologians which permits a condonation of divergency in the higher interests of the Christian commonwealth; and he seems also to have hinted that the whole question could be reopened when the crisis was over. Gennadius was bitterly distressed. Before Isidore's arrival he had delivered a passionate harangue to the people, begging them not to desert the faith of their fathers in the hope of material assistance that would be of little value. But the sight of the Cardinal's soldiers had made them waver. He therefore retired to his cell in the Pantocrator, after affixing to the monastery gate an angry manifesto in which he warned the people once more of the criminal folly of their abandonment of true religion. Lucas Notaras wrote to him to say that his opposition was vain; but his influence began to be felt again. There were anti-Latin riots in the streets; and as the weeks passed and no more troops arrived from the West the enemies of union recovered their strength.

Cardinal Isidore, himself a Greek, behaved with forbearance and tact, so much so that the Emperor's confidant, Phrantzes, suggested that it might be wise to appoint him Patriarch in the place of the absentee Gregory Mammas. But Constantine knew that Isidore would never agree to that. Archbishop Leonard, however, with a Latin's contempt for the Greeks, was dissatisfied. He demanded that the Emperor should arrest the leaders of the opposition and appoint judges to condemn them. It was a foolish suggestion; for it would only have created martyrs. Constantine contented himself with summoning the members of the Synaxis to meet him at the Palace, on 15 November, to explain their objections. At his request they drew up and signed a document giving reasons for their refusal to accept the union of Florence. They reiterated their theological disapproval of its formula on the Holy Spirit; but they would, they said, welcome another Council, to be held at Constantinople and to be attended by qualified representatives of all the Eastern churches. The only obstacle to this was the ill-will of the Latins. They would, they added, gladly receive back the Patriarch Gregory if he would assure them that he shared their faith. It is not known whether Gennadius was present at the meeting with the Emperor. He was not among the fifteen signatories of the document, who included five bishops, three high dignitaries of the Patriarchate and seven abbots and monks. Their attitude was not unreasonable, if the union was not to provoke a schism between the Church of Constantinople and all the other Orthodox Churches. But to the politicians unity with the West, which might bring material help, took precedence over unity with Eastern Churches which could provide no assistance.

A few days later there occurred the sinking of the Venetian merchant-ship by the guns of Rumeli Hisar. A new wave of panic swept through the city; the need for Western aid seemed more urgent than ever. The unionist party won back supporters. Gennadius, fearing, as he admitted, that the desire for help would spread like a forest fire, issued another broadsheet, to emphasize that Western help involved union. He repeated in it that he at least would not allow his faith to be sullied in the hope of help the efficiency of which was very doubtful. His words were read and noted.

On 12 December 1452 a solemn liturgy was held in the great cathedral of the Holy Wisdom, in the presence of the Emperor and the Court. The Pope and the absent Patriarch were commemorated in the prayers, and the decrees of the Union of Florence were read out. Cardinal Isidore, anxious to show that his fellow-Greeks had been won over, reported that the church was thronged; only Gennadius and eight other monks were absent. But other members of his party painted a different picture. There was no enthusiasm among the Greeks; and henceforward few of them would enter the cathedral, where only priests who had accepted union were allowed to serve. To Archbishop Leonard even the Emperor seemed to be lukewarm and weak in his efforts to enforce the union, while Lucas Notaras was, he thought, its open foe. If Notaras did indeed make his oft-quoted remark preferring the Sultan's turban to the Cardinal's hat, it was doubtless provoked by irritation with the intransigence of such Latins as Leonard, who would not understand his efforts at reconciliation.

After the union had been proclaimed there was no more open opposition. Gennadius kept silence in his cell. The bulk of the people accepted the accomplished fact with sullen passivity; but they worshipped only in the churches whose priests were untainted. Even many of its supporters hoped that if the city were spared the decree would be amended. Had the union been followed quickly by the appearance of ships and soldiers from the West its practical advantages might have won it general support. The Greeks, with the doctrine of economy in their minds, could have reflected that the abandonment of their religious loyalties would be well compensated by the preservation of the Christian Empire. But, as it was, they had paid the price demanded for Western aid, and they were cheated.[1]

CHAPTER V

PREPARATIONS FOR THE SIEGE

Throughout the last months of 1452 the Sultan brooded over his plans. No one even among his ministers knew exactly what he intended. Was he to be content now that his fortress at Rumeli Hisar gave him control of the Bosphorus and would enable him to blockade Constantinople so completely that in time it would have to surrender? He had plans drawn for a splendid new palace at Adrianople, on an island in the river Maritsa. Did that mean that he had no thought for the present of moving his government to the ancient Imperial capital? So his Vizier Halil hoped. Halil, whether or not he was receiving regular presents from the Greeks, as was generally suspected, disliked the idea of a campaign against Constantinople. A siege would be expensive; and should it fail the humiliation to Ottoman prestige would be disastrous. Moreover, Constantinople in its present state was politically powerless and commercially convenient. Halil had his supporters amongst others of Murad's old ministers. But there was a vigorous party opposed to him, led by soldiers such as Zaganos and Turahan Pasha, with the eunuch Shehab ed-Din behind them; and it was they who had the Sultan's ear.[1]

Mehmet himself spent many sleepless nights that winter as he thought about his campaign. It was said that he might be seen at midnight tramping through the streets of Adrianople dressed as a simple soldier; and anyone who recognized him and saluted him was straightway put to death. One night, about the second watch, he suddenly ordered Halil to be brought before him. The old vizier came trembling, fearing to hear of his dismissal. To appease his master he brought with him a dish hastily filled with gold coins. 'What is this, my teacher?' asked the Sultan. Halil

murmured that it was customary for ministers summoned suddenly to the Presence to bring gifts with them. Mehmet brushed the
dish aside. He had no use for such gifts. 'Only one thing I want',
he cried. 'Give me Constantinople.' He then revealed that his
mind was finally made up. He would attack the city as soon as
possible. Halil, nervous and despondent, promised his loyal
support.[1]

A few days later, towards the end of January, the Sultan
assembled all his ministers and made them a long speech in which
he reminded them of the achievements of their ancestors. But,
he declared, the Turkish Empire would never be secure until it
held Constantinople. The Byzantines might be weak, but, all the
same, they had shown how well they could plot with the enemies
of the Turks, and in their weakness they might put the city into
the hands of allies who would not be so ineffectual. Constantinople was not impregnable. Earlier sieges had failed because of
extraneous causes. But now the moment had come. The city was
torn by religious dissension. The Italians were unreliable as allies,
and many of them were traitors. Moreover, the Turks were at
last in command of the seas. For himself, he said, if he could not
rule an empire which contained Constantinople, he would sooner
not rule an empire at all.

His audience was stirred. Even those of his Council who disapproved of his intentions dared not voice their misgivings.
Unanimously his ministers followed his lead and voted for war.[2]

As soon as the war was sanctioned the Sultan ordered the
military governor of the European provinces, Dayi Karadja Bey,
to collect an army and attack the Byzantine cities and towns on
the coasts of Thrace. The towns on the Black Sea coast, Mesembria, Anchialus and Byzus, surrendered at once and so escaped
pillage. But some of the towns on the Marmora coast, such as
Selymbria and Perinthus, attempted to resist. They were taken
by storm and sacked and their fortifications dismantled.[3] Already,
in the previous October, Turahan Bey and his sons had been

stationed on the isthmus of Corinth, to make raids into the Peloponnese and so to distract the Emperor's brothers that they would
never be able to send him assistance.[1]

In his speech to his Council the Sultan had emphasized that he
now had command of the sea. Previous attempts against the city
had been made from the land only. The Byzantines had always
been able to receive supplies by water; and, until recently, the
Turks had been obliged to hire Christian ships for the transport
of their armies between Europe and Asia. Mehmet was determined to alter that. Throughout the month of March 1453, ships
of all sorts began to assemble off Gallipoli. There were old ships,
many of which had been repaired and re-caulked; but many more
were new, hastily constructed during the last few months in ship-
yards in the towns of the Aegean coast. There were triremes, in
which, unlike the ancient triremes, the benches were all on one
level. Each row, placed at a slightly oblique angle to the side of
the ship, contained three rowers, each with a single short oar on
its own thole-pin but all three projecting through one rowlock-
port. The boat lay low in the water and was two-masted, the
sails being used when the wind was favourable. There were
biremes, slightly smaller boats with a single mast, where the
rowers sat in pairs on either side. There were *fustae*, or long boats,
lighter than the biremes and swifter, with single rowers on each
side forward of the mast and pairs aft. There were galleys, a term
which was often loosely used to mean any large vessel, whether
a trireme or a bireme or a sailing boat devoid of rowers, but which
technically meant a large boat, higher out of the water, with a
single bank of long oars. There were also *parandaria*, heavy
sailing-barges used for transport.[2]

The size of the Sultan's armada is variously given. Figures
given by the Byzantine historians are wildly exaggerated; but,
from the evidence of the Italian sailors who were present at Constantinople, it seems to have included six triremes and ten biremes,
about fifteen galleys with oars, about seventy-five *fustae* and

twenty *parandaria*, together with a number of sloops and cutters, used mainly for carrying messages. The governor of Gallipoli, the Bulgarian-born renegade Suleiman Baltoghlu, was placed in command. The oarsmen and sailors were some of them prisoners or slaves but many of them volunteers, lured by handsome wages. The Sultan himself took a personal interest in the appointment of the officers, considering his fleet to be of even greater import-ance than his army.[1]

About the end of March this armada made its way up the Dardanelles into the Sea of Marmora, to the consternation of the Christians, Greeks and Italians alike. They had not realized till that moment the strength of the Sultan's naval power.[2]

While the fleet cruised in the Sea of Marmora the Turkish army assembled in Thrace. As with the navy, the Sultan himself saw to its outfitting. Throughout the winter armourers all over his dominions had been at work, making shields, helmets, breast-plates, javelins, swords and arrows, while engineers constructed ballistas and battering-rams. Mobilization was rapid but com-plete. Regiments from every province were collected, as well as all the soldiers on furlough in their military fiefs. Irregulars were enrolled in their thousands. Only the garrisons needed to protect the frontiers and to police the provinces were left behind, as well as the forces that Turahan maintained in Greece. The size of the army was awe-inspiring. The Greeks declared that three or four hundred thousand men were assembled in the Sultan's camp; and even the soberer Venetians spoke of a hundred and fifty thousand. In probability, to judge from Turkish sources, the regular troops numbered some eighty thousand, excluding the irregulars, the Bashi-bazouks, who may have added another twenty thousand, and the non-combatant camp-followers, of whom there must have been several thousand. The pride of place was held by the Janissary regiments. Since their re-organization by Sultan Murad II some twenty years earlier they numbered twelve thousand, of whom a small proportion were technicians or civil servants and the kennelmen and falconers whom Mehmet himself had added. Every Janissary was at this time of Christian origin; but he had been brought up from childhood to be a devout Moslem, to regard his regiment as his family and the Sultan as his commander and father. A few Janissaries might remember their families and perform occasional acts of kindness to them; but their fanaticism for the Faith was unquestioned and their discipline superb. They had not greatly approved of Mehmet in the past; but they welcomed eagerly a campaign against the infidel.[1]

The army in itself was impressive. Still more alarming were the new-fangled machines with which it was equipped. Mehmet's decision to make his attack on Constantinople in the spring of 1453 was largely due to the recent triumphs of his cannon-founders. Cannon had been used in western Europe for over a hundred years, ever since a German friar called Schwartz had constructed a gun whose balls were impelled by gun-powder. The value of cannon in siege-warfare was quickly realized; but the experiences of the Germans at the siege of Cividale in northern Italy in 1321 and of the English at Calais in 1347 has not been very successful. The cannons were not powerful enough to harm solid masonry. For the next hundred years the new arm was mainly used for dispersing enemy troops in the field or for breaking down light barricades. The Venetians had attempted to use cannon in naval warfare, against the Genoese in 1377.[2] But the ships of the time could not take the weight of heavy machines; and cannon-balls fired by the naval guns of the time were seldom powerful enough to sink a ship, though they might do considerable damage. Sultan Mehmet, whose interest in the sciences had been stimulated by his doctor, the Italian Jew, Jacobo of Gaeta, was alive to the importance of artillery. Early in his reign he had ordered his foundries to experiment in producing larger cannon.[3]

In the summer of 1452 a Hungarian engineer called Urban came to Constantinople and offered his services as a maker of artillery to the Emperor. Constantine could not, however, pay him the salary that he thought to be his due, nor could he provide him with the raw material that he needed. Urban therefore left the city and approached the Sultan. He was at once admitted to the Presence and cross-questioned. On declaring that he could construct a cannon that would blast the walls of Babylon itself, he was given a salary four times greater than that which he would have been willing to accept and provided with all the technical assistance that he needed. Within three months he built the huge cannon which the Sultan placed on the walls of his castle at Rumeli Hisar and which sank the Venetian ship that had attempted to run the blockade. Mehmet then ordered him to make a cannon twice the size of the first. It was cast at Adrianople and completed in January. The length of its barrel was estimated to be forty spans, that is, twenty-six feet and eight inches. The thickness of the bronze round the barrel was one span, that is, eight inches, and the circumference of the barrel four spans at the rear, where the powder was inserted, and twelve spans for the front half, where the balls were inserted. The balls were said to weigh twelve hundredweight. As soon as it was ready a company of seven hundred men, to whom its care was assigned, placed it upon a cart drawn by fifteen pairs of oxen. They dragged it with some difficulty to the neighbourhood of Mehmet's palace, where its powers were to be tested. The citizens of Adrianople were warned that there would be a fearful noise and that they must not panic. Indeed, when the fuse was lit and the first ball fired, the reverberation was heard for a hundred stadia, and the ball hurtled through the air for a mile, then buried itself six feet deep in the earth. Mehmet was delighted. Two hundred men were sent to level the road that led to Constantinople and to strengthen the bridges; and in March the cannon set out on its journey, drawn by sixty oxen, with two hundred men marching beside it, to keep the gun-carriage steady. Meanwhile under Urban's direction the foundries produced other cannon, though none was to be so huge or so famous as this monster.[1]

Throughout the month of March the Sultan's great army moved in detachments through Thrace towards the Bosphorus. It was not easy to provide for all the needs of so vast a host; but everything had been carefully planned. Discipline was good, and the morale of the troops very high. Every Moslem believed that the Prophet himself would accord a special place in Paradise to the first soldier who should force an entry into the ancient Christian capital. 'They shall conquer Qostantiniya', the Tradition had declared. 'Glory be to the prince and to the army that shall achieve it.' Another Tradition, adapted by the preachers to fit the occasion, told of the Prophet asking his disciples: 'Have you heard of a city of which one side is land and the two others sea? The hour of Judgement shall not sound until seventy thousand sons of Isaac shall capture it.' Of the Sultan's own enthusiasm there could be no doubt. Many times he was heard to declare his determination to be the prince who should achieve this supreme triumph for Islam.[1] He himself left Adrianople on 23 March. On 5 April he arrived with the last detachments of the army outside the walls of the city.[2]

Within the city the atmosphere was very different. The sight of the huge Turkish fleet cruising in the Sea of Marmora and of the vast cannons, headed by Urban's monster, lumbering towards the land-walls, showed the citizens what they were to expect. There were one or two slight earthquakes and some torrential rains, all of them interpreted as evil omens, while men and women reminded themselves of all the prophecies that foretold the end of the Empire and the coming of Anti-Christ.[3] Yet, for all the feeling of despair, there was no lack of courage. Even those thinkers who wondered whether in the end absorption into the Turkish Empire might prove less harmful to the Greek people than the present state of division, poverty and impotence, joined whole-heartedly in the preparations for the defence. Throughout the winter months, with the Emperor encouraging them, men, and women, too, could be seen repairing the walls and clearing out the moats.

All the arms within the city were collected together to be re-distributed where they would be most needed. A fund was set aside, to which not only the state but churches and monasteries and private persons all contributed, to meet the special expenses. There was still considerable wealth in the city; and it seemed to some of the Italians that more might have been given by certain of the Greeks. But, in fact, it was not so much money that was needed as man-power, armaments and food; and money could not buy them now.[1]

The Emperor did all that he could. Ambassadors had been sent to Italy in the autumn of 1452 to beg for urgent help. The response was poor.[2] A new embassy was sent to Venice; but the Senate replied on 16 November that it was indeed deeply distressed by the news from the East, and, if the Pope and other powers were going to take action, it would gladly co-operate. The Venetians had not yet heard of the fate of Rizzo's galley the previous week; but even that news and urgent messages from the Venetian colony at Constantinople could not induce them to take definite action.[3] An envoy sent that same month to Genoa received the promise of one ship; and the government offered to appeal for further aid to the King of France and the Republic of Florence. King Alfonso of Aragon's promises were even vaguer; but he gave the Byzantine ambassadors permission to collect wheat and other foodstuffs in Sicily for transmission to Constantinople. They were busy on their task when the siege began, and they never saw their native land again. Pope Nicholas was anxious to help, but he was unwilling to commit himself too far until he felt certain that the union of the Churches had really been achieved; and he could do little without the Venetians. His attention had moreover been distracted by a revolt in Rome in January 1453. Till the city was pacified he could not contemplate action abroad.[4]

The letters that passed between Rome and Venice make sorry reading. The Venetians would not forget that the Papacy still owed them money for the hire of galleys in 1444; and the

Pope had no confidence in Venetian good-will. It was not till 19 February 1453 that the Venetian Senate, on the receipt of the latest news from the East, voted to send at once to Constantinople two transports, each with four hundred men on board, and to order that fifteen galleys now being re-equipped should follow them when they were ready. Five days later the Senate passed a decree exacting special taxes from merchants engaged in the Levant trade to pay the expenses of this flotilla. On the same day letters were sent to the Pope, the Western Emperor and the Kings of Hungary and Aragon, to say that unless help was provided at once Constantinople was doomed. Yet on 2 March the Senate was still discussing the organization of this flotilla. It was decided to place it under the command of Alviso Longo but under the supreme authority of the Captain-General of the Sea, Giacomo Loredan. A week later another resolution was passed in the Senate urging the utmost speed. But the days went by and nothing was done. Early in April letters were at last received from Rome, telling of the Pope's intention to send five galleys to the East. A reply from Venice, dated 10 April, congratulated the Cardinals on this decision but reminded them of the previous Pope's failure to pay his debts. It added that, according to the latest information from Constantinople, foodstuffs were more urgently needed now than men; and it reminded Rome, rather belatedly, that ships should reach the Dardanelles before 31 March, as thenceforward the prevailing north wind made the passage of the Straits more difficult. The departure of the Venetian flotilla was finally decided for 17 April; but then there were further delays and postponements. When at last the ships sailed from Venice Constantinople had already been besieged for a fortnight.[1]

Pope Nicholas was genuinely worried by these delays. Already he had bought at his own expense a cargo of arms and foodstuffs. He dispatched it to Constantinople in three Genoese ships, which sailed about the end of March.[2]

No other government paid any attention to the Emperor's

appeals. In the hope of luring Genoese merchants to bring food to the city he had announced that imports would be duty-free. But there was no response. The Genoese authorities persisted in a policy of equivocal neutrality. It had been hoped that that great Christian warrior, John Hunyadi, Regent of Hungary, would take advantage of a moment when the Turks had almost denuded the Danube frontier of troops. But the Hungarians had been crippled by their disasters at the end of Murad's reign; and Hunyadi himself was in a difficult position, as his ward, King Ladislas V, had come of age on 14 February and resented his tutelage. None of the Orthodox princes could give help.[1] The Grand Prince of Russia was too far away and with troubles of his own; appeals had been made to him in vain.[2] Besides, Russia had been deeply shocked by the proclamation of the union of the Churches. The princes of Moldavia, Peter III and Alexander II, were quarrelling with each other. The Prince of Wallachia, Vladislav II, was the Sultan's vassal and would certainly not move against him without the help of Hungary.[3] George, Despot of Serbia, was an even more dutiful vassal, and even sent a detachment of soldiers to join Mehmet's army. They fought bravely for their overlord, in spite of the sympathy that they felt for their co-religionists in Constantinople.[4] In Albania Scanderbeg was still a thorn in the Sultan's side. But he was on bad terms with the Venetians; and the Turks had stirred up rival chieftains against him. The Aegean lords and the Knights of St. John at Rhodes were none of them in a position to intervene except as members of some great coalition. The Despots of the Morea were kept in check by Turahan Bey's forces. The King of Georgia and the Emperor of Trebizond were each of them hard put to defend their own frontiers. The Anatolian emirs, much as they resented the Sultan, had received too recent a taste of his power to move so soon against him again.[5]

Yet, though the governments defaulted, there were men who were ready to fight for Christendom at Constantinople. The Venetian colony in the city offered unstinted support to the

Emperor. At a meeting attended by Constantine and his Council and by Cardinal Isidore, the Venetian Bailey, Girolamo Minotto, undertook to share fully in the defence and to see that no Venetian ship left the harbour without permission. He also guaranteed that a flotilla would be sent from Venice and wrote there urgently demanding immediate help. Two Venetian merchant-captains, Gabriele Trevisano and Alviso Diedo, whose ships were anchored in the Golden Horn on their return from a Black Sea voyage, promised to remain to join in the struggle. In all, six Venetian vessels and three from the Venetian colony of Crete were retained in the harbour with the consent of their commanders, and were transformed into warships, 'for the honour of God and the honour of all Christendom', as Trevisano proudly said to the Emperor. Amongst the Venetians who pledged themselves to defend the great city which their ancestors had sacked two and a half centuries before were many that bore the most eminent surnames of the Republic, Cornaro, Mocenigo, Contarini and Venier. They were all to be recorded in a roll of honour written by their compatriot, the sailor-surgeon Nicolo Barbaro, whose unvarnished diary gives probably the most honest account of the siege.[1]

These Venetians offered their services because they found themselves at Constantinople when the war began and were too honourable and proud to make their escape. But there were Genoese who were ashamed of their government's timidity and who came of their own will from Italy to fight for Christendom. Among them were Maurizio Cattaneo, the two brothers Geronimo and Leonardo di Langasco, and the three Bocchiardo brothers Paolo, Antonio and Troilo, who equipped and brought at their own expense a small company of soldiers. On 29 January 1453, the city was cheered by the news of the arrival of a famous Genoese soldier, Giovanni Giustiniani Longo, a youngish man belonging to one of the greatest families of the Republic and a kinsman of the powerful house of Doria. He brought with him seven hundred well-armed soldiers, four hundred that he had recruited at Genoa and three hundred recruited at Chios and Rhodes. The Emperor received him gladly, offering him the lordship of Lemnos, should the Turks be driven off. He was reputed to be particularly skilled at the defence of walled cities; so he was at once appointed to take command of the whole area of the landwalls. He wasted no time in setting about his duties, carefully inspecting them all and seeing to their strengthening wherever it seemed necessary. Though it was hard to persuade Venetians to work with a Genoese, such was his personality that he won their co-operation. At his request Trevisano reopened and cleared the moat that ran in from the Golden Horn in front of the walls of Blachernae until the ground began to rise. Many citizens from Pera joined the defence, believing, as their Podestà later wrote, that the fall of Constantinople would mean the end of their colony.[1]

A few soldiers belonged to more distant lands. The Catalan colony in the city organized itself under its Consul, Péré Julia; and some Catalan sailors joined them.[2] From Castile there came a gallant nobleman, Don Francisco de Toledo, who claimed descent from the Imperial house of Comnenus and so called the Emperor his cousin.[3] In Giustiniani's company there was an engineer called Johannes Grant, usually described as a German but who may well have been a Scottish adventurer who had found his way through Germany to the Levant.[4] The Ottoman pretender, Orhan, who had been living since his childhood at Constantinople, offered his services and those of his household to the Emperor.[5]

Not all the Italians in the city showed the courage of Minotto or of Giustiniani. On the night of 26 February seven ships, six from Crete and one from Venice, under the command of Pietro Davanzo, slipped out of the Golden Horn with seven hundred Italians on board. Their flight was a serious blow to the defence. No one else, Greek or Italian, followed their example.[6]

There remained when the siege opened twenty-six ships equipped for fighting in the Golden Horn, apart from small craft and the merchant-ships of the Genoese of Pera, anchored beneath their colony's walls. Five were Venetian, five Genoese, three Cretan, one from Ancona, one from Catalonia and one from Provence, and ten belonging to the Emperor. Nearly all were high-decked boats, without oars and dependent on their sails. It was a small fleet in comparison with the Turkish armada.[1] The disparity in man-power on land was even greater.

At the end of March, when the Turkish army was moving through Thrace, Constantine sent for his secretary Phrantzes and told him to make a census of all the men in the city, including monks, who were capable of bearing arms. When Phrantzes added up the lists he found that there were only four thousand, nine hundred and eighty-three available Greeks and slightly under two thousand foreigners. Constantine was appalled by the figure and charged Phrantzes not to publish it. But Italian witnesses came to a similar conclusion.[2] Against the Sultan's army of some eighty thousand men and his hordes of irregulars, the great city, with its fourteen miles of walls, had to be defended by less than seven thousand men.

CHAPTER VI

THE SIEGE BEGINS

Easter is the great festival of the Orthodox Church, when every Christian rejoices in the knowledge of his Saviour's resurrection. But there was little joy in the hearts of the people of Constantinople on Easter Sunday, 1453. It fell upon 1 April. After a stormy winter spring was coming to the Bosphorus. In the orchards throughout the city the fruit-trees were bursting into flower. The nightingales were returning to sing in the copses and the storks to build their nests on the roof-tops. The sky was streaked with long lines of migratory birds flying to their summer homes away in the north. But Thrace was rumbling with the sounds of a great army on the move, of men and horses and of oxen pulling their creaking wagons.

For many days past the citizens had been praying that at least they might be allowed to perform the rites of Holy Week in peace. That much was granted to them. It was on Monday, 2 April, that the first detachment of the enemy came into sight. A small company of the defenders made a sortie against them, killing some men and wounding many others. But, as more and more Turkish troops appeared, the company withdrew into the city; and the Emperor ordered the bridges across the moats to be destroyed and the gates of the city to be closed.[1] That same day, too, he gave instructions to have a great boom stretched across the entrance to the harbour of the Golden Horn. It consisted of a chain fixed at one end of the Tower of Eugenius, under the acropolis, and at the other to a tower on the sea-walls of Pera; and it was supported on wooden floats. A Genoese engineer, Bartolomeo Soligo, was responsible for putting it in place.[2]

By Thursday, 5 April, the whole Turkish army had arrived

86

outside the walls, with the Sultan himself in command. He camped temporarily about a mile and a half away. Next day he moved his troops nearer, into their final positions. The defenders likewise took up their appointed stations.[1]

The city of Constantinople occupies a peninsula roughly triangular in shape, with slightly curved sides. The land-walls stretched from the Blachernae quarter on the Golden Horn to the Studion quarter on the Sea of Marmora in a gently convex curve; they were some four miles in length. The walls along the Golden Horn were about three and a half miles in length; they ran in a concave curve from Blachernae to the Acropolis Point, now usually known as Seraglio Point, which faces northward up the Bosphorus. From the Acropolis point to Studion was a distance of about five and a half miles; the walls went round the blunt apex of the peninsula, facing the entrance to the Bosphorus, then in a slightly concave curve along the Marmora shore. The walls along the Golden Horn and the Marmora were single. Along the Marmora they rose fairly straight out of the sea. Eleven gates opened through them on to the water; and there were two small fortified harbours, to accommodate light craft that could not round the point into the Golden Horn against the prevailing north wind. Along the shore of the Golden Horn a foreshore had emerged in the course of the centuries, which was now covered with warehouses. Sixteen gates opened on to it. At the west end, to protect the vulnerable Blachernae quarter John Cantacuzenus had constructed a moat through the silt, running directly under the wall. These sea-walls were in fairly good repair. It was unlikely that they would be severely attacked. Though the Franks and Venetians had forced their way into the city in 1204 from the Golden Horn, such an assault would only be possible for an enemy in full control of the harbour. Round the apex of the city the current ran too fast for landing-craft to come up easily to the base of the walls, while shoals and reefs provided additional protection to the Marmora walls.

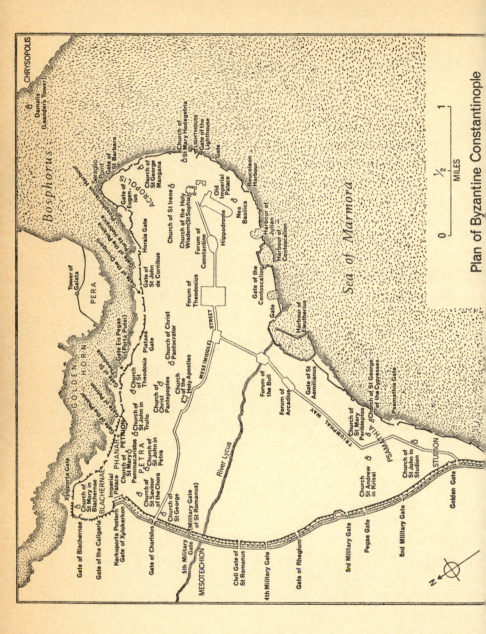

Plan of Byzantine Constantinople

It was along the land-walls that the main attack was to be expected. At the northern end the Blachernae quarter jutted out from the main line. It had originally been a suburb but had been enclosed in the seventh century by a single wall. This had been repaired in the ninth and twelfth centuries and had been strengthened by the fortifications of the Imperial palace which Manuel I had built against it. At its lower end it was protected by John Cantacuzenus's moat, which seems to have run round the corner where the wall reached the Golden Horn, as far as the beginning of a steep slope, up which the wall climbed, before turning at right angles to meet the main line of the walls. It was pierced by two gates, known as the Gates of Caligaria and of Blachernae, and by a small postern gate, which had been closed, called the Kerkoporta, at the angle where it joined the old Theodosian wall. The Theodosian wall, erected by the Prefect Anthemius in the reign of Theodosius II, ran from this point in an unbroken line to the Sea of Marmora. It was a triple wall. On the outside was a deep ditch, a foss, some sixty feet in width, sections of which could be flooded if necessary. On the inside of the ditch there was a low crenellated breastwork, within which was a passage some forty to fifty feet in breadth, running the whole length of the walls and known as the Peribolos. Then there rose the wall usually described as the outer wall, about twenty-five feet in height, with square towers placed along it at intervals varying from fifty to a hundred yards. Within it was another space known as the Parateichion, which varied from forty to sixty feet in width. Then there rose the inner wall, about forty feet in height, with towers, some square and some octagonal, about sixty feet in height, spaced so as to cover the interstices between the towers of the outer wall. This line of walls was pierced by a number of gates, some used by the general public, the others reserved to the military. There was a small postern gate on the Marmora shore. Then, going northward, there was the Golden Gate, which ranked as the First Military Gate and which

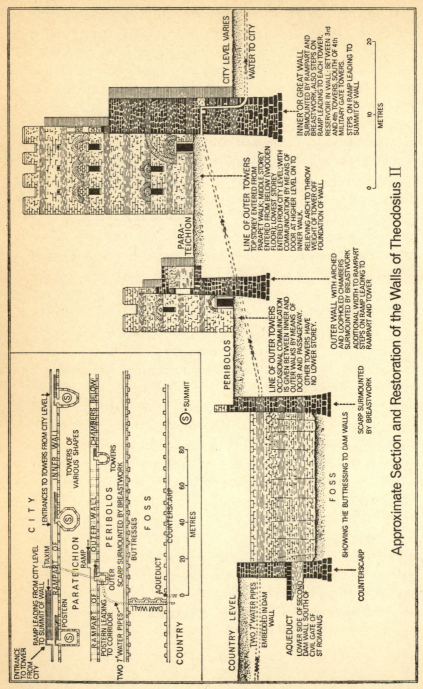

Approximate Section and Restoration of the Walls of Theodosius II

Fig. 2

was traditionally used by the Emperor when he made a ceremonial entry into the city. Next was the Second Military Gate, then the civil Gate of Pegae, now known as the Silivria Gate. Close to it was the Third Military Gate. The terrain rose now, to the Rhegium Gate and the Fourth Military Gate beyond. The Gate of Saint Romanus, the present Top Kapusi, was at the highest point of the ridge. The ground then dropped about a hundred feet into the valley of the little river Lycus, which passed through a conduit under the walls two hundred yards south of the Fifth Military Gate. This gate, which was thus on the floor of the valley, had been known to the Byzantines as the Gate of Saint Kyriake, from the name of a nearby church. But it seems to have been called popularly the Military Gate of Saint Romanus; and writers describing the siege continually confuse it with the civil Gate of Saint Romanus. From there the ground rose again to another ridge, at the top of which was the Charisian Gate, the Adrianople Gate of today. The stretch of the walls crossing the Lycus valley was known as the Mesoteichion and had always been considered to be their most vulnerable section. The Charisian Gate was sometimes called the Polyandrion; and the stretch of the walls that continued along the ridge to the Xylokerkon Gate, just before the junction with the Blachernae wall, was known as the Myriandrion.[1]

When Sultan Murad had attacked the city in 1422 the Byzantines had concentrated their defence on the outer wall, which the Turks had been unable to breach. Giustiniani and the Emperor agreed, in view of the few troops at their disposal, that this would again be the proper strategy. The inner wall could not be manned as well, though heavier missiles could be fired from its towers. The damage done to the outer wall in 1422 had been largely repaired during the following years; and Giustiniani had made it his business to see that the repairs were complete. Archbishop Leonard, who fancied himself as a strategist, declared afterwards that the military strategists were all wrong; they should have defended the inner wall. But these, he adds, with typical malice against the Greeks, had been badly repaired, as the money set aside for the purpose had been misappropriated by two Greeks, whom he calls Jagarus and the monk Neophytus. It was a monstrous libel. Jagarus, whose real name was Manuel Palaeologus Iagrus, was a kinsman of the Emperor's and a respected statesman whose name actually appears on several inscriptions at points where the walls have been carefully repaired. There was a well-known monk Neophytus at the time, who was a friend of the Emperor but an enemy to union. He was now living quietly and piously at the Charsianites monastery and taking no part in public affairs. It is hard to see how he could have intercepted a building contract. But the Archbishop believed that there was no enormity of which schismatic clergy were incapable.[1]

On 5 April the defenders took up the positions allotted to them by the Emperor. The Emperor stationed himself with his best Greek troops at the Mesoteichion, where the walls crossed the Lycus valley, with Giustiniani on his right at the Charisian Gate and the Myriandrion; but when it became clear that the Sultan was going to concentrate his attack on the Mesoteichion, Giustiniani and his Genoese moved down to join him there; and the Myriandrion was taken over by the Bocchiardi brothers and their men. The Venetian Bailey, Minotto, and his staff took up quarters in the Imperial Palace at Blachernae and were responsible for its defence, their first task being to clear and refill the moat. An elderly compatriot, Teodoro Caristo, saw to the section of the walls between the Caligarian Gate and the Theodosian wall. The Langasco brothers, with Archbishop Leonard, were stationed behind the moat that ran into the Golden Horn. On the Emperor's left was Cattaneo with his Genoese troops, and next to him the Emperor's kinsman, Theophilus Palaeologus, with Greek troops, guarding the Pegae Gate. The Venetian, Filippo Contarini, was in charge from the Pegae Gate to the Golden Gate, which was defended by a Genoese called Manuel. On his left, by the sea, was Demetrius Cantacuzenus.

The sea-walls were more thinly manned. Jacobo Contarini was in charge at Studion. Next to him, along a section that was un-likely to be attacked, the walls were guarded by Greek monks, who, presumably, were to keep watch and summon reserves should an emergency 'occur. Near them, by the harbour of Eleutherius, were Prince Orhan and his Turks. At the east end

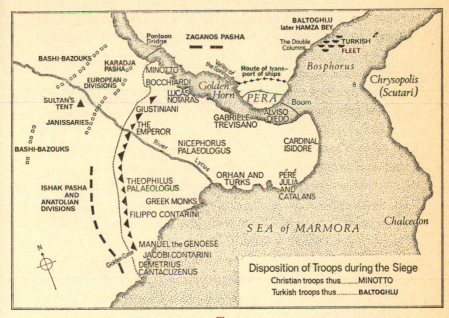

Fig. 3

of the Marmora shore, under the Hippodrome and the old Sacred Palace, were the Catalans under Péré Julia. Cardinal Isidore was stationed with two hundred men at the Acropolis Point. The shores of the Golden Horn were guarded by Venetian and Genoese sailors under the command of Gabriele Trevisano, while his com-patriot, Alviso Diedo, was made commander of the ships in the harbour. Two detachments of reserves were kept in the city, one under the command of the Megadux, Lucas Notaras, stationed in the Petra quarter, close behind the land-walls, with a supply of mobile guns, and the other, under Nicephorus Palaeologus, near the Church of the Holy Apostles, on the central ridge. Ten ships were detached from the fleet to serve at the boom; five of these were Genoese, three Cretan, one from Ancona and one Greek. The command here was given to a Genoese, probably to Soligo who had fixed the boom. It was essential to have someone there who would be on good terms with the Genoese of Pera, as the chain was attached at one end to their walls. In general the Emperor seems to have tried to intermix his Greek, Venetian and Genoese troops, so that they would realize their interdependence and avoid nationalistic quarrels.[1]

The defence was adequately equipped with javelins and arrows and a few culverines and with mangonels for casting stones. There were also several cannons in the city; but they proved to be of little value. There was a shortage of saltpetre for them; and it was found that when they were fired from the walls and towers, which was necessary if their missiles were to reach the enemy lines, the reverberation damaged the fortifications. The individual soldiers seem to have had good suits of armour, better than those of most of the Turkish troops.[2]

By the morning of 6 April the soldiers were at their posts; and the garrisons on the walls could watch the Turkish army take up its stations. The Sultan had already detached a large section of his army, under Zaganos Pasha, to the northern shore of the Golden Horn, where it spread out over the hills to the Bosphorus, thus isolating Pera and keeping watch on any move that the Genoese there might make. A road was constructed over the marshy ground at the head of the Horn, so that Zaganos could communicate quickly with the main force. Opposite the walls of Constantinople, from the Golden Horn up the hill to the Charisian Gate, were placed the regular European troops of the army, under Karadja Pasha, who had at his disposal a number of heavy guns, for use against the single Blachernae wall, and especially against the vulnerable corner where the wall joined the Theodosian wall.

From the southern slopes of the Lycus valley down to the Sea of
Marmora there were the regular Anatolian troops, under Ishak
Pasha, assisted, no doubt because the Sultan did not entirely trust
him, by Mahmud Pasha, a half-Greek, half-Slav renegade, descended from the old Imperial family of the Angeli, who was
becoming the Sultan's most intimate friend and counsellor. The
Sultan himself took command of the section in the Lycus valley,
opposite to the Mesoteichion. He pitched his red and gold tent
about a quarter of a mile from the walls. In front of it were his
Janissaries and other selected regiments, together with the best of
his guns, including Urban's great masterpiece. The Bashi-bazouks
were encamped in various groups just behind the main lines,
ready to be moved wherever they might be needed. In front of
their positions, for the whole length of the walls, the Turks dug
a trench, backed by a rampart made with the earth, on top of
which they erected a low wooden palisade, pierced at frequent
intervals by posterns.[1]

The fleet, under Baltoghlu, had orders to see that no supplies
could reach the city by sea. There was a constant patrol off the
Marmora shore, so that no boat could approach the small harbours
there. But Baltoghlu's main task was to force his way through the
boom that guarded the Golden Horn. He made his headquarters in
the Bosphorus, off the quay known as the Double Columns, where
the Palace of Dolma Bahçe now stands. There he was joined,
ten days after the siege began, by a number of large ships from the
northern Anatolian ports, all of them equipped with heavy guns.[2]

As soon as the Emperor saw that the Turkish troops were
assembled before the walls, he suggested to Trevisano that his
sailors, clad in their distinctive costumes, should parade, nearly a
thousand strong, along the whole length of the walls, so that the
Sultan should be quite certain that there were Venetians, too,
among his enemies. The Venetians gladly complied.[3] The Sultan
for his part, in conformance with Islamic law, sent a last message
under a flag of truce to the city. He would, he said, as the Law

commanded, spare the citizens, harming neither their families nor their belongings, if they voluntarily surrendered to him. Otherwise they would be shown no mercy. But the citizens had little faith in his promises, nor would they now desert their Emperor.[1]

As soon as this formality was over and the guns were in position, the Turks opened the fighting with a heavy bombardment of the walls. By dusk on that first day, 6 April, a portion of the wall near the Charisian Gate had been severely damaged; and a steady bombardment the following day brought it down in ruins. But after nightfall the defenders managed to make adequate repairs. Mehmet then decided to wait until he could bring more guns to bear on the weaker parts of the walls. In the meantime his soldiers were ordered to set to work to fill up the great foss, so that they could advance at once to occupy any breach that the artillery might make. He also ordered mining operations to be undertaken against the parts of the wall where the terrain seemed to be suitable. At the same time Baltoghlu was told to test the defences of the boom. It was probably on 9 April that his ships made their first attack there. They had no success; and Baltoghlu decided to await the coming of the Black Sea squadron.[2]

During this time of waiting the Sultan took some of his best troops and some artillery to attack two small castles outside the walls, which were still holding out for the Emperor. One was at Therapia, on a hill above the Bosphorus, the other at the village of Studius, near the Marmora coast. The castle at Therapia resisted for two days, till its walls had been shattered by gun-fire and the bulk of its garrison killed. The survivors, forty of them, then surrendered unconditionally. They were all put to death by impalement. The smaller castle at Studius was demolished in a few hours. The thirty-six survivors of the garrison were captured in the ruins and likewise impaled. This was done within sight of the walls, that the citizens might see what befell those who opposed the Sultan. Meanwhile Baltoghlu was sent to occupy the Princes' Islands, in the Sea of Marmora. Only on the largest of the islands,

Prinkipo, was there any attempt at resistance. There, on a hill-top beside the main monastery of the island, was a solid tower built by the monks as a refuge against pirates, probably at the time when the Catalan Company was raiding the Empire. Its small garrison of thirty men refused now to surrender. Baltoghlu had brought some cannon with him; but the cannon-balls made no impression on the thick masonry. So, as soon as the wind was favourable, he collected brushwood which he placed close to the walls and set alight, adding sulphur and pitch to the fire. The flames soon engulfed the building. Some of the defenders perished within the walls; and those that escaped through the flames were taken and put to death. Baltoghlu then rounded up the civilian inhabitants of the island and sold them all into slavery, to punish them for having permitted resistance on their soil.[1]

On 11 April the Sultan was again in his tent before the walls, and all his great guns had been placed to his liking. The following day the bombardment began, to last with ceaseless monotony for more than six weeks. The cannons were unwieldly. It was difficult to keep them in position on their platforms of planks and rubble. They continually slid off into the mud caused by the April rains. The largest of them, including Urban's monster, needed so much attention that they could only be fired seven times in a day. But each of those seven shots did enormous damage. The cannon-balls. coming from just across the foss, in a cloud of black smoke and with a deafening roar, broke into a thousand pieces as they hit the walls; and the masonry could not stand up to them. The defenders attempted to lessen their impact by hanging sheets of leather and bales of wool over the walls, but with little effect. Within less than a week the outer wall across the Lycus valley had been completely destroyed in many places and the foss in front largely filled up, so that the task of repair was very difficult. Nevertheless Giustiniani and his helpers managed to erect a stock-ade. Men, and women too, from the city came every night after dark with planks and barrels and sacks of earth. The stockade was made mainly of wood, with barrels filled with earth placed on it to serve as crenellations. It was ramshackle and fragile; but at least it provided some protection for the defenders.[1]

At the harbour boom things were better. On 12 April, as soon as his reinforcements from the Black Sea had arrived, Baltoghlu brought up his larger ships towards the chain. As he approached his archers let loose a hail of arrows at the ships that lay at anchor guarding it, and his guns fired their cannon-balls. Then, as they closed, his marines hurled flaming brands on to the Christian ships, while others tried to cut their anchor-ropes, and others to board them by means of grappling irons and ladders. They had little success. The cannon-balls could not achieve sufficient elevation to harm the tall Christian galleys. The Megadux Lucas Notaras had been sent with his reserves to help in the defence. It was well organized. Pails of water, carried by relays of men, put out the fires. The Christian arrows and javelins, fired from the greater height of their decks and the crows-nests, were far more effective than the Turks'; and their stone-throwing machines did great damage. Cheered by their successes and aided by navigators more skilful than the enemies', the Christian fleet began to move out to encircle the Turkish ships nearest to the boom. In order to save them Baltoghlu called off the attack and sailed back to his anchorage off the Double Columns.[2]

The defeat humiliated the Sultan. His active mind saw at once that unless his cannons could aim higher they would be of little use against the tall ships of the Christians. His foundries were ordered to improve their designs. It was difficult to calculate the necessary trajectory; but after a few days they made improvements that satisfied the Sultan. A cannon with a higher trajectory was placed just beyond Galata Point and began to fire at the ships anchored along the boom. The first shot failed, but the second landed on the very centre of a galley and sank her, with considerable loss of life. The Christian ships were forced to keep within the boom, where the walls of Pera offered protection.

It was, however, on land that Mehmet was most hopeful. He calculated that the damage done to the land-walls would enable him to take the city without the necessity of forcing the boom. On 18 April, two hours after sunset, he ordered an assault on the Mesoteichion. To the light of flares, with their drums beating and their cymbals clanging, and shouting their battle-cries, detachments of heavy infantry-men and javelin-throwers and archers and the footmen of the Janissary Guard rushed over the filled-in foss up to the stockade. They brought torches with which to set fire to the wooden planks of which it was made, and they had fixed hooks at the end of their lances with which to bring down the barrels full of earth which topped it. Some had ladders to place against the parts of the wall that still stood. The fighting was confused. In the narrow terrain on which the assault was launched the Turks' superiority in numbers was valueless: while the armour worn by the Christians was more efficient than that of the Turks and enabled them to risk their persons more boldly. Giustiniani was in command and proved his value as a leader. Greeks as well as Italians were inspired by his energy and courage and loyally supported him. The Emperor himself was not present. He had feared that this was to be an attack along the whole line of the walls and was on a hasty tour of inspection, to see that everyone was prepared.

The fighting lasted for four hours. Then the Turks were called back to their lines. The Venetian diarist Barbaro calculated that they had lost about two hundred men. Not one of the Christians had been killed.[1]

The failure of this first assault on the walls, coming so soon after the failure of the attack on the boom, gave new confidence to the defenders. Though the bombardment continued relentlessly, they set about the repair of the walls with freshened enthusiasm. If only help would soon arrive from the outside world the city might yet be saved.

Two days later their hopes were given further encouragement.

CHAPTER VII

THE LOSS OF THE GOLDEN HORN

Throughout the first two weeks of April the wind had been blowing strong from the north. The three Genoese galleys which the Pope had hired and filled with arms and provisions were storm-bound at Chios. On 15 April the wind changed suddenly to the south; and the ships set sail at once for the Dardanelles. As they approached the Straits they were joined by a large Imperial transport, laden with corn bought by the Emperor's ambassadors in Sicily and commanded by an experienced sailor called Phlatanelas. The Dardanelles were unguarded, as the whole Turkish fleet was now off Constantinople. The ships sailed swiftly through into the Sea of Marmora. In the morning of Friday, 20 April, watchers on the sea-walls saw them approach towards the city. They were seen, too, by Turkish watchmen who hastened to inform the Sultan. He leapt on to his horse and rode over the hills to give orders to Baltoghlu. The admiral was instructed to capture the ships if possible, otherwise to sink them. On no account must they be allowed to reach the city. If he failed in this task he was not to return alive.

Baltoghlu at once prepared his ships. He decided not to use the boats dependent on sails alone, as they could not run against the fresh southerly wind; all the rest of his fleet was to join him. The Sultan had brought some of his best soldiers with him. These were loaded on to the larger transports. Some of the ships were fitted with guns. Others were protected with erections of shields and bucklers. Within two or three hours the great armada set out, propelled by thousands of oars, to capture the helpless victims. They advanced, confident of victory, drums beating and trumpets sounding. In the city all the citizens who could be spared from the defence of the walls crowded to the slopes of the Acropolis or on to the summit of the huge ruined Hippodrome, with anxious eyes fixed on the Christian ships, while the Sultan and his staff watched from the shores of the Bosphorus, just beyond the walls of Pera.

In the early afternoon, when the Turks came up to them, the Christian ships were already off the south-eastern corner of the city. Baltoghlu from the leading trireme shouted to them to lower their sails. They refused and kept to their course. Thereupon the leading Turkish ships closed in on them. A heavy sea was now running, with the wind blowing against the Bosphorus current. It was difficult to manoeuvre the triremes and biremes in such weather. Moreover, the Christian ships had the advantage of height and were well-armed. From their decks, their high poops and prows and their crows-nests the sailors were able to pour down their arrows and javelins and stones on to the Turkish ships below them; and the Turks could do very little except try to board or set fire to the hulls. For nearly an hour the Christian ships sailed on, impeded by the Turks but continually shaking them off. Then suddenly, just as they were about to round the point below the Acropolis, the wind dropped and their sails flapped idly. Here a branch of the current that sweeps southward down the Bosphorus hits the point and curves northward toward the Pera shore; and its pull is particularly strong after a southerly wind. The Christian ships were caught in it. After almost touching the walls of the city they began slowly to drift towards the very spot where the Sultan was watching the battle.

It seemed easy now for Baltoghlu to take his prey. He had noted the damage that the Christians' fire could do to his ships if they came too close. He therefore brought up his larger vessels to surround the enemy at a slight distance, to fire cannon-balls and flame-bearing lances at them, intending to close in again when they were weakened. His efforts were vain. His light cannon lacked the necessary elevation; and any fires that were started were quickly put out by the well trained Christian crews. He therefore called out to his men to advance and board. He himself took as his target the Imperial transport. It was the largest of the Christian vessels and the least well-armed. He ran the bow of his trireme into her poop, while others of his ships came up and tried to fasten themselves to her with grappling-irons or with hooks flung at her anchor-chains. Of the Genoese ships one was seen to be surrounded by five triremes, another by thirty *fustae*, and the third by forty *parandaria* filled with soldiers; but in the confusion no one could tell from a distance what was happening. The discipline on the Christian ships was superb. The Genoese wore effective armour, and they had supplied themselves with ample tuns of water with which to put out fires and with axes that were used to lop off the heads and hands of the boarding-parties. The Imperial transport, though less well suited for war-fare, carried barrels filled with the inflammable liquid known as Greek Fire, the arm which had saved Constantinople in many sea-battles during the last eight hundred years. These were used with a devastating effect. The Turks on their side were handi-capped by their oars. Those of one ship would be entangled with another's; and many were broken by the missiles that poured down from above. But whenever a Turkish ship was disabled there was always another to take her place.

It was round the Imperial ship that the fighting was most desperate. Baltoghlu would not let go of her. Wave after wave of his men attempted to board her, only to be driven back by Phlatanelas and his crew. But she was running short of weapons. The Genoese captains, despite their own difficulties, noticed her plight. They somehow brought their ships close alongside; and soon the four ships were lashed together. To the watchers on the shore they gave the appearance of a great four-towered fortress rising out of the confusion of the Turkish fleet.

All through the afternoon the citizens watched the battle with growing anxiety from their walls and towers. The Sultan too

watched excitedly from the shore, now shouting words of encouragement, now curses, and now instructions which Baltoghlu
pretended not to hear; for His Majesty, for all his appreciation of
sea-power, had no knowledge at all of seamanship. In his eagerness Mehmet kept urging his horse into the sea, riding out into
the shallow water till his robe was trailing in it, as though he
wished to take part in the fighting himself.

As evening approached it seemed that the Christian ships could
not survive much longer. They had done great damage; but there
were still fresh Turkish ships to come up to the attack. Then
suddenly, as the sun began to set, the wind rose again in gusts from
the north. The great sails of the Christian ships filled once more;
and they were able to crash their way through the Turkish craft
towards the safety of the boom. In the gathering darkness Baltoghlu could not reorganize his fleet. With the Sultan still hurling
commands and imprecations at him, he ordered a withdrawal to
the anchorage off the Double Columns. When night had fallen
the boom was opened, and three Venetian galleys, under Trevisano's command, sailed out with a loud noise of trumpets, so that
the Turks would believe that they were to be attacked by the
whole Christian fleet and would remain on the defensive. The
victorious ships were then escorted to anchorages in the security
of the Golden Horn.

It had been a great and heartening victory. In their delight the
Christians declared that ten or twelve thousand Turks had perished
and not one Christian, though two or three sailors died of their
wounds a few days later. A soberer estimate gave the Turkish
losses as slightly more than a hundred killed and more than three
hundred wounded, and the Christian losses as twenty-three
killed and almost half the crews suffering from some sort of
wound. Nevertheless, the ships had brought a welcome increase
in man-power and valuable supplies of armaments and foodstuffs. They had shown, too, the superiority of Christian seamanship.[1]

The Sultan was enraged. Though his losses had not been large, the humiliation and the damage to Turkish morale were serious. A letter written to him at once by one of the chief religious authorities in his camp, Sheikh Ak Shemseddin, told him that people were blaming him for his misjudgement and lack of authority and sternly ordered him to punish the responsible culprits, lest similar disasters should occur among his land-forces as well.[1] Next day Mehmet summoned Baltoghlu before him and publicly upbraided him as a traitor, a coward and a fool, and ordered his beheading. The unhappy admiral, who had been severely wounded in the eye by a stone hurled from one of his own ships, was only saved from death by the testimony given by his officers to his personal tenacity and courage. He was sentenced to be deprived not only of his offices of Admiral and Governor of Gallipoli, which were given to one of the Sultan's intimates, Hamza Bey, but also of all his private possessions, which were distributed among the Janissaries. He was then bastinadoed and released, to spend the rest of his days in impoverished obscurity.[2]

Ever since the first failure of his ships to force the boom Mehmet had been wondering how to obtain control of the Golden Horn. This bitter defeat determined him to act at once. While the sea-battle had been raging on 20 April the bombardment of the walls had never ceased. On the 21st it recommenced more relentlessly than ever. Within the course of the day a great tower near the Lycus valley, known as the Bactatinian, was brought down in ruins and a large portion of the outer wall below it destroyed. Had the Turks then ordered a general assault it would have been impossible, so the defenders believed, to have held them. But the Sultan was not present at the walls that day; and the order to attack was not given. After dark the breach was repaired with beams and earth and rubble.[3]

Mehmet had spent the day at the Double Columns. His ingenious mind had worked out the answer to his problem. It was probably an Italian in his service who suggested to him that ships could be transported overland. The Venetians in one of their recent Lombard campaigns had triumphantly carried a whole flotilla on wheeled platforms from the river Po to Lake Garda. But there the country had been flat. To transport ships from the Bosphorus into the Golden Horn, over a ridge that rose nowhere less than two hundred feet above sea-level, was a harder problem. But the Sultan lacked neither man-power nor material. During the early days of the siege his engineers had been constructing a road which seems to have run from Tophane up the steep valley which leads to the present Taksim Square, then to have turned a little to the left and come down the valley below the present British Embassy to the low ground by the Golden Horn which the Byzantines called the Valley of the Springs and which is now known as Kasimpaşa. If the sailors in the Golden Horn or the citizens of Pera had noticed the construction of the road, they doubtless assumed that the Sultan merely wished to have easier access to his naval base at the Double Columns. There timber had been amassed to make wheeled cradles for the ships and a sort of tramway; metal wheels had been cast, and teams of oxen collected. Meanwhile a number of guns were placed in the Valley of the Springs.

On 21 April work was speeded up. While thousands of artisans and labourers made the last preparations, the Sultan ordered his cannon behind Pera to play continuously on the boom, so that the ships stationed there should be distracted, while the black smoke would obscure the view up the Bosphorus and veil his activities there. By a deliberate error some of the cannon-balls fell on the walls of Pera itself, to keep the citizens away from them so that they could not pry.

It was at the first glimmering of dawn on Sunday, 22 April, that the strange procession of boats began. The cradles were lowered into the water and the ships tied on to them there; then pulleys dragged them ashore and teams of oxen were harnessed in front of each, with teams of men to help over the steeper and more difficult parts of the road. In every boat the oarsmen sat in their places, moving their oars in the empty air while the officers walked up and down giving the beat. Sails were hoisted exactly as though the vessels were at sea. Flags were flown, drums beaten and fifes and trumpets played while ship after ship was hauled up the hill, as it were in a fantastic carnival. A small *fusta* led the way. Once it had negotiated the first steep slope successfully, some seventy triremes, biremes, *fustae* and *parandaria* followed in rapid succession.[1]

Long before noon the Christian sailors on the Golden Horn and the watchmen on the walls above the harbour saw to their horror this extraordinary movement of ships down the hill opposite to them into the waters of the Horn by the Valley of the Springs. There was consternation in the city. Before the last vessel had slithered into the harbour the Venetian Bailey had consulted with the Emperor and Giustiniani and, on their advice, had summoned the Venetian sea-captains to an intimate discussion, at which Giustiniani was the only outsider to be present. Various suggestions were made. One proposal was to induce the Genoese at Pera to join in a general attack on the Turkish fleet in the harbour. With the help of their boats, which had hitherto taken no part in the war, the Turks might easily be beaten in open battle. But Pera was unlikely to wish to abandon its neutrality; and in any case time would be lost over the necessary negotiations. Another proposal was to land men on the opposite bank to destroy the Turkish guns at the Valley of the Springs and then to attempt to burn their ships. But there were not enough fighting men in the city to risk so hazardous an operation. Finally, the captain of a galley that had come from Trebizond, Giacomo Coco by name, proposed that an immediate attempt should be made by night to burn the ships; and he offered to lead the expedition himself. His offer was accepted by the council, who decided to act without informing the Genoese in the city. Secrecy was essential; and the Venetians were prepared to supply the necessary boats.

Coco's scheme was to send two large transports ahead, with their sides protected against cannon-balls with bales of cotton and wool. Two large galleys were to follow, to drive off any opposition. Hidden by these great ships two small *fustae*, propelled by oarsmen, would creep unnoticed into the midst of the Turkish ships, cutting their anchor-ropes and flinging combustibles on to them. To Coco's disappointment it was decided to wait until the night of the 24th to make the attempt, in order that the Venetian ships might be prepared. Unfortunately the secret was not kept; somehow the Genoese in the city heard of it and were furious at being excluded, suspecting that the Venetians wished to steal the glory. To pacify them it was agreed that they could supply one of the boats. But they had none ready; so they insisted that there should be another postponement, till the 28th. It was a disastrous decision. The Turks were all the while adding to their number of guns at the Valley of the Springs; and it was impossible to keep all the preparations unnoticed. The news reached Pera and a Genoese there who was in the Sultan's pay.

On Saturday, 28 April, two hours before dawn, two great transports, one Venetian and one Genoese, well padded with their bales, crept out from the protection of the walls of Pera, accompanied by two Venetian galleys, each with forty oarsmen, under the command of Trevisano himself and his deputy, Zaccaria Grioni. They were followed by three light *fustae*, each with seventy-two oarsmen, with Coco in the leading boat, and with them a number of small boats carrying combustible materials. As they started out, the sailors noticed a bright light flaring from one of the towers of Pera. They wondered whether this was a signal for the Turks; but as they drew near to the Turkish fleet everything seemed to be quiet. The heavy transports and galleys moved slowly through the still water; and Coco grew impatient. He knew that his boat could outpace them, so, eager for action and for glory, he brought the *fustae* through the line and made straight for the Turks. There was a sudden roar as the Turkish guns opened fire from the shore. They had been warned. Coco's boat was hit by one of the first shots. A few minutes later she was struck amidships and sank. A few sailors were able to swim ashore, but most of them, including Coco himself, perished. The other *fustae*, with the small boats trailing round them, made for the protection provided by the galleys. But by the time that they came up the Turkish guns were keeping a continuous fire, directing their aim by the light of flares and by their own flashes. The two transports in front were struck many times. Their bales saved them from serious damage; but their sailors were too busily engaged in putting out the smouldering fires caused by the shots to do anything for the small boats, many of which were sunk. The Turks concentrated their main attention on Trevisano's galley. Two balls fired from the slope of the hill struck her with such force that she began to fill with water. Trevisano and his crew had to take to their boats and abandon her. After this success, in the faint light of dawn, the Turkish ships put out to the attack. But the Christians were able to disentangle themselves. After an hour and a half of fighting both squadrons returned to their anchorages.

Forty Christian sailors had swum ashore to the Turkish lines. Later in the day they were slaughtered in full sight of the city. In revenge the two hundred and sixty prisoners that were in the city were brought to the walls and beheaded before the eyes of the Turks.

The battle had shown once more that the Christians outmatched the Turks in the quality of their ships and their seamanship. But they had none the less suffered a costly defeat. They had lost a galley and a *fusta* and about ninety of their best sailors. Only one Turkish ship had been destroyed. The depression in the city was deep. It was clear that the Turks could not now be displaced from the Golden Horn. They had not obtained complete mastery of it; the Christian fleet still floated. But the harbour was no longer secure, and the long line of walls that faced it was no longer free from the danger of attack. To the Greeks, who remembered that it had been over these walls that the Crusaders had entered the city in 1204, the outlook seemed especially threatening; and the Emperor and Giustiniani were in despair to know how now they could man all the defences.

By moving half his fleet into the Golden Horn and by defeating the attempt of the Christians to dislodge the intruders, Mehmet had won a great victory. It seems that he still believed that the city would have to be captured by breaking through the land-walls; but he could now perpetually threaten the harbour-walls while still keeping enough ships outside the boom to blockade the city. Moreover, should a relieving fleet arrive and manage to force the blockade, it would find no peace in the harbour. The new situation also gave him a tighter control of Pera. The part played by the Genoese there had been shamefully equivocal. The government at Genoa had given the local authorities a free hand, while probably advising them to pursue a policy of neutrality. This they had officially done. The general sympathies of the colony were with their fellow-Christians across the harbour. Several of the citizens had joined Giustiniani. The colony's merchants continued to trade with the city, sending what goods they could spare to it. Others did, indeed, trade also with the Turks; but many of these acted as spies, reporting to Giustiniani the information that they gathered in the Turkish camp. The authorities had so far endangered their neutrality as to allow the harbour boom to be fixed at one end to their walls; and though their ships had taken no part in the fighting it seems that the sailors used to render small services to the ships at the boom. But it was hard for any Genoese to like a Greek and still harder for him to like a Venetian. A few heroic soldiers like Giustiniani or the Bocchiardi brothers might fling themselves whole-heartedly into the struggle; but at Pera, where the average man did not see himself to be immediately threatened, such heroism seemed a little extravagant.

The Greeks and Venetians returned the dislike. Though they genuinely admired Giustiniani and were ready to follow his command, and though they gave generous praise to the other valiant Genoese, Pera appeared to them to be a nest of traitors to Christendom. The Sultan certainly had his spies there, as the story of the last battle showed. Surely, too, it was thought, someone in Pera must have been aware of the Sultan's preparations to move his ships along a road so close to the town walls. Even though it doubtless could not have been prevented, at least some warning of the operation might have been sent across the harbour. Archbishop Leonard, himself a Genoese, wrote with some embarrassment of his countrymen's behaviour.[1]

But, if the Christians in Constantinople were dissatisfied with the citizens of Pera, so too was the Sultan. He could not well attempt to occupy the colony while he had the siege of Constantinople itself on his hands. To storm it would use up more men and machines than he could spare for the moment; and any move that he might make against it would probably bring a Genoese fleet to the Levant, and he would lose his command of the seas. But now that his ships were in the Golden Horn he encircled Pera. Its merchants could no longer easily row their goods across the harbour to Constantinople, bringing the latest information about the Turkish camp. Unless Pera was prepared to break its neutrality there was little more that it could do to help the Christian cause; and the Sultan seems to have been satisfied from the agents that he maintained there that the authorities were not going to take such a risk.[2]

Also, the Sultan could now improve his communications with Zaganos's army on the heights behind Pera and with the naval headquarters on the Bosphorus. Hitherto the only road had made a long detour round the marshy head of the Golden Horn, though there was a short cut through an inconvenient ford across its upper waters. Now, with his ships in the Horn to protect him, he could build a bridge across the harbour, just above the city walls. It was a pontoon, constructed of about a hundred wine barrels lashed securely together in pairs joined lengthways, to form the width of the passage, with a slight space between each pair. Over the barrels were beams and over them planks. Five men could walk abreast on them; and they could support heavy carts. Attached to the pontoon were floating platforms, each strong enough to bear the weight of a cannon. Troops could thus be moved quickly from the Pera shore to the walls of the city under the protection of the guns, while the guns could pound at a new angle against the walls of the Blachernae quarter.[1]

The Christians still kept most of their ships at the boom, to prevent the junction of the two Turkish fleets and to welcome any relieving flotilla that might arrive; and the Turks did not venture to attack them for several days. But their presence there could not disguise the fact that the defence had lost control of the Golden Horn.

CHAPTER VIII

FADING HOPE

The Sultan did not follow up his victory with any attempt to assault the city. He preferred for the time being to harass and wear out the defence. The bombardment of the land-walls never ceased. Every night teams of citizens had to come and make what repairs they could. The guns from the new pontoon platforms hammered at the Blachernae quarter. Every now and then Turkish ships would put out from their anchorage across the Horn and make as if to attack the walls above the harbour. Greek and Venetian ships had to keep on the alert to intercept them. There was scarcely any hand-to-hand fighting for a week, and no loss of life. But the city had other problems to face. Provisions were running short. Men who should be at their stations on the walls continually asked permission to go back to the city to find food for their wives and children. By the first days of May the shortage was so acute that the Emperor made a fresh collection of funds from the churches and from private individuals and with the money bought up whatever provisions he could find, setting up a committee to see that they were evenly distributed. It did its job well. Though the rations were small every family had its share; there were no more serious complaints. But the gardens in the city produced little at that season, and fishing boats could no longer put out safely to sea, even in the Golden Horn. The number of cattle and sheep and swine within the walls had never been large and was quickly diminishing, as were the stores of grain. Unless provisions, even more than men, were soon sent from outside, the soldiers and the citizens would be starved into surrender.[1]

V   The Triple Wall of Constantinople
The view looks northward across the Mesoteichion, where
the wall was breached

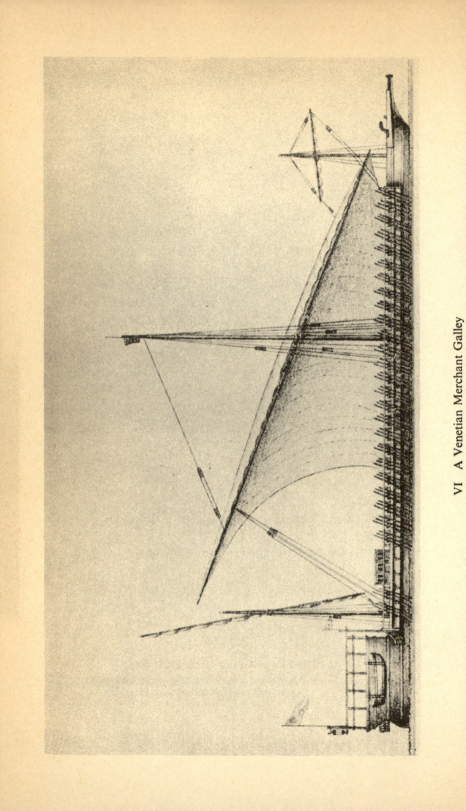

VI   A Venetian Merchant Galley

With this in mind the Emperor summoned the leading Venetians as well as his own notables and suggested that a swift ship be sent out of the harbour down the Dardanelles to seek the fleet that Minotto had promised that Venice would dispatch. It had been on 26 January that Minotto had written to Venice to beg for it; and nothing had been heard in reply. At Constantinople no one knew of the delays that had occurred at Venice, where, though Minotto's letter had been in the Senate's hands by 19 February, exactly two months passed before the relieving fleet set sail. The Emperor had great faith in the Captain-General, Loredan, who, he had heard, was a brave Christian commander. He did not know of the instructions that were given to the Admiral Alviso Longo on 13 April: that he was to take his fleet as speedily as possible to Tenedos, stopping only for one day at Modon to revictual. At Tenedos he was to remain at anchor till 20 May, informing himself about the strength and movements of the Turkish fleet. On that date he would be joined by the Captain-General with his own galleys and with galleys from Crete. Then the whole fleet would sail up the Dardanelles and force its way to the beleaguered city. Nor was it known at Constantinople that Loredan was only ordered to leave Venice on 7 May. He was to sail to Corfu, where the governor's galley would meet him and take him to Negropont. There two Cretan galleys would meet him; and they would all sail for Tenedos. If Longo had already left for Constantinople, a galley would have been left behind to inform him and escort him up the Straits. But he was not to provoke any action by the Turks until he reached Constantinople, where he was to put himself at the Emperor's disposal, emphasizing to him the great sacrifices that Venice was making in coming to his aid. If Constantine had already made peace with the Turks, the Captain-General was to go to the Morea and use his forces to oblige the Despot Thomas to restore some villages that he had illegally annexed. On 8 May the Senate passed supplementary resolutions. If Loredan heard on his journey that the Emperor had not made peace, he was to see that Negropont was placed in a proper state of defence. He was moreover to be accompanied by an ambassador, Bartolomeo Marcello, who was to proceed at once to the Sultan's court and assure Mehmet of the Republic's peaceable intentions; the Captain-General and his forces had merely come to escort back the merchant-ships engaged in the Levant trade and to see to Venice's legitimate interests. The Sultan should be urged to make peace with the Emperor and the Emperor to accept any reasonable terms. But if Mehmet was determined to continue with his enterprise the ambassador was not to insist but was to report back to the Senate.

The Senate's instructions were carefully thought out and might have been effective had there been limitless time. But no one at Venice understood as yet the tenacity of the Sultan's character nor the superb quality of his weapons of war. The threat to Constantinople was known; but everyone believed that somehow the great fortress-city could hold out indefinitely.[1]

The Pope, despite his anxiety, was still more leisurely. It was not until 5 June, a week after all was over, that his representative, the Archbishop of Ragusa, informed the Senate of His Holiness's proposal about the five galleys that the Venetians were to loan to him for the rescue of the city. He would pay fourteen thousand ducats, which should cover the salaries of the crews for four months. The Archbishop was told that this was not enough. He returned to Rome with a demand that the Pope must also pay for part of the armament; but in the meantime the galleys would be made ready for the voyage.[2]

In ignorance of all the delays and in the hope of soon making contact with a Venetian fleet, a Venetian brigantine from the flotilla in the Golden Horn, with twelve volunteers on board, all disguised to look like Turks, was towed to the boom on the evening of 3 May. At midnight the chain was moved to let her through. Hoisting the Turkish colours she sailed unintercepted on the north wind across the Marmora and out into the Aegean.[1]

In the city itself the strain was beginning to tell on the defenders' nerves. The mutual dislike of the Venetians and the Genoese broke out into open quarrels. The Venetians blamed the Genoese for the disaster of 28 April. The Genoese retorted that it was all the fault of Coco's imprudence. They then accused the Venetians of sending away ships to safety whenever an occasion arose. The Venetians pointed out that they had unshipped the rudders from many of their galleys and had stored them and the sails in the city. Why had the Genoese not done the same? The Genoese remarked that they had no intention of lessening the efficiency of their vessels, particularly as many of them had wives and children at Pera to consider. When the Venetians further upbraided the Genoese for keeping in touch with the Sultan's camp, they answered that any negotiations that they had conducted there had been done with the full knowledge of the Emperor, whose interests were similar to their own. The recriminations were so public that the Emperor in despair summoned the leaders of both sides and begged them to keep the peace. 'The war outside our gates is enough for us', he cried. 'For the pity of God do not start a war between yourselves.' His words had some effect. Outward co-operation was restored; but the ill-will remained.[2]

It is probable that during these days the Emperor had tried to negotiate with the Sultan. It seems that the Genoese of Pera had made tentative inquiries on his behalf. But the Sultan's offer was unchanged. The city must be surrendered to him uncon-ditionally, then he would personally guarantee the citizens their lives and personal possessions. The Emperor could retire if he wished to the Morea. The terms were unacceptable. No one in the city, whatever his political views, would now contemplate the humiliation of surrender; nor had anyone much faith in the Sultan's clemency. There were, however, among the Emperor's advisers several who believed that he should escape from the city.

He would be better able to organize a campaign against the Turks from without than from within. His brothers and many sympathizers from all over the Balkans would surely flock to his banner, including, perhaps, the valiant Scanderbeg himself; and he could rouse Western Europe to its duty. But Constantine quietly and firmly refused to listen to them. He feared that if he abandoned the city the defence would disintegrate; if the city had to perish he would perish with it.[1]

The Genoese of Pera had good reasons for wishing for peace. On 5 May the Turkish guns began to fire over the city at the Christian ships by the boom. They aimed particularly at the Venetians; but a ball, two hundred pounds in weight, fell upon a Genoese merchant-ship, laden with a valuable cargo of silk, and sank her. She belonged to a trader of Pera and had been anchored close under the walls. The municipality sent at once to the Sultan to complain, pointing out how useful the neutrality of Pera was to him. His ministers received the mission with some truculence. Their gunners could not know, they said, that the ship was not a hostile ship, a 'pirate' come to help their enemies. But if the owner could prove his case the Sultan, as soon as he had captured Constantinople, would look into the matter and give full compensation.[2]

During the first days of May Urban's great cannon had been out of order. By 6 May it was repaired; and the bombardment of the land-walls showed renewed vigour, while the Turkish ships were obviously being prepared for battle. The defence rightly suspected an assault on the following day and made its own preparations. When the assault came, four hours after sunset on 7 May, it was, however, directed only against the Mesoteichion section of the land-walls. A vast number of Turks, armed as usual with scaling ladders and hooks attached to their lances, poured in over the filled-up foss. There was bitter fighting for about three hours; but they could not force an entry over the ruined walls and the stockade. Prodigies of valour were attributed to a Greek soldier called Rhangabe, who was said to have cut in two the Sultan's own standard-bearer, Amir Bey, though he himself was soon surrounded and slain.[1]

Though the Turkish navy had not attacked that night, conditions in the Golden Horn seemed so insecure that next day the Venetians decided to unload all the war material kept in their ships and store it in the Imperial arsenal. On the 9th they further resolved that all their ships apart from those required to guard the boom should be moved into the small harbour known as the Neorion, or the Prosphorianus, just within the boom under the Acropolis, and that the crews should be brought to help defend the Blachernae quarters, where the walls had been badly damaged by the fire of the guns on the pontoon. Some of the sailors were at first unwilling to agree. It was not till 13 May that this re-arrangement was completed. The sailors' main task was to see to the repair of the wall that protected the quarter.[2]

They nearly arrived too late. On the previous evening the Turks had launched another full-scale attack, this time on the high ground near the junction of the Blachernae and Theodosian walls. It was nearly midnight when the assault began. It was repulsed and was soon called off; the walls here were still in too strong a state.[3]

On 14 May the Sultan, satisfied in view of the Venetians' move that his ships in the Golden Horn would not now be attacked, moved his batteries from the hills behind the Valley of the Springs and took them across his new bridge to bombard the Blachernae wall at the section where it began to mount the slope. They did small damage there; so a day or two later he moved them again, to join his main batteries in the Lycus valley. He could see that this was the most promising section to attack. Henceforward the bombardment of other sections of the walls was only intermittent, but there with the increased number of guns it could be carried on without a pause.[4]

On the 16th and again on the 17th the main Turkish fleet sailed down from the Double Columns to make a demonstration against the boom. It was still well defended; and on both occasions the ships retired without firing an arrow or a shot. A similar manoeuvre was made on the 21st. The whole fleet came with drums and trumpets sounding. It appeared so menacing that bells were rung in the city to put everyone on the alert. Once again after promenading up and down in front of the boom the ships sailed back quietly to their anchorage. This was the last occasion on which the boom was threatened. It is probable that the morale of the sailors, few of whom were Turks by birth, was not very high; and neither the Sultan nor his Admiral wished to risk the humiliation of another defeat.[1]

Meanwhile the land operations had been supplemented by attempts to dig mines under the walls. The Sultan had begun such operations during the first days of the siege, but he lacked sufficiently experienced miners. Now Zaganos Pasha produced from among his troops a number of professional miners from the silver-mines at Novo Brodo in Serbia. They were ordered to dig a mine under the walls somewhere near to the Charisian Gate, where the ground was thought to be favourable. They started on their work far in the rear, in the hope of escaping notice; but the task of digging under the foss as well as the walls was too difficult. This mine was abandoned. Instead, they began to dig under the single Blachernae wall, near the Caligarian Gate. On 16 May their operation was discovered by the defence. The Megadux, Lucas Notaras, whose business it was to deal with such an emergency, called upon the services of the engineer Johannes Grant. At his request Grant dug a countermine and succeeded in entering the Turkish mine, where he burnt the wooden props. The roof fell in, burying many of the miners. This failure discouraged the Turkish sappers for several days; but by 21 May they were digging mines at various parts of the wall, concentrating mainly on the section near the Caligarian Gate. The countermining was done by Notaras's Greek troops, with Grant to direct them. In some cases it was possible to smoke the enemy miners out of their caverns, in others to flood the mines from cisterns intended to provide water for the foss.[1]

The Sultan had already made use of another device. On the morning of 18 May the defence was horrified to see a great wooden tower on wheels standing outside the walls of the Mesoteichion. The Turks had assembled it during the night. It consisted of a wooden framework protected with layers of bullocks' and camels' hides, with steps inside which led to an upper platform, itself as high as the outer wall of the city. On the platform were stored scaling ladders, to be used when the turret should be moved up against the wall; but its primary purpose was to provide protection for the workmen engaged in filling up the foss. Experience gained by his earlier attempts at an assault had taught the Sultan that the foss was still an obstacle and that it must have solid pathways built across it. All day on the 18th his men worked to build a road over the foss, while the turret stood over them, on the edge of the ditch, opposite to a tower which his artillery had destroyed and from which the masonry had fallen forward into the ditch. By dark the task was almost complete, in spite of fierce opposition. Part of the foss had been filled with the fallen masonry and stones and earth and brushwood, and the turret had been edged on to the causeway to test its strength. But during the night some of the defenders crept out and placed kegs of powder into the fillings. When they were set alight there was a great explosion, and the wooden turret burst into flames and collapsed, killing the men on it. By morning the foss was half-cleared again and the nearby wall and stockade repaired. Other turrets built by the Turks proved equally unsuccessful. Some were destroyed and the rest withdrawn.[2]

Such successes kept the spirits of the Christians from falling. On 23 May they had their last heartening experience. That day, as on previous days, the Turks attempted to mine under the Blachernae wall; but on this occasion the Greeks were able to surround and capture a number of miners, including a senior officer. Under torture he revealed to them where all the Turkish mines were placed. Grant was able to destroy them one by one, that day and the next. The last to be destroyed was one whose entrance had been cunningly concealed by one of the Sultan's wooden turrets; had the plans not been betrayed it would never have been discovered. From that time the Turks abandoned their mining activities.[1]

They may have realized that the strain on the defence was doing their work for them. Remarkably few Christians had as yet been killed; but many had been wounded, and all were tired and hungry. Supplies of arms, particularly of powder, were falling low; and food was shorter than ever. And on the 23rd, the day of the mining victory, Christian hopes suffered a terrible blow. That afternoon a boat was sighted tacking up the Marmora with a number of Turkish vessels in pursuit. She shook them off; and under cover of darkness the boom was opened to let her in. It was thought at first that she was the forerunner of a relieving fleet. But she was the brigantine that had sailed twenty days before to search for the Venetians. She had cruised to and fro through the islands of the Aegean; but no Venetian ships had been found nor were there even any rumours of ships in the offing. When it seemed useless to search any longer the captain asked the sailors what their wishes were. One man said that it was foolish to return to a city that was probably already in Turkish hands. But the others silenced him. It was their duty, they declared, to go back and tell the Emperor, whether it was to life or to death. When they came to his presence he wept as he thanked them. No Christian power was coming to join in the battle for Christendom. The city could now only put its faith, he said, in Christ and His Mother, and Saint Constantine its founder.[2]

Even this faith was to be tested. There were signs that Heaven itself was turning against the city. During these days everyone remembered again the prophecies that the Empire would perish.

The first Christian Emperor had been Constantine, son of Helena; the last would be similarly named. Men remembered, too, a prophecy that the city would never fall while the moon was waxing in the heavens. This had cheered the defenders when they faced the assault during the previous week. But on 24 May the moon would be at the full; and under the waning moon peril would come. On the night of the full moon there was an eclipse and three hours of darkness. It was probably on the following day, when the citizens all knew of the hopeless message brought by the brigantine, and when the eclipse had lowered their spirits still deeper, that a last appeal was made to the Mother of God. Her holiest icon was carried on the shoulders of the faithful round the streets of the city, and everyone who could be spared from the walls joined in the procession. As it moved slowly and solemnly the icon suddenly slipped off the platform on which it was borne. When men rushed to raise it it seemed as though it were made of lead; only the greatest effort could replace it. Then, as the procession wound on, a thunder-storm burst on the city. It was almost impossible to stand up against the hail, and the rain came down in such torrents that whole streets were flooded and children nearly swept away. The procession had to be abandoned. Next day, as if such omens had not been enough, the whole city was blotted out by a thick fog, a phenomenon unknown in those lands in the month of May. The Divine Presence was veiling itself in cloud, to conceal its departure from the city. That night, when the fog had lifted, it was noticed that a strange light played about the dome of the great Church of the Holy Wisdom. It was seen from the Turkish camp as well as by the citizens; and the Turks, too, were disquieted. The Sultan himself had to be reassured by his wise men who interpreted the sign as showing that the light of the True Faith would soon illumine the sacred building. For the Greeks and their Italian allies there was no such comforting interpretation.

Lights, too, could be seen from the walls, glimmering in the distant countryside far behind the Turkish camp, where no lights should be. A few hopeful watchmen declared that these were the camp-fires of troops coming with John Hunyadi to rescue the beleagured Christians. But no army appeared. The strange lights were never explained.[1]

Now once again the Emperor's ministers went to him to beg him to escape while still it might be possible and organize the defence of Christendom from some safer spot where he might find support. He was so weary that while they talked to him he fainted. When he revived he told them once more that he could not desert his people; he would die with them.[2]

The month of May was drawing to a close; and in the gardens and the hedgerows the roses were now in bloom. But the moon was waning; and the men and women of Byzantium, the ancient city whose symbol had been the moon, prepared themselves to meet the crisis that all knew to be upon them.

CHAPTER IX

THE LAST DAYS OF BYZANTIUM

Among the Christians hope was fading. But in the Turkish camp, too, there was pessimism and a general feeling of frustration. The siege had lasted for seven weeks; and yet the huge Turkish army with its magnificent war-engines had achieved very little. The defence might be weary and short of men and materials; and the walls of the city had been badly damaged. But no soldier had yet penetrated through them. There was still a danger that help might arrive from the West. Mehmet's agents had informed him that a fleet had been ordered to sail from Venice; and there were rumours that it had even reached Chios.[1] There was always the possibility that the Hungarians might cross the Danube. During the early days of the siege an embassy from John Hunyadi had arrived at the Turkish camp and had suggested that as Hunyadi was now no longer Regent of Hungary the armistice that he had signed for three years with the Sultan was no longer binding.[2] Moreover, morale amongst the Sultan's own troops was beginning to sink. His sailors had suffered humiliating reverses. His soldiers had won as yet no victories. The longer that the city eluded him the more his own prestige declined.

At his Court the old Vizier Halil and his friends still disapproved of the whole venture. Mehmet had gone against their advice in undertaking it. Was it possible that they were justified? It was, perhaps, partly to show them that he was not unreasonable and partly to satisfy his own conscience as a good Moslem who should avoid fighting unless the infidel obstinately refused to surrender, that he made one last overture for peace; though it would be peace on his own terms. There was in his camp a young noble called Ismail, the son of a renegade Greek whom he had made vassal-prince of Sinope. This was the envoy whom he now sent to the city. Ismail had friends among the Greeks, and he did his best to persuade them that it was not too late to save themselves. On his urging they appointed an ambassador to go back to the Turkish camp with him. The man's name was not recorded; we only know that he was of no high rank or family. The Sultan's treatment of ambassadors was notoriously uncertain; and it was doubtless felt that none of the notables could be spared on so risky a mission. He was however received not ungraciously by Mehmet, who sent him back with the message that the siege would be raised if the Emperor would undertake to pay an annual tribute of a hundred thousand gold bezants; or, if it were preferred, the citizens could abandon the city with all their movable possessions, and none of them would be harmed. When the offer came before the Emperor's Council one or two members believed that it might be possible to gain time by promising to pay the tribute. But the majority knew that so great a tribute could never be raised and that if it were not immediately forthcoming the Sultan would merely continue with the siege; and none of them now was willing to allow him to take over Constantinople without further effort. It may be that, as Turkish sources report, the Emperor answered by offering to surrender everything that he owned, except for the city, which was in fact his only remaining possession. To this the Sultan retorted that the only choice left to the Greeks lay between the surrender of the city, death by the sword, or conversion to Islam.[1]

These hollow negotiations probably took place on Friday, 25 May. On the Saturday Mehmet summoned his inner Council. The Vizier, Halil Pasha, relying on his record of long and distinguished public service, rose to his feet and demanded that the siege be abandoned. He had never approved of the campaign, and events had shown him to be right. The Turks had made no headway; instead, they had suffered some humiliating setbacks. At any time the princes of the West would come to the city's rescue. Venice had already dispatched a great fleet. Genoa, however unwillingly, would be forced to do likewise. Let the Sultan offer terms that would be acceptable to the Emperor and retire before worse disasters occurred. The venerable Vizier commanded respect. Many of his hearers, remembering how ineffectual the Turkish warships had shown themselves in their battles against the Christians, must have shuddered at the thought of great Italian navies bearing down on them. The Sultan, after all, was only a boy of twenty-one. Was he imperilling his great heritage with the impetuous recklessness of youth?

The next to speak was Zaganos Pasha. He disliked Halil, and he knew that the Sultan shared his dislike. Seeing his master's look of angry despair at the effect of Halil's speech he declared that he had no faith in the Grand Vizier's fears. The European powers were too bitterly divided amongst themselves ever to undertake joint action against the Turks; and even if a Venetian fleet was approaching, which he disbelieved, its ships and men would be far outnumbered by the Turks. He spoke of the omens that foretold the doom of the Christian Empire. He spoke of Alexander the Great, that youth who with a far smaller army had conquered half the world. The attack should be pressed forward, with no thought of retreat. Many of the younger generals rose to support Zaganos; the commander of the Bashi-bazouks was particularly vehement in his demand for stronger action. Mehmet's spirits rose; this was what he wished to hear. He told Zaganos to go out amongst the troops and ask them what they wished. Zaganos soon returned with the desired answer. Every man, he said, insisted that there should be an immediate attack. The Sultan then announced that the assault should take place as soon as it could be prepared.

From that moment Halil must have known that his days were numbered. He had always been a kindly friend to the Christians, with the tolerance of a pious Moslem of the old school, unlike such upstart renegades as Zaganos and Mahmud. Whether he had actually received presents from the Greeks is uncertain. But his enemies now insinuated that this was so; and the Sultan was glad to believe them.[1]

News of the Sultan's decision soon reached the city. Christians in his camp shot arrows over the walls, with letters describing the meeting of the Council wrapped round them.[2]

Throughout the Friday and the Saturday the bombardment of the land-walls had been heavier than ever. But the damage done was still quickly repaired. By the Saturday evening the stockade was as strong as it had ever been. But through the night the Turks could be seen by the light of their flares to be bringing up material of all sorts to fill the foss up solidly, and moving their guns forward on to the platforms that they built. On the Sunday the bombardment was concentrated on the stockade across the Mesoteichion. Three direct shots by the great cannon brought a portion down. Giustiniani, who had been supervising the repair-work, was slightly wounded by a splinter and retired for a few hours while his wound was dressed. He returned to his post before nightfall.[3]

On that same day of 27 May the Sultan rode through his whole army to announce that the great assault would take place very soon. His heralds followed him, pausing here and there to pro-claim that, as the customs of Islam ordered, the soldiers of the Faith would be allowed three days in which they might freely sack the city. The Sultan had sworn by eternal God and His Prophet and by the four thousand prophets and by the souls of his father and his children that all the treasure found in the city would be fairly distributed among the troops. The proclamation was received with shouts of joy. From within the city walls men could hear the Moslem hosts cry out in jubilation: 'There is no God but God, and Mohammed is His Prophet'.[4]

That night, as on the Saturday night, flares and torches lit up swarms of workmen pouring more and more material into the foss and piling stocks of arms beyond it. This night they worked in high excitement, shouting and singing, while fifes and trumpets, pipes and lutes encouraged them on. So bright were the flames that for one hopeful moment the besieged believed that the Turkish camp had caught fire and hurried on to the walls to see the conflagration. When they realized the true cause of the light they could only kneel down and pray.[1]

At midnight, quite suddenly, the work ceased and all the lights went out. The Sultan had commanded that the Monday should be a day of rest and atonement, that his warriors might be prepared for the final assault on the Tuesday. He himself spent the day inspecting all his troops and giving them their orders. First he rode with a grand escort over the bridge across the Golden Horn out to the Double Columns, to see his Admiral, Hamza Bey. Hamza was told that on the morrow his ships must be spread out across the boom and round against the whole Marmora shore of the city. The men should be given scaling-ladders and should attempt wherever possible, either from the ships themselves or from small boats, to make a landing and scale the walls, or, if that proved impracticable, at least to feign attacks so constantly that none of the defence would dare to leave the spot. As he rode back to give similar orders to his ships within the Golden Horn Mehmet stopped outside the chief gate of Pera and summoned the magistrates of the town to him. They were sternly commanded to see that none of their citizens gave any help to Constantinople the following day. If they disobeyed he would punish them at once. He then returned to his tent, to emerge again in the afternoon, when he rode down the whole length of the land-walls, talking to the officers and haranguing the men as they sat about the encampment.[2] When he had seen that all was to his liking, he summoned his ministers and the army leaders to his tent and spoke to them.

His speech is given to us by the historian Critobulus, who, like all educated Byzantines, was a student of Thucydides and therefore put into the mouths of his heroes the speeches which he

thought they would and should have given. But though the
words are the historian's they give us the sense of what the Sultan
must have said. He reminded the assembly of the riches that the
city still contained and of the booty that would soon be theirs.
He reminded them that for centuries it had been the sacred duty
of the Faithful to capture the Christian capital and that the Traditions promised success. The city was not impregnable, he said.
The enemy were few and exhausted and short of arms and
provisions, and divided between themselves; the Italians would
certainly not wish to die for a land that was not their own. To-
morrow, he declared, he would send wave after wave of his men
to the attack till out of weariness and despair the defenders would
yield. He urged his officers to show courage and keep discipline.
He then bade them go to their tents and rest and to be ready for
the signal of attack when it came. The chief commanders stayed
with him to receive his final instructions. The Admiral Hamza
already knew his allotted task. Zaganos, after providing men to
supplement the sailors who were to attack the walls along the
Golden Horn, was to bring the rest of his army across the bridge
for the assault on Blachernae. Karadja Pasha would be on his
right, as far as the Charisian Gate. Ishak and Mahmud, with the
Asiatic troops, were to attack the stretch from the Civil Gate of
Saint Romanus down to the Marmora, concentrating on the area
round the Third Military Gate. He himself, with Halil and
Saruja, would direct the main attack, which would be in the
Lycus Valley. Having made his wishes known he retired to have
supper and to sleep.[1]

All day long there was a strange stillness outside the walls.
Even the great cannons were silent. There were some in the city
who declared that the Turks were preparing to withdraw; but
their optimism was only a vain attempt to raise their own spirits.
Everyone knew that in fact the moment of crisis had come.
During the last few days the nervous exhaustion of the defenders
had been shown in bickering and mutual accusations between

VII   The City Walls

The view shows the stretch of the walls running northward from the
Charisian Gate. The tower from which the Emperor took his final look
at the Turkish camp is on the left.

VIII   View of Trebizond

Greeks, Venetians and Genoese. To the Venetians and the Greek alike the neutrality of Pera suggested that no Genoese was to be trusted. The arrogance of the Venetians offended both the Genoese and the Greeks. The Venetians had been constructing wooden shields and mantles in the workshops of their own quarter; and Minotto ordered Greek workmen to carry them to the defence lines at Blachernae. The workmen refused to do so unless they were paid, not from reasons of greed, as the Venetians chose to believe, but because they resented such summary orders from an Italian and because they genuinely needed to have money or spare time if they were to find food for their hungry families. Few Venetians had their families with them; and the Genoese women and children were living in comfort at Pera. The Italians never realized the strain imposed upon the Greeks by the certainty that their wives and children would all be involved in their fate. Sometimes there were disputes over strategy. As soon as it was clear that the great attack was coming, Giustiniani demanded from the Megadux Lucas Notaras that he should move the cannons that he controlled to the Mesoteichion, where every gun would be needed. Notaras refused. He believed, not without cause, that the harbour walls also were to be attacked; and they were already inadequately defended. There were angry words; and the Emperor had wearily to intervene. Giustiniani seems to have won his point. Archbishop Leonard, in his hatred of the Orthodox, declared that the Greeks were jealous lest the credit for the defence should go to the Latins and that henceforward they were sullen and half-hearted. He chose to forget that there were as many Greeks as Italians fighting in the Lycus valley; nor, as he admitted, did any Greek show lack of zeal when the battle began.[1]

On this Monday, with the knowledge that the crisis was upon them, the soldiers and citizens forgot their quarrels. While the men at the walls worked on to repair the shattered defences a great procession was formed. In contrast to the silence in the

Turkish camp, in the city the bells of the churches rang and their wooden gongs sounded as icons and relics were brought out upon the shoulders of the faithful and carried round through the streets and along the length of the walls, pausing to bless with their holy presence the spots where the damage was greatest and the danger most pressing; and the throng that followed behind them, Greeks and Italians, Orthodox and Catholic, sang hymns and repeated the Kyrie Eleison. The Emperor himself came to join in the procession; and when it was ended he summoned his notables and commanders, Greek and Italian, and spoke to them. His speech was recorded by two men present, his secretary Phrantzes and the Archbishop of Mitylene. Each of them wrote down the Emperor's speech in his own way, adding pedantic allusions and pious aphorisms, to give it a rhetorical form that in all probability it lacked. But their accounts agree sufficiently for us to know its substance. Constantine told his hearers that the great assault was about to begin. To his Greek subjects he said that a man should always be ready to die either for his faith or for his country or for his family or for his sovereign. Now his people must be prepared to die for all four causes. He spoke of the glories and the high traditions of the great Imperial city. He spoke of the perfidy of the infidel Sultan who had provoked the war in order to destroy the True Faith and to put his false prophet in the seat of Christ. He urged them to remember that they were the descendants of the heroes of ancient Greece and Rome and to be worthy of their ancestors. For his part, he said, he was ready to die for his faith, his city, and his people. He then turned to the Italians, thanking them for the great services that they had rendered and telling of his trust in them for the fighting that was to come. He begged them all, Greeks and Italians alike, not to fear the vast numbers of the enemy and the barbarous devices of fires and of noise designed to alarm them. Let their spirits be high; let them be brave and steadfast. With the help of God they would be victorious.

All that were present rose to assure the Emperor that they were ready to sacrifice their lives and their homes for him. He then walked slowly round the chamber, asking each one of them to forgive him if ever he had caused offence. They followed his example, embracing one another, as men do who expect to die.[1]

The day was nearly over. Already crowds were moving towards the great Church of the Holy Wisdom. For the past five months no pious Greek had stepped through its portals to hear the Sacred Liturgy defiled by Latins and by renegades. But on that evening the bitterness was ended. Barely a citizen, except for the soldiers on the walls, stayed away from this desperate service of intercession. Priests who held union with Rome to be a mortal sin now came to the altar to serve with their Unionist brothers. The Cardinal was there, and beside him bishops who would never acknowledge his authority; and all the people came to make confession and take communion, not caring whether Orthodox or Catholic administered it. There were Italians and Catalans along with the Greeks. The golden mosaics, studded with the images of Christ and His Saints and the Emperors and Empresses of Byzantium, glimmered in the light of a thousand lamps and candles; and beneath them for the last time the priests in their splendid vestments moved in the solemn rhythm of the Liturgy. At this moment there was union in the Church of Constantinople.[2]

When the Emperor's Council was dismissed the ministers and commanders rode through the city to join in the worship. After confessing and taking communion each then went to his station, resolved to conquer or to die. When Giustiniani and his Greek and Italian comrades came to their allotted places and passed through the inner wall to the outer wall and the stockade, orders were given for the gates of the inner wall to be closed behind them, that there might be no retreat.[3]

Later in the evening the Emperor himself rode on his Arab mare to the great cathedral and made his peace with God. Then he returned through the dark streets to his Palace at Blachernae and summoned his household. Of them, as he had done of his ministers, he asked forgiveness for any unkindness that he might have shown them, and he bade them good-bye. It was close on midnight when he mounted his horse again and rode, accompanied by the faithful Phrantzes, down the length of the land-walls, to see that everything was in order and that the gates through the inner wall were closed. On their way back to Blachernae the Emperor dismounted near the Caligarian Gate and took Phrantzes with him up a tower, at the outmost angle of the Blachernae wall, from which they could peer out into the darkness both ways, across to the Mesoteichion on the left and down to the Golden Horn on the right. Below them they could hear noises as the enemy brought up their guns over the filled-in foss. This activity had been going on since sunset, so the watchmen told them. In the distance they could see flickering lights as the Turkish ships moved across the Golden Horn. Phrantzes waited with his master for an hour or so. Then Constantine dismissed him; and they never met again. The battle was beginning.[1]

CHAPTER X

THE FALL OF CONSTANTINOPLE

The afternoon of Monday, 28 May, had been clear and bright. As the sun began to sink towards the western horizon it shone straight into the faces of the defenders on the walls, almost blinding them. It was then that the Turkish camp had sprung into activity. Men came forward in thousands to complete the filling of the foss, while others brought up cannons and war-machines. The sky clouded over soon after sunset, and there was a heavy shower of rain; but the work went on uninterrupted, and the Christians could do nothing to hinder it. At about half-past one in the morning the Sultan judged that everything was ready and gave the order for the assault.[1]

The sudden noise was horrifying. All along the line of the walls the Turks rushed in to the attack, screaming their battle-cries, while drums and trumpets and fifes urged them on. The Christian troops had been waiting silently; but when the watchmen on the towers gave the alarm the churches near the walls began to ring their bells, and church after church throughout the city took up the warning sound till every belfry was clanging. Three miles away, in the Church of the Holy Wisdom the worshippers knew that the battle had begun. Every man of fighting age returned to his post; and women, nuns amongst them, hurried to the walls to help bring up stones and beams to strengthen the defences and pails of water to refresh the defenders. Old folk and children came out of their houses and crowded into the churches, trusting that the saints and angels would protect them. Some went to their parish church, others to the tall Church of Saint Theodosia, by the Golden Horn. It was her feast-day on the Tuesday; and the building was decked with roses gathered from the gardens and the hedgerows. Surely she would not abandon her wor-shippers. Others went back to the great cathedral, remembering an old prophesy that said that though the infidel might penetrate through the city right into the holy building, there the Angel of the Lord would appear and drive them back with his bright sword to perdition. All through the dark hours before dawn the con-gregations waited and prayed.

There was no time for prayer at the walls. The Sultan had made his plans with care. Despite his arrogant words to his army experience had taught him to respect the enemy. On this occasion he would wear them down before risking his best troops in the battle. It was his irregulars, the Bashi-bazouks, whom he first sent forward. There were many thousands of them, adventurers from every country and race, many of them Turks but many more from Christian countries, Slavs, Hungarians, Germans, Italians and even Greeks, all of them ready enough to fight against their fellow-Christians in view of the pay that the Sultan gave them and the booty that he promised. Most of them provided their own arms, which were an odd assortment of scimitars and slings, bows and a few arquebuses; but a large number of scaling-ladders had been distributed amongst them. They were unreliable troops, excellent at their first onrush but easily discouraged if they were not at once successful. Knowing this weakness Mehmet placed behind them a line of military police, armed with thongs and maces, whose orders were to urge them on and to strike and chastise any who showed signs of wavering. Behind the military police were the Sultan's own Janissaries. If any frightened irregular made his way through the police they were to cut him down with their scimitars.

The Bashi-bazouks' attack was launched all along the line, but it was only pressed hard in the Lycus valley. Elsewhere the walls were still too strong; and they were attacked chiefly with the purpose of distracting the defenders from going to re-inforce their comrades in the vital section. There the fighting was fierce. The

Bashi-bazouks were up against soldiers far better armed and far better trained than themselves; and they were further handicapped by their numbers. They were continually in each other's way. Stones hurled against them could kill or disable many at a time. Though a few attempted to retreat, most of them kept on, fixing their ladders to the walls and the stockade and clambering up, only to be cut down before they reached the top. Giustiniani and his Greeks and Italians were supplied with all the muskets and culverins that could be found in the city. The Emperor came himself to encourage them. After nearly two hours of fighting Mehmet ordered the Bashi-bazouks to retire. They had been checked and repulsed, but they had served their purpose in wearying the enemy.

Some of the Christians hoped that this might be just an isolated night-attack, intended to test their strength; and all of them hoped for a moment of rest. It was not granted to them. They scarcely had time to reform their lines and replace beams and barrels of earth on the stockade before a second attack was launched. Regiments of Anatolian Turks from Ishak's army, easily recognized by their special uniforms and breastplates, came pouring down the hill from outside the Civil Gate of Saint Romanus into the valley and wheeled round to face the stockade. Once more the bells of the churches near the walls rang out to give the alarm. But the sound was drowned by the booming of Urban's great cannon and its fellows as they began afresh to pound the walls. Within a few minutes the Anatolians had rushed in to the assault. Unlike the irregulars they were well armed and well disciplined, and all of them devout Moslems eager for the glory of being the first to enter the Christian city. With the wild music of their trumpeters and pipers to encourage them they hurled themselves at the stockade, climbing over each other's shoulders in their efforts to fix their ladders on to the barrier and hack their way over the top. In the faint light of flares, with clouds continually veiling the moon it was hard to see what was happening. The

Anatolians, like the irregulars before them, were at a disadvantage on that narrow front because of their numbers. Their discipline and their tenacity only made their losses the heavier as the defenders flung stones down on them and pushed back their ladders or fought with them hand to hand. About an hour before dawn, when this second attack was beginning to falter, a ball from Urban's cannon landed fully upon the stockade, bringing it down for many yards of its length. There was a cloud of dust as the rubble and earth were flung into the air; and the black smoke of the gunpowder blinded the defence. A band of three hundred Anatolians rushed forward through the gap that had been made, shouting that the city was theirs. But, with the Emperor at their head, the Christians closed around them, slaughtering the greater part and forcing the others back to the foss. The check discomfited the Anatolians. The attack was called off, and they retired to their lines. With cries of triumph the defence once more set about repairing the stockade.

The Turks had been no more successful on other sectors. Along the southern stretch of the land-walls Ishak was able to keep up enough pressure to prevent the defence from moving men to the Lycus valley, but, with his own best troops gone to fight there, he could not make a serious attack. Along the Marmora Hamza Bey had difficulty in bringing his ships close in shore. The few landing parties that he was able to send were easily repulsed by the monks to whom the defence had been entrusted or by Prince Orhan and his followers. There were feints along the whole line of the Golden Horn but no real attempt at an assault. Around the Blachernae quarter the fighting was fiercer. On the low ground by the harbour the troops that Zaganos had brought across the bridge kept up a constant attack, as did Karadja Pasha's men higher up the slope. But Minotto and his Venetians were able to hold their section of the walls against Zaganos, and the Bocchiardi brothers against Karadja.

The Sultan was said to be indignant at the failure of his Anatolians.

But it is probable that he intended them, like the irregulars before them, to wear out the enemy rather than themselves to enter the city. He had promised a great prize to the first soldier who should successfully break through the stockade; and he wished the privilege to go to some member of his own favourite regiment, his Janissaries. The time had now come for them to enter the battle. He was anxious; for if they failed him it would scarcely be possible to continue the siege. He gave his orders quickly. Before the Christians had time to refresh themselves and do more than a few rough repairs to the stockade, a rain of missiles, arrows, javelins, stones and bullets, fell upon them; and behind the rain, the Janissaries advanced at the double, not rushing in wildly as the Bashi-bazouks and the Anatolians had done, but keeping their ranks in perfect order, unbroken by the missiles of the enemy. The martial music that urged them on was so loud that the sound could be heard between the roar of the guns from right across the Bosphorus. Mehmet himself led them as far as the foss and stood there shouting encouragement as they passed him. Wave after wave of these fresh, magnificent and stoutly armoured men rushed up to the stockade, to tear at the barrels of earth that surmounted it, to hack at the beams that supported it, and to place their ladders against it where it could not be brought down, each wave making way without panic for its successor. The Christians were exhausted. They had fought with only a few minutes' respite for more than four hours; but they fought with desperation, knowing that if they gave way it would be the end. Behind them in the city the church bells were clanging again, and a great murmur of prayer rose to heaven.

The fighting along the stockade was hand-to-hand now. For an hour or so the Janissaries could make no headway. The Christians began to think that the onslaught was weakening a little. But fate was against them. At the corner of the Blachernae wall, just before it joined the double Theodosian wall, there was, half-hidden by a tower, a small sally-port known as the Kerkoporta.

It had been closed up many years earlier; but old men remembered it. Just before the siege began it had been reopened, to allow sorties into the enemy's flank. During the fighting the Bocchiardis and their men had made effective use of it against Karadja Pasha's troops. But now someone returning from a sortie forgot to bar the little gate after him. Some Turks noticed the opening and rushed through it into the courtyard behind it and began to climb up a stairway leading to the top of the wall. The Christians who were just outside the gate saw what was happening and crowded back to retake control of it and to prevent other Turks from following. In the confusion some fifty Turks were left inside the wall, where they could have been surrounded and eliminated if at that moment a worse disaster had not occurred.

It was just before sunrise that a shot fired at close range from a culverin struck Giustiniani and pierced his breastplate. Bleeding copiously and obviously in great pain, he begged his men to take him off the battle-field. One of them went to the Emperor who was fighting near by to ask for the key of a little gate that led through the inner wall. Constantine hurried to his side to plead with him not to desert his post. But Giustiniani's nerve was broken; he insisted on flight. The gate was opened, and his body-guard carried him into the city, through the streets down to the harbour where they placed him on a Genoese ship. His troops noticed his going. Some of them may have thought that he had retreated to defend the inner wall; but most of them concluded that the battle was lost. Someone shouted out in terror that the Turks had crossed the wall. Before the little gate could be shut again the Genoese streamed headlong through it. The Emperor and his Greeks were left on the field alone.

From across the foss the Sultan noticed the panic. Crying: 'The city is ours', he ordered the Janissaries to charge again and beckoned on a company led by a giant called Hasan. Hasan hacked his way over the top of the broken stockade and was deemed to have won the promised prize. Some thirty Janissaries followed him. The Greeks fought back. Hasan himself was forced to his knees by a blow from a stone and slain; and seventeen of his comrades perished with him. But the remainder held their positions on the stockade; and many more Janissaries crowded to join them. The Greeks resisted tenaciously. But the weight of numbers forced them back to the inner wall. In front of it was another ditch which had been deepened in places to provide earth for reinforcing the stockade. Many of the Greeks were forced back into these holes and could not easily clamber out, with the great inner wall rising behind them. The Turks who were now on top of the stockade fired down on them and massacred them. Soon many of the Janissaries reached the inner wall and climbed up it unopposed. Suddenly someone looked up and saw Turkish flags flying from the tower above the Kerkoporta. The cry went up: 'The city is taken.'

While he was pleading with Giustiniani the Emperor had been told of the Turks' entry through the Kerkoporta. He rode there at once, but he came too late. Panic had spread to some of the Genoese there. In the confusion it was impossible to close the gate. The Turks came pouring through; and the Bocchiardis' men were too few now to push them back. Constantine turned his horse and galloped back to the Lycus valley and the breaches in the stockade. With him was the gallant Spaniard who claimed to be his cousin, Don Francisco of Toledo, and his own cousin Theophilus Palaeologus and a faithful comrade-at-arms, John Dalmata. Together they tried to rally the Greeks, in vain; the slaughter had been too great. They dismounted and for a few minutes the four of them held the approach to the gate through which Giustiniani had been carried. But the defence was broken now. The gate was jammed with Christian soldiers trying to make their escape, as more and more Janissaries fell on them. Theophilus shouted that he would rather die than live and disappeared into the oncoming hordes. Constantine himself knew now that the Empire was lost, and he had no wish to survive it. He flung off his imperial insignia and, with Don Francisco and John Dalmata still at his side, he followed Theophilus. He was never seen again.[1]

The cry that the city was lost went echoing through the streets. From the Golden Horn and from its shores Christians and Turks alike could see Turkish flags flying on the high towers of Blachernae, where the Imperial Eagle and the Lion of Saint Mark had flown only a few minutes earlier. Here and there the fighting continued for a while. On the walls near the Kerkoporta the Bocchiardi brothers and their men battled on; but soon they realized that no more could be done. So they cut their way through the enemy down to the Golden Horn. Paolo was captured and killed; but Antonio and Troilo reached a Genoese boat which ferried them across, unnoticed by the Turkish ships, to the safety of Pera. On their flank, in the Palace of Blachernae, Minotto and his Venetians had been surrounded. Many were slain; the Bailey himself and his leading notables were taken prisoners.[2]

Signals reporting the entry through the walls were flashed round the whole Turkish army. The Turkish ships in the Golden Horn hastened to land their men on the foreshore and to attack the harbour walls. They met with little resistance, except by the Horaia Gate, near the Aivan Serai of today. There the companies of two Cretan ships blockaded themselves in three towers and refused to surrender. Elsewhere the Greeks had fled to their homes in the hope of protecting their families, and the Venetians took to their ships. It was not long before a company of Turks had forced their way through the Plataea Gate, at the foot of the valley still dominated by the great aqueduct of Valens. Another company came through the Horaia Gate. Wherever they entered detachments were sent along within the walls to fling open other gates for their comrades who were waiting outside. Nearby, seeing that all was lost, local fishermen opened the gates of the Petrion quarter themselves, on the promise that their houses would be spared.[3]

Along the stretch of the land-walls south of the Lycus the Christians had repelled all the Turkish attacks. But now regiment after regiment was entering through the gaps in the stockade and fanning out on either side to open all the gates. The soldiers on the walls found themselves surrounded. Many were killed in trying to escape from the trap; but most of the commanders, including Filippo Contarini and Demetrius Cantacuzenus, were captured alive.[1]

Off the Marmora shore Hamza Bey's ships too saw the signals and sent landing parties to the walls. At Studion and Psamathia there seems to have been no resistance. The defenders surrendered at once, in the hope that their homes and churches would escape pillage.[2] On their left Prince Orhan and his Turks fought on, knowing what fate would await them if they fell into the Sultan's hands;[3] and the Catalans stationed below the old Imperial Palace resisted until they were all captured or slain.[4] On the Acropolis Cardinal Isidore judged that it would be prudent to abandon his post. He disguised himself and attempted to escape.[5]

The Sultan kept control of some of his regiments to act as his escort and as military police. But most of his troops were already eager to begin the looting. The sailors were especially impatient, fearing that the soldiers would forestall them. Hoping that the boom would prevent the Christian ships from escaping out of the harbour and that they could capture them at their leisure they abandoned their ships to scramble ashore. Their greed saved many Christian lives. While a number of the Greek and Italian sailors, including Trevisano himself, were captured before they could escape from the walls, others were able to join the skeleton crews left on their ships, unimpeded by any Turkish action, and prepare them for battle, if need be. Others were able to scramble on to the ships before they sailed, or to swim out to them like the Florentine Tetaldi. When he saw that the city had fallen Alviso Diedo, as commander of the fleet, sailed over in a small boat to Pera to ask the Genoese authorities there whether they intended to advise their fellow-Genoese to stay in the harbour and fight or to make for the open sea. His Venetian ships, he promised, would co-operate with whatever decision they made. The Podestà of Pera recommended that an embassy should go to the Sultan to inquire whether he would let all the ships go free or whether he would risk war with Genoa and Venice. The suggestion was hardly practicable at such a moment; but meanwhile the Podestà had locked the gates of Pera, and Diedo, with whom was the diarist Barbaro, was unable to rejoin his ships. But the Genoese sailors in the ships anchored below the walls of Pera made it known that they intended to sail away and they wished to have the support of the Venetians. On their insistence Diedo was allowed to leave in his sloop. He made straight for the boom, which was still closed. Two of his sailors hacked with axes at the thongs that bound it to the walls of Pera, and it drifted away on its floats. Signalling to the ships in the harbour to follow him Diedo sailed through the gap. Seven Genoese ships from Pera sailed close behind him, and soon afterwards they were joined by most of the Venetian warships, by four or five of the Emperor's galleys and by one or two Genoese warships. They had all waited as long as they dared to pick up refugees who swam out to them; and after they had passed through the boom the whole flotilla remained for an hour or so at the entrance to the Bosphorus to see if any more ships would escape. Then they took advantage of the strong north wind that was blowing to sail down the Sea of Marmora through the Dardanelles to freedom.[1]

So many of Hamza Bey's ships had been deserted by his sailors in their rush for plunder that he was powerless to stop the flight of Diedo's fleet. With those of his ships that were still manned he sailed round over the broken boom into the Golden Horn. There in the harbour he trapped the ships that were left, another four or five Imperial galleys, two or three Genoese galleys and all the unarmed Venetian merchantmen. Most of them were crowded with refugees so far beyond their capacity that they would never have been able to put out to sea. A few small boats still managed to slip across to Pera. But in the full light of day it was no longer easy to elude the Turks. By noon the whole harbour and everything in it were in the hands of the conquerors.[1]

There remained one small pocket of resistance in the city. The Cretan sailors on the three towers near to the entrance of the Golden Horn still held out and could not be dislodged. Early in the afternoon, seeing that they were completely isolated, they grudgingly surrendered to the Sultan's officers on condition that their lives and property were untouched. Their two ships were beached below the towers. Unmolested by the Turks, whose admiration they had won, they launched them and set sail for Crete.[2]

Sultan Mehmet had already known for many hours that the great city was his. It was at dawn that his men had broken through the stockade; and soon afterwards, with the waning moon still high in the sky, he came himself to examine the breach through which they had entered.[3] But he waited till afternoon before making his own triumphant entry into the city, when the first excesses of massacre and pillage should be over and some sort of order restored. In the meantime he returned to his tent, where he received delegations of frightened citizens and the Podestà of Pera in person.[4] He also wished to discover what had been the fate of the Emperor. That was never clearly known. A story was circulated later round the Italian colonies in the Levant that two Turkish soldiers who claimed to have killed Constantine brought a head to the Sultan which captured courtiers who were present recognized as their master's. Mehmet set it for a while on a column in the Augustean Forum, then stuffed it and sent it to be exhibited round the leading courts of the Islamic world. Writers who were present at the fall of the city told different stories. Barbaro reported that some claimed to have seen the Emperor's body among a pile of the slain but that others maintained that it was never found. The Florentine Tetaldi wrote similarly that some said that his head was sliced off and others that he died at the gate after being struck to the ground. Either story could be true, he added; for he certainly died in the crowd, and the Turks decapitated most of the corpses. His devoted friend Phrantzes tried to find out more details; but he only learnt that when the Sultan sent to search for the body a number of corpses and heads were washed in the hope of identifying him. At last a body was found with an eagle embroidered on the socks and stamped on the greaves. It was assumed to be his; and the Sultan gave it to the Greeks for them to bury. Phrantzes himself did not see it, and he was a little doubtful whether it was really his master's; nor could he find out where it was buried. In later centuries a nameless grave in the Vefa quarter was shown to the pious as the Emperor's burial-place. Its authenticity was never proved, and it is now neglected and forgotten.[1]

Whatever the details may have been, Sultan Mehmet was satisfied that the Emperor was dead. He was now not only Sultan but heir and possessor of the ancient Roman Empire.

CHAPTER XI

THE FATE OF THE VANQUISHED

Since the days of the Caliph Omar and the first great conquests for the Faith, Islamic tradition has prescribed the proper treatment to be given to conquered peoples. If a city or a district surrenders of its own will to the conqueror it is not to be pillaged, though it may have to pay an indemnity; and its Christian and Jewish inhabitants may retain their places of worship, subject to certain regulations about the buildings themselves. Even if the capitulation is due to dire necessity because the defence can hold out no longer, the rule is still held to be valid, though the conqueror can now insist upon harsher terms, exacting heavier fines and demanding the punishment of his more obdurate enemies. But when a city is taken by storm its inhabitants have no rights. The conquering army is allowed three days of unrestricted pillage; and the former places of worship, with every other building, become the property of the conquering leader; he may dispose of them as he pleases.

Sultan Mehmet had promised to his soldiers the three days of pillage to which they were entitled. They poured into the city. After his first troops had broken through the walls he insisted on a certain discipline. The regiments marched in one by one, with music playing and colours flying. But once they were within the city all joined in the wild hunt for loot. At first they could not believe that the defence was finished. They slew everyone that they met in the streets, men, women and children without discrimination. The blood ran in rivers down the steep streets from the heights of Petra towards the Golden Horn. But soon the lust for slaughter was assuaged. The soldiers realized that captives and precious objects would bring them greater profit.[1]

Of the soldiers that entered over the stockade or through the Kerkoporta many turned aside to sack the Imperial Palace at Blachernae. They overpowered its Venetian garrison and started to snatch at all its treasures, burning books and icons once the jewelled covers and frames had been wrenched off, and hacking at the mosaics and marbles round the walls. Others made for the small but splendid churches by the walls, Saint George by the Charisian Gate, Saint John in Petra, and the lovely church of the monastery of the Holy Saviour in Chora, to strip them of their stores of plate and their vestments and everything else that could be torn from them. In the Chora they left the mosaics and frescoes undamaged, but they destroyed the icon of the Mother of God, the Hodigitria, the holiest picture in all Byzantium, painted, so men said, by Saint Luke himself. It had been taken there from its own church beside the Palace at the beginning of the siege, that its beneficent presence might be at hand to inspire the defenders on the walls. It was taken from its setting and hacked into four pieces. The soldiers then rushed on, some to enter the nearby houses, others towards the bazaars and the great buildings at the eastern apex of the city.[1]

The sailors from the ships in the Golden Horn had already entered through the Plataea Gate and were emptying the warehouses along the walls. Soon some of them came upon a pathetic procession of women moving towards the church of Saint Theodosia, to pray for her protection on this her feast-day. The women were rounded up and distributed among their captors; who then went on to sack the rose-hung church and take the worshippers there.[2] Others climbed the hill to join the soldiers from the land-walls in despoiling the triple church of the Pantocrator and the monastery buildings attached to it, and the neighbouring church of the Pantepoptes.[3] Others that had entered through the Horaia Gate paused to sack the bazaar quarter before climbing the hill towards the Hippodrome and the Acropolis. Sailors from the ships in the Marmora had meanwhile made their way through the old Sacred Palace. Its halls were deserted and half-ruined; but there were still splendid churches there, such as the Nea Basilica that Basil I had built nearly five centuries before. They were all thoroughly pillaged. Then the sailors from both fleets and the first batches of soldiers from the land-walls converged on the greatest church of all Byzantium, the Cathedral of the Holy Wisdom.[1]

The church was still thronged. The Holy Liturgy was ended, and the service of matins was being sung. At the sound of the tumult outside the huge bronze gates of the building were closed. Inside the congregation prayed for the miracle that alone could save them. They prayed in vain. It was not long before the doors were battered down. The worshippers were trapped. A few of the ancient and infirm were killed on the spot; but most of them were tied or chained together. Veils and scarves were torn off the women to serve as ropes. Many of the lovelier maidens and youths and many of the richer-clad nobles were almost torn to death as their captors quarrelled over them. Soon a long procession of ill-assorted little groups of men and women bound tightly together was being dragged to the soldiers' bivouacs, there to be fought over once again. The priests went on chanting at the altar till they too were taken. But at the last moment, so the faithful believed, a few of them snatched up the holiest vessels and moved to the southern wall of the sanctuary. It opened for them and closed behind them; and there they will remain until the sacred edifice becomes a church once more.[2]

The pillage continued all day long. Monasteries and convents were entered and their inmates rounded up. Some of the younger nuns preferred martyrdom to dishonour and flung themselves to death down well-shafts; but the monks and the elder nuns now obeyed the old passive tradition of the Orthodox Church and made no resistance. Private houses were systematically plundered; each plundering party left a little flag by the entrance to show when a house had been thoroughly emptied. The inhabitants were carried off along with their possessions. Anyone who collapsed from frailty was slaughtered, together with a number of infants who were held to be of no value; but in general lives were now spared. There were still great libraries in the city, some secular and many more attached to monasteries. Most of the books were burnt; but there were Turks astute enough to see they were marketable objects and saved a number that were later sold for a few pence to anyone who might be interested. There were scenes of ribaldry in the churches. Many jewelled crucifixes were borne away with Turkish turbans rakishly surmounting them. Many buildings were irreparably damaged.[1]

By evening there was little left to plunder; and no one protested when the Sultan proclaimed that the looting now should cease. The soldiers had enough to occupy them during the next two days sharing out the loot and counting the captives. It was rumoured that there were about fifty thousand of them, of which only five hundred were soldiers. The rest of the Christian army had perished, apart from the few men who had escaped by sea. The dead, including the civilian victims of the massacre, were said to number four thousand.[2]

The Sultan himself entered the city in the late afternoon. Escorted by the finest of his Janissary Guards and followed by his ministers, he rode slowly through the streets to the Church of the Holy Wisdom. Before its gates he dismounted and bent down to pick a handful of earth which he poured over his turban, as an act of humility towards his God. He entered the church and stood silent for a moment. Then, as he walked towards the altar, he noticed a Turkish soldier trying to hack up a piece of the marble pavement. He turned on him angrily, and told him that permission to loot did not involve the destruction of buildings. Those he reserved for himself. There were still a few Greeks cowering in corners whom the Turks had not yet bound and taken away. He ordered that they should be allowed to go in peace to their homes. Next, a few priests came out from the secret passages behind the altar and begged him for mercy. Them too he sent away under his protection. But he insisted that the church should at once be transformed into a mosque. One of his *ulema* climbed into the pulpit and proclaimed that there was no God but Allah. He himself then mounted on to the altar slab and did obeisance to his victorious God.[1]

When he left the Cathedral the Sultan rode across the square to the old Sacred Palace. As he moved through its half-ruined halls and galleries it was said that he murmured the words of a Persian poet: 'The spider weaves the curtains in the palace of the Caesars; the owl calls the watches in Afrasiab's towers.'[2]

With the Sultan's progress through the city order was restored. His army was sated with booty, and his military police saw to it that the men returned to their bivouacs. He rode back to his camp through quiet streets.

Next day he ordered all the booty that had been taken to be displayed before him and selected from it the proportion to which he as commander was entitled; and he saw that a proper share was given to those of his troops whose duties had not allowed them to take part in the pillage. He reserved for himself all the captive members of the great families of Byzantium and such of its high officials as had survived the massacre. He freed at once most of the noble ladies, giving many of them money so that they might redeem their families; but he retained the fairest of their young sons and daughters for his own seraglio. Many other youths were offered liberty and commissions in his army on condition that they renounced their religion. A few of them apostasized; but the greater part preferred to accept the penalties of loyalty to Christ. Amongst the Greek captives he discovered Lucas Notaras the Megadux and some nine others of the Emperor's ministers. He himself redeemed them from their captors and received them graciously, releasing the Megadux and two or three others. But many of Constantine's other officials, among them Phrantzes, were not identified and remained in captivity.[3]

No such mercy was shown to the Italian prisoners. Minotto, the Venetian Bailey, was put to death with one of his sons and seven of his leading compatriots. Among them was Catarino Contarini, who had already been ransomed from Zaganos Pasha's troops but who was retaken, and another seven thousand gold pieces demanded for his release. This was a sum that none of his friends could pay. The Catalan Consul, Péré Julia, was also executed, with five or six of his fellow-Catalans. Archbishop Leonard had been captured but was not recognized, and was soon ransomed by merchants from Pera who had hastened to the Turkish camp to rescue Genoese compatriots. Cardinal Isidore was even luckier. He had abandoned his ecclesiastical robes, giving them to a beggar and wearing the beggar's rags in their place. The beggar was captured and slain, his head being displayed as the Cardinal's, while Isidore was sold for practically nothing to a Pera merchant who had recognized him. The Turkish prince Orhan had also tried to escape in disguise; he had borrowed the habit of a Greek monk, hoping that his perfect knowledge of Greek would save him from suspicion. But he was captured and betrayed by a fellow-prisoner, and was decapitated on the spot.

The Genoese galley to which the wounded Giustiniani had been borne was one of those that managed to escape from the Golden Horn. He was landed at Chios, and there he died a day or two later. To his own followers he remained a hero; but the Greeks and Venetians, greatly though they had admired his energy, his gallantry and his leadership throughout the siege, considered that in the end he had proved himself a deserter. He should have had the courage to face pain and death rather than risk the whole collapse of the defence by his flight. Many even of the Genoese felt shame for him. Archbishop Leonard blamed him bitterly for his untimely terror.

The fate of the Greek captives was diverse. After three days, when the official period for plunder was ended, the Sultan issued a proclamation, telling those of the Greeks who had avoided capture or who had been ransomed to go to their homes where their lives and their possessions would now be undisturbed. But there were not very many of them; nor were many of their houses habitable. Mehmet was said himself to have sent four hundred Greek children as a gift to each of the three leading Moslem potentates of the time, the Sultan of Egypt, the King of Tunis and the King of Grenada.[1] Many Greek families were never to be reunited. Matthew Camariotes, in his lament on the city, tells of the desperate search that he and his friends made to find their relatives. He himself lost sons and brothers. Some he knew later to have been killed; others merely vanished; and he had the shame of discovering that his nephew had survived by renouncing his faith.[2]

The kindness that Mehmet had shown to the Emperor's surviving ministers was of short duration. He had talked of making Lucas Notaras governor of the conquered city. If it had ever been his real intention he soon changed his mind. His generosity was always curtailed by suspicion; and counsellors warned him not to trust the Megadux. He put his loyalty to the test. Five days after the fall of the city he gave a banquet. In the course of it, when he was well flushed with wine, someone whispered to him that Notaras's fourteen-year old son was a boy of exceptional beauty. The Sultan at once sent a eunuch to the house of the Megadux to demand that the boy be sent to him for his pleasure. Notaras, whose two elder sons had been killed fighting, refused to sacrifice the boy to such a fate. Police were then sent to bring Notaras with his son and his young son-in-law, the son of the Grand Domestic Andronicus Cantacuzenus, into the Sultan's presence. When Notaras still defied the Sultan, orders were given for him and the two boys to be decapitated on the spot. Notaras merely asked that they should be slain before him, lest the sight of his death should make them waver. When they had both perished he bared his neck to the executioner. The following day nine other Greek notables were arrested and sent to the scaffold.

The Sultan later was said to have regretted their deaths and to have punished the counsellors who had roused his suspicions. But it is probable that his repentance was deliberately belated. He had decided to eliminate the leading lay officials of the old Empire.[1]

Their womenfolk were sent back into captivity and formed part of the long procession of prisoners that accompanied the Court on its return to Adrianople. Notaras's widow died on the way at the village of Messene. She had been of Imperial blood and the greatest lady in Byzantium after the death of the Empress-Mother, deeply respected even by her husband's opponents for her dignity and her charity.[2] One of her daughters, Anna, had already escaped to Italy with some of the treasures of the family.[3]

Phrantzes, whose hatred of the Megadux was unassuaged even by their mutual sorrows and who gave a bitterly unkind and untruthful account of his death, himself had to undergo a similar tragedy. He was a slave for eighteen months in the household of the Sultan's Master of the Horse before he could redeem himself and his wife; but his two children, both of them god-children of the Emperor Constantine, were taken into the Sultan's seraglio. The girl, Thamar, died there while still a child; the boy was slain by the Sultan for refusing to yield to his lusts.[4]

On 21 June the Sultan and his Court left the conquered city for Adrianople. It was now half in ruins, emptied and deserted and blackened as though by fire, and strangely silent. Wherever the soldiers had been there was desolation. Churches had been desecrated and stripped; houses were no longer habitable and shops and stores battered and bare. The Sultan himself as he rode through the streets had been moved to tears. 'What a city we have given over to plunder and destruction', he murmured.

He had, however, seen to it that not all the city was reduced to ruins. The populous quarters along the central ridge, the commercial quarters along the eastern half of the Golden Horn shoreline, the Palace of Blachernae and the noble houses nearby, and the older palaces and churches near the Hippodrome and the

Acropolis, all had suffered. But, after we have read the ghastly story of the pillage told us by woeful contemporary Christian writers, it is oddly surprising to discover that there were districts in which the churches were apparently untouched. The Christians continued to use them without interruption. Yet in a city taken by storm no shrine should have been left to them. The contradiction is explained if we remember the nature of the city, with great open spaces separating the villages and quarters from each other. When it was known that the Turks had broken through the walls the local officials in certain districts prudently surrendered at once to the attackers and admitted them through their gates. It seems that they were then sent under escort, with the keys of their townships, to the Sultan's camp and that he accepted their submission and provided reliable police to see that their churches, and, perhaps, their houses, were protected from pillage. Thus it was that the churches in Petrion, where the fishermen had voluntarily opened the gates, and in the neighbouring quarter of the Phanar were not touched; nor were the churches in the whole area of Psamathia and Studium, by the Sea of Marmora, where the defence had promptly offered its submission to the sailors of Hamza Bey's fleet. It was doubtless, too, the citizens in those districts who were able to raise the money which ransomed many of their compatriots from less fortunate areas. Had they not been left unplundered it would have been impossible to find ransom-money for the captives.[1]

Still more remarkable was the fact that the great cathedral of the Holy Apostles, the second largest and second most venerable church in the city, survived the sack with its treasury intact. It stood near to the main street leading from the Charisian Gate; and innumerable Turkish soldiers must have passed in front of it. The Sultan had presumably decided already that he would reserve it for his Christian subjects when he had taken the Church of the Holy Wisdom from them and therefore at once sent guards to protect it.[2]

Later Sultans were to be less indulgent towards the Christians; and one by one their churches were taken from them. But Mehmet the Conqueror, once his conquest was complete, wished to show that he regarded the Greeks as well as the Turks as his loyal subjects. The Christian Empire was ended; but he saw himself as the heir to its emperors, and as such he was mindful of his duties.[1]

First among these duties was to see to the welfare of the Orthodox Church. Mehmet was well aware of its difficulties during recent years, and he could now fully inform himself about its details. He learnt that the Unionist Patriarch, Gregory Mammas, had fled from the city in 1451 and that in the general opinion of the Greeks he had thus forfeited his throne. A new Patriarch must be elected; and it was obvious that there was one man fitted for the post, the revered leader of the opposition to Union, the scholar George Scholarius Gennadius.

When the city fell George Scholarius was in his cell at the monastery of the Pantocrator. Its great triple church had at once attracted the invading hordes. While some of them sacked the buildings others rounded up the monks to sell them into slavery. When the Sultan sent to summon George to his presence he could not be found. Eventually it was discovered that he had been bought by a rich Turk of Adrianople, who was impressed and somewhat embarrassed by his acquisition of so venerable and learned a slave and who was treating him with the utmost courtesy. His capture was reported to the Sultan; and a few days later envoys arrived at his house to escort George back to Constantinople.

Mehmet had already decided on the general lines of his policy towards his Greek subjects. They were to form a *milet*, a self-governing community within his empire, under the authority of their religious head, the Patriarch, who would be responsible for their good behaviour before the Sultan. After some discussion George Scholarius was persuaded to accept the Patriarchate. Such bishops as could be found nearby were assembled to form the Holy Synod; and, at the Sultan's request, they formally elected George, under his monastic name of Gennadius, to the Patriarchal throne. This was probably done before the Sultan left Constantinople at the end of June; but the dating is a little uncertain. Some months seem to have elapsed before Gennadius was officially enthroned. The ceremony probably took place on 6 January 1454. The procedure was copied from that of Byzantine times. In his role of Emperor the Sultan received the new Patriarch in audience and handed to him the insignia of office, the robes, the staff and the pectoral cross. The old cross had disappeared; either it had been lost in the sack of the city or the previous Patriarch, Gregory Mammas, had absconded with it to Rome; so the Sultan himself provided a new and splendid cross. A formula for the Sultan to utter was evolved. It ran: 'Be Patriarch, with good fortune, and be assured of our friendship, keeping all the privileges that the Patriarchs before you enjoyed.' The new Patriarch then mounted on a fine horse, the gift of the Sultan, and rode to the Church of the Holy Apostles, which was to be the Patriarchal Church, now that the Church of the Holy Wisdom was a mosque. There, according to the ancient custom, he was enthroned by the Metropolitan of Heraclea. He then moved in procession round the city, returning to take up his residence in the precincts of the Holy Apostles.

Meanwhile the Sultan and Patriarch worked out together the new constitution for the Greek *milet*. According to Phrantzes, who probably obtained his information while he was still in captivity, Mehmet gave Gennadius a written document promising him personal inviolability, exemption from paying taxes, complete security from deposition, complete freedom of movement, and the right to transmit these privileges to his successors for evermore; and similar privileges were to be enjoyed by the senior metropolitans and Church officials who formed the Holy Synod. There is no reason for doubting this evidence; though the freedom from deposition naturally did not cancel the right of the Holy Synod to depose a Patriarch by declaring his election to have been uncanonical, as had often happened in Byzantine times. The Patriarchal chroniclers of the next century claimed that in another written document the Sultan promised Gennadius that the customs of the Church with regard to marriage and burial should be legally sanctioned, that the Orthodox should celebrate Easter as a feast and be allowed freedom of movement during the three days of the feast, and that no more churches were to be converted into mosques. The right of the Church to administer the Christian community seems to have been taken for granted, to judge from later *berats* issued by the Turkish authorities to confirm the election of bishops and to state their duties. Ecclesiastical courts were empowered to hear all cases between the Orthodox that had a religious significance, including those that concerned marriage and divorce, testaments and the guardianship of minors. Lay courts set up by the Patriarch dealt with all other civil cases between Orthodox litigants. Only criminal cases and cases in which a Moslem was involved went to the Turkish courts. The Church itself did not collect the taxes due from the Greek communities to the State. That was the duty of the local headman. But the Church might be required to threaten excommunication and other religious penalties against Christians who did not pay their taxes or who in other ways failed to obey the commands of the State. The clergy were free from the obligation to pay taxes, though they could make contributions that were nominally voluntary. They alone among the Christians were allowed to wear beards; and every Christian had to wear a distinctive dress; and none could bear arms. The taking of male children to form the corps of Janissaries was to continue.[1]

In general these were the terms that Christian communities traditionally could expect from Moslem conquerors. But the Greeks of Constantinople were granted one special concession. The pathetic little embassies that had hastened to the Sultan's presence with the keys of their districts as he waited to enter the conquered city were rewarded for their enterprise. Officially the Conqueror seems only to have demanded that the great Cathedral of the Holy Wisdom should be converted into a mosque. Elsewhere, except in the protected districts of Petrion and Phanar, Studium and Psamathia, the Christians did in fact lose their churches. Nearly all of them had been thoroughly sacked and desecrated and the quarters in which they stood had been devastated. It would have been pointless to have tried to restore and reconsecrate them even if permission had been granted. It was enough, and more, indeed, than the optimists could have expected, that so many churches were left to them, to puzzle Turkish lawyers of a later date who could not understand why in a city that had been stormed the vanquished should have retained any of their shrines.

The arrangement suited the conquering Sultan; for he decided that these were the quarters in which his Greek subjects in Constantinople should dwell; and they would have to have buildings in which to carry on their worship. But as time went on his settlement was forgotten. One by one the old Christian churches were taken from them to be converted into mosques, till by the eighteenth century only three Byzantine shrines remained in Christian hands, the church known as Saint Mary of the Mongols, preserved by a special decree of the Conqueror granted to his favourite architect, Christodulus the Greek, and two chapels so tiny as to be overlooked, Saint Demetrius Kanavou and Saint George of the Cypresses. Elsewhere the Christians worshipped in newer buildings, of unobtrusive design, so as not to offend the eyes of the victorious Moslems.[1]

The Patriarch Gennadius himself had begun the process. The Church of the Holy Apostles, assigned to him by Mehmet, was in a state of disrepair; and it would have been costly to put it in order, if, indeed, the Christians would have been allowed to redecorate so grand an edifice. The district in which it stood was settled by Turks who resented its presence. Then one day, probably in the summer of 1454, the corpse of a Turk was found in its courtyard. It had doubtless been planted there; but its presence justified the Turks in making hostile demonstrations. Gennadius prudently asked permission to move his seat. Collecting all the treasures and relics that were preserved in the church he took them to the Phanar quarter, to the convent church of the Pammacaristos. The nuns were moved to buildings attached to the nearby church of Saint John in Trullo; and Gennadius and his staff moved into the nunnery. The Pammacaristos remained the Patriarchal church for more than a century. There the Conquering Sultan would come to visit his friend Gennadius, for whom he developed a high regard. He would not enter the church itself for fear that zealous followers would later use that as an excuse for taking over the building; but he and Gennadius would converse in the side-chapel, whose exquisite mosaics are now once more being revealed to the world. They discussed politics and religion; and at the Sultan's request Gennadius wrote for him a short and eirenical treatise, explaining and justifying the points on which Christian doctrine differed from that of Islam. The Sultan's tact was wasted. In 1586 his descendant Murad III annexed the church and converted it into a mosque.[1]

In the meantime Sultan Mehmet had set about the rebuilding of Constantinople. At first its desolation had appalled him. His architects continued with the great palace that he had planned at Adrianople, on an island in the river Maritsa, as though he intended to make that his chief residence. But soon he changed his mind. He was the heir now of the Caesars; he must live in the Imperial city. He made himself a small palace on the central ridge of the city, near where the University now stands, and he began to draw plans for a greater palace on the site of the ancient acropolis. Turks from all over his dominions were encouraged to settle in the city. The government provided help for the building of houses and shops for them. The Greeks who had remained there and the captives that they had redeemed were promised security; and they too seem to have received governmental aid. A number of noble Byzantine families who had fled in recent years to the provinces were persuaded to return by hints that they would enjoy the privileges due to their rank; though the only privileges that their rank secured for many of them were imprisonment and even death, lest their eminence might make them leaders of subversion. When the last pockets of Greek freedom were extinguished most of their inhabitants were forcibly moved to Constantinople. Five thousand families were brought there from Trebizond and its neighbouring cities. These included not only the noble families but shop-keepers and artisans, and, in particular, masons to help in the construction of new houses, new bazaars, new palaces and new fortifications. Then, as tranquillity returned and with it prosperity, more and more Greeks came of their own free will to take advantage of the openings for merchants and for craftsmen that the splendid reborn city provided. On the heels of the Greeks and specially encouraged by the Sultan came Armenians, rivalling the Greeks in their desire to dominate the commercial and financial life of the city, and with them, equally hopefully, numbers of Jews. Turks too kept pouring in, to enjoy the amenities of the capital that they had conquered.[1] Long before his death in 1481 Sultan Mehmet could look with pride on the new Constantinople, a city where new buildings were daily rising and where workshops and bazaars hummed with activity. Since the conquest its population had increased fourfold; within a century it would number more than half a million.[2] He had destroyed the old crumbling metropolis of the Byzantine Emperors, and in its place he had created a new and splendid metropolis in which he intended his subjects of all creeds and all races to live together in order, prosperity and peace.

CHAPTER XII

EUROPE AND THE CONQUEROR

On Saturday, 9 June 1453, three ships sailed into the harbour of Candia in Crete. Two of them carried the Cretan sailors who had been the last to give up the fight at Constantinople. They brought with them the news that the city had fallen eleven days ago. Throughout the island there was consternation. 'There has never been and there never will be a more dreadful happening', wrote a scribe at the monastery of Agarathos.[1]

Other refugees had reached the Venetian colonies of Chalcis and Modon; and their governors hastened to send messages to Venice. The messengers arrived there on 29 June. The Senate was hastily summoned; and the Secretary read out the governors' letters to the horrified Senators. Next morning a courier left to carry the news on to Rome. On 4 July he paused at Bologna to break the news to Cardinal Bessarion who was in residence there. Four days later he was received in audience by Pope Nicholas V. Another courier had gone to Naples, to warn King Alfonso of Aragon.[2]

It was not long before all Western Christendom had learnt that the great city was in infidel hands. The horror was all the greater because no one in the West had really expected it. Men knew that the city was in danger, but, immersed in their own local worries, they had not understood how acute the danger was. They had heard of its vast fortifications; they had heard too of the gallant companies that had set out to its rescue and of the armada from Venice that was sailing eastward. They had not noticed how pathetically small was its garrison in comparison with the hordes of the infidel, nor that the Sultan was provided with artillery against which no ancient wall could survive. Even the Venetians, for all their sources of information and their practical experience, had believed, as the Pope believed, that the defence could well be maintained until the relieving forces should arrive.[1]

In fact the Venetian galleys which the Pope had helped to equip had reached the coast of Chios and were anchored there waiting for a favourable wind when Genoese ships that had escaped from Pera sailed up to tell them that it was too late. The Venetian admiral, Loredan, promptly moved his fleet back across the Aegean to Chalcis till new orders should arrive from Venice.[2]

He received them in mid-July. On 4 July the Collegio, the Doge's special Privy Council, was summoned to an extraordinary session. Lodovico Diedo, captain of the galleys at Constantinople, had arrived the previous day, and he now gave an eye-witness account of the disaster. The government decided upon a policy of prudence. While orders were sent to the governors of Crete, of Chalcis and of Lepanto, telling them urgently to see that their defences were sound and to lay in provisions against a possible Turkish attack, a letter was dispatched on 5 July to Loredan, bidding him to prepare a ship to take the ambassador Bartolomeo Marcello, who was still with him, to the Sultan's court. A week later the Senate voted to provide Marcello with a sum of up to twelve hundred ducats, to be used as presents for the Sultan and his ministers. On 17 July full instructions were transmitted to Marcello. He was to tell the Sultan that Venice had no wish to cancel the treaty made between the Republic and Sultan Murad II. He was to demand the release of the galleys captured in the Golden Horn, none of which, he must emphasize, were warships. If the Sultan refused to renew the treaty on the old terms, he must refer back to Venice; but if the Sultan seemed amenable he must press for the return of Venetian merchants to Constantinople with the privileges that they had enjoyed under the Byzantines, and he must secure the release of all Venetian prisoners held by the Turks.

A few days later permission was given by the Senate for the son of the Venetian Bailey, Minotto, to go to Constantinople to arrange for the ransom of his father, his mother, and his brother. He may have rescued his mother; but the others were dead. About the same time it was decreed that the money and possessions lodged by Greeks in Venetian ships which had survived the disaster were to be confiscated and used to pay the debts still owing to Venetians by Greeks. Venice needed what reparation she could find. Her losses at Constantinople were estimated at two hundred thousand ducats; and another hundred thousand had been lost by her Cretan subjects.[1]

In Genoa the panic was even greater. The Genoese, worn out by their long war against Alfonso of Aragon and with the French and the Milanese each aiming to reduce them to vassaldom, were in no position to send forces to relieve their Levantine colonies. Their distress was enhanced when they received the report written on 17 June by Angelo Lomellino, Podestà of Pera. In it he told of the fate of his town. He described how at the moment of the fall of Constantinople he had opened his gates to Zaganos Pasha and how, to please the Sultan, he had done his best to persuade the citizens not to sail away in their ships. Immediately afterwards he had sent two envoys, Luciano Spinola and Baldassare Maruffo, to the Sultan's presence, with orders to express to him cordial congratulations on his victory and to ask that the privileges given to Pera by the Byzantines should be confirmed. Mehmet received them angrily. He was irritated by the flight of so many ships from Pera and he taunted the citizens with the equivocal part that they had been playing. A second embassy sent a day or two later under Babilano Pallavicini and Marco de' Franchi was more successful. On Mehmet's orders Zaganos Pasha handed them an Imperial *firman*. It promised that the town would not be destroyed. The citizens could keep their houses and shops, vines and mills, warehouses and ships. Their women and children would not be touched nor would their sons be taken for the Janissary corps. Their churches could remain in use; but no bells must be rung and no new churches built. No Turk was to live amongst them apart from the Sultan's officials. They might travel and trade freely throughout the Sultan's dominions, by land and sea; and Genoese subjects might have free access to Pera. They were excused from special taxes and duties; but every male citizen would have to pay a capitation-tax. They could retain their commercial customs but otherwise must obey the Sultan's laws. They were to elect their own headman or Elder to supervise their trade and deal with the Turkish authorities.

Pera was thus reduced to the status of any Christian town which submitted voluntarily to Moslem rule. The terms could have been worse. In any case the Podestà had to accept them. On 3 June the Sultan himself visited Pera. He ordered all the citizens' arms to be handed over, and he insisted on the destruction of the land-walls, including the citadel, the Tower of the Holy Cross. A Turkish governor was installed. Lomellino gave up his post as Podestà but was asked by his fellow-citizens to remain as their Elder till he returned to Genoa the following September.[2]

The loss of Pera and the Turkish control of the Straits endangered the existence of the Genoese colonies on the northern shore of the Black Sea, in particular the town of Caffa in the Crimea. This had been the port for Tartary and the lands of central Asia; and, were the Republic to abandon it, the many Genoese citizens with wealth invested there would sue for compensation which the Treasury could no longer afford to pay. Happily for the Genoese government the powerful financial house of the Consilio of Saint George agreed to take over the administration of these distant colonies. The directors of the Consilio believed that there were still profits to be made from them. But in fact fewer and fewer sailors were prepared to make the voyage through the Straits and fewer and fewer merchants were prepared to pay the tolls demanded by the Sultan's officials there. It was anyhow impossible to give the colonies adequate military support. Within half a century the whole empire of Genoa in the Black Sea had vanished, conquered by the Turks and their Tartar allies.[3]

The one other important Genoese colony in the Levant was the island of Chios. It had been administered for many years by its Mahona, a chartered company formed by the leading Genoese merchants and land-owners in the island. After the loss of Pera, and with the impending loss of the Black Sea colonies, Chios became the main outpost of the Genoese empire; but its strategic value was diminishing with the decline of the far eastern trade. Here too the Genoese government could afford neither to abandon nor to maintain it. The Mahona was instructed to make its own arrangements with the Sultan.[1]

The smaller Western merchant cities which had dealings with Constantinople were better able to adjust themselves. Unlike Genoa and Venice they were interested in the local rather than the far eastern trade. The Anconitan colony had suffered losses estimated at more than twenty thousand ducats when the city was sacked; but the Anconitans were personally unharmed, apparently because Mehmet knew and liked their leading citizen, Angelo Boldoni. They were able to continue their trade with Turkey, even though their overlord the Pope disapproved of it.[2] The Florentines, whose losses were estimated at about the same figure, soon established good relations with the Sultan. They were his favourites amongst the Italians; he had a particular admiration for the Medici family.[3] The Catalans, who had fought well and suffered severely, were soon back at Constantinople, though it seems that their consulate was never reopened.[4] The Ragusans had been about to open a consulate there on very favourable terms arranged with the Emperor Constantine. But, fortunately for them, there had been administrative delays; and they were thus not involved in the siege. But they had to wait five years before they could negotiate a commercial agreement with the Sultan. Thenceforward they played a prominent part in the Levantine trade.[5]

To many pious Christians the readiness of the merchant cities to trade with the infidel seemed to be a betrayal of the Faith.

Venice in particular was playing an equivocal role, trying on the one hand to organize a crusade against the Turks and on the other hand sending friendly embassies to the Sultan in order to safeguard its trade. Her ambassador, Marcello, succeeded after a year of negotiation in arranging a truce which allowed for the redemption of remaining Venetian captives and ships; and he stayed on for another two years in Constantinople, vainly seeking to recover commercial privileges for his countrymen. In 1456 he was recalled and thrown into prison for a year on the excuse that he had consented to the release of a few Turkish prisoners held at Chalcis. He was sacrificed in a graceless attempt to show Christendom that the Republic was truly the enemy of the infidel.[1]

In Roman eyes the issue was clearer. There must be a strong and sincere crusade with all the Western powers in alliance. Pope Nicholas, weary and disillusioned though he was, roused himself to take the lead. Ever since he had heard the fatal news from Constantinople he had been writing letters pleading for action. On 30 September 1453, he issued a Bull to all the princes of the West preaching the Crusade. Each potentate was enjoined to shed his blood and the blood of his subjects for the cause, and each was to provide a tithe of his revenues.[2] The two Greek cardinals, Isidore and Bessarion, strenuously supported him. Bessarion himself wrote to the Venetians, half scolding them and half beseeching them that they should cease from their wars in Italy and concentrate their strength on a campaign against Anti-Christ.[3] Even greater activity was shown by the Papal Legate in Germany, the Sienese humanist, Aeneas Sylvius Piccolomini, who throughout 1454 attended diets all over his territory at which he eloquently urged the need for a crusade. On his insistence many fine resolutions were passed. But nothing was done.[4] The Emperor Frederick III was fully conscious of the Turkish menace. He understood the threat to Hungary, where his young cousin Ladislas was king. If Hungary fell all Western Christendom would be in danger. He had already written to the Pope, using the Legate as his secretary, to express his horror at the fall of Constantinople; and Aeneas Sylvius added a personal note bewailing, as he termed it, 'the second death of Homer and of Plato'.[1]

Nevertheless there was no Crusade. Though princes hastened to collect reports on the fall of the city and writers wrote horrified laments, though the French composer Guillaume Dufay set a dirge to music that was sung throughout French lands, no one was ready to take action. Frederick was poor and powerless with no real authority over the German princes. Neither politically nor financially could he afford to go crusading. Charles VII of France was busy rehabilitating his country after the long and expensive war with England. The Turks were a long way off; he had greater problems nearer home. In England, which was suffering even more greatly from the effects of the Hundred Years' War, the Turks seemed still more remote. King Henry VI could do nothing. He had just lost his reason; and the whole country was slipping towards the chaos of the Wars of the Roses. King Alfonso of Aragon, whose Italian possessions would certainly be threatened by any Turkish move towards the west, contented himself with a few small defensive measures. He was an old man now; he only wanted to preserve his hegemony in Italy. No other king showed any interest, except for King Ladislas of Hungary. He had good reason to be alarmed. But he was on bad terms with his great Captain-General, the ex-Regent John Hunyadi. Without him and without allies he could not venture upon action.[2]

The Pope had hopes of the richest prince in Europe, Philip the Good, Duke of Burgundy; for Philip had often talked of his wish for a crusade. In February 1454, Philip presided at a banquet at Liège, where a live pheasant garlanded in precious stones was brought in to the royal table, while a huge man dressed as a Saracen threatened the guests with a toy elephant and young Oliver de la Marche, dressed as a damsel, mimed the sorrows of Our Lady Church. All the company swore solemnly to go to the Holy War. But the pretty pantomime was meaningless. The Oath of the Pheasant, as it was called, was never fulfilled.[1]

So, though Western Europe mourned piously, no Papal Bull could rouse it to action. Nicholas V died early in 1455. His successor, the Catalan Calixtus III, was unpopular in Italy because of his race and was himself a dying man. He valiantly equipped a fleet which he sent to the Aegean, where it captured the islands of Naxos, Lemnos and Samothrace. But no Christian power was willing to receive the islands as a gift; and they soon reverted into Turkish hands.[2] Aeneas Sylvius, who followed him in 1458 as Pope Pius II, was still more energetic. Relying on promises that he had obtained, he hoped that a great Christian expedition would indeed start out for the East. He died in 1464 on his way to Ancona, to bid God-speed to a crusade that never assembled.[3]

The West remained unmoved when it came to deeds. Aeneas Sylvius might grieve sincerely; and there were a few historically minded romantics such as Oliver de la Marche, to whom the Emperor that fell at Constantinople had been the one authentic emperor, the true heir of Augustus and of Constantine, unlike the upstart in Germany.[4] But there was nothing that they could do. The Papacy itself was largely to blame for this apathy. For more than two centuries the popes had denounced the Greeks as being wilful schismatics, and of recent years they had complained loudly that Byzantine adherence to the Union of the Churches was insincere. Western peoples to whom the Turks were a very distant threat might well wonder why they should be asked to give their money and their lives to rescue those recalcitrants. They were conscious, too, of the angry ghost of Virgil, who ranked in the West as an honorary Christian and a Messianic prophet. He had told of the horrors of the Greek sack of Troy. The sack of Constantinople was its retribution. Literary-minded authors with a taste for Classical phraseology, such as Cardinal Isidore himself, were apt to call the Turks the Teucri. Were they not therefore the heirs of the Trojans, if not actual Trojans themselves? A letter supposed to have been written by Mehmet II to Pope Nicholas was circulating in France a few decades later; and in it the Sultan was made to express his surprise that the Italians should show him enmity, since they were descended from the same Trojan stock as the Turks.[1] Laonicus Chalcocondylas complained bitterly that at Rome it was generally believed that the Greeks were being punished for their atrocities at Troy;[2] and Pope Pius II, whose name of Aeneas should have given him special authority, was at pains to point out that the Teucri and the Turcae were not identical. The legend was harming his efforts for the Crusade.[3]

Eastern Christendom could not show such indifference. During the late summer of 1453 the Sultan's court at Adrianople was crowded with ambassadors from all the neighbouring Christian states. Early in August envoys arrived from George Brankovitch, Despot of Serbia, well provided with money not only to be presented to the Sultan and his ministers but also to be used, more charitably, on the redemption of prisoners. They were followed by embassies from the late Emperor's brothers, Demetrius and Thomas, Despots of the Morea, from John Comnenus, Emperor of Trebizond, from Imaret Dadian, King of Mingrelia, from Dorino Gattilusi, lord of Lesbos and Thasos, and his brother Palamede, lord of Enos, from the Mahona of Chios and from the Grand Master of the Knights of Saint John. They found the Sultan in an affable mood. He merely demanded from each of the princes a recognition of his suzerainty and an increased tribute. The Serbian Despot was to pay him twelve thousand ducats annually, the Despots of the Morea ten thousand, the Mahona of Chios six thousand and the lord of Lesbos three. The Emperor of Trebizond was let off with two thousand. Ambassadors were to bring the sums to him once a year. Only the Knights of Saint John refused to acknowledge his suzerainty or to pay a tribute. They could not do so, they said, without permission from their own overlord, the Pope. Mehmet did not feel able at the moment to enforce his will upon Rhodes. He let the Knights' envoys go in peace.[1]

The Gattilusi brothers were particularly fortunate. Soon after the fall of Constantinople the Sultan had sent troops against Palamede's city of Enos, on the Thracian mainland; and Palamede had hastened to proclaim his submission. About the same time the Turkish fleet occupied the Byzantine islands of Imbros and Lemnos. The Byzantine officials all fled, with the exception of a judge on Imbros, the historian Critobulus. He made friends with the Turkish admiral, Hamza Bey; and, as a result of his ingenious intrigues, the lord of Lesbos was given Lemnos by the Sultan, for an annual tribute of 2325 ducats, and the lord of Enos Imbros, for an annual tribute of 1200 ducats.[2]

The East Christian world breathed again. Though Constantinople was lost the Sultan seemed to be willing to allow the minor states to live on in peace. But they had to pay heavily for their immunity; and money was not easily found. Moreover there had been ominous changes in the Sultan's court.

In August 1453 the Vizier Halil Chandarli was suddenly arrested and stripped of his offices. A few days later he was put to death. Mehmet had never forgiven Halil for the part that he had played in 1446. Hitherto he had been too powerful and too widely respected as Sultan Murad's trusted friend and the leading Elder Statesman in the realm. Till Constantinople was safely in his hands the Sultan could not afford to dismiss him; it would have been dangerous to alienate the old Turkish families who regarded him as their leader. But his advice had been proved wrong. He had tried first to prevent and then to raise the siege of Constantinople. Whether he honestly feared that the enterprise would fail or would involve the Turks in a great war against the Western powers or whether, as his enemies said, he was heavily bribed by the Greeks, with whom he was known to be friendly, we cannot now tell. The accusation of treason had to be made, to justify his downfall. Even the most highly revered of oriental statesmen are apt to be fond of receiving gifts. It may well be that Halil, while genuinely devoted to the welfare of his countrymen, was at the same time a pensioner of the Greeks. But he had mis-calculated and was punished for it. With him fell the other ministers that had survived from Murad II's time, except for Ishak Pasha; and he had been relegated to Anatolia. Zaganos Pasha now became Chief Vizier, and his friends filled the govern-ment. They were nearly all of them aggressive converts to Islam, men without vested interests and wholly dependent upon the Sultan's favour, and all of them eager to urge their master on to further conquests as soon as the time should be ripe.[1]

When that time came the Christian princes were themselves largely to blame. The Serbians were the first to suffer. In 1454 George Brankovich was obliged, by a show of force, to yield some of his territory to the Sultan. He was in a delicate position. The Hungarians, just across his northern frontier, were as eager to dominate his lands as were the Turks. Serbia became the theatre of their wars. The Sultan's failure to capture Belgrade from John Hunyadi in June 1456 added to his embarrassment. Hunyadi died on the morrow of his victory; and a few weeks later George was wounded in a fracas in the Hungarian camp. He lingered on for a few months, dying on Christmas Eve, aged ninety. His long diplomatic experience and the influence of his daughter Mara, the Sultan's revered step-mother, had enabled him to maintain himself. His heir was not so wise. George be-queathed the Despotate to his widow and his youngest son, Lazar. Lazar resented his mother's share in the inheritance. Her sudden and suspicious death a few months later obliged the Lady Mara to flee to the Sultan's court, while her elder brothers, both blinded many years previously by Murad II's orders, escaped, one with her to Constantinople and the other to Rome. Mehmet had other preoccupations at the moment; and Lazar died in January 1458, leaving a disputed inheritance. But in 1459 a Turkish army marched into the Despotate, welcomed by many of the Serbs who were weary of disorder. Within a few weeks all Serbia was in Turkish hands, with the exception of Belgrade, which the Hungarians held till 1521. The neighbouring kingdom of Bosnia, where Lazar's daughter Maria was Queen, was conquered four years later. The King, Stephen Tomashevich, was beheaded and Maria entered a Turkish harem.[1]

Meanwhile the last remnants of Greek independence were disappearing. First to go were the lands entrusted to the semi-Greek Gattilusi princes. Dorino and Palamede both died in 1455. The former's son and heir was weak and the latter's wicked. The Sultan was provided with excuses for annexing their lands. By 1459 Imbros, Tenedos, Lemnos and the town of Enos were in Turkish hands, though Imbros was given a Christian governor in the person of Critobulus. Lesbos survived precariously till 1462, when Niccolo Gattilusi, Dorino's younger son, who had already strangled his brother, was forced to surrender his lands and was himself strangled.[2]

The Duchy of Athens was overrun in 1456. Its Florentine Duke, Franco, whose youthful beauty the Sultan had admired, was allowed to remain for four more years as lord of Thebes. Then he was put to death and his lands absorbed and his sons enlisted among the Janissaries.[3]

In the Morea, where the brother Despots Demetrius and Thomas only interrupted their quarrels when a foreign danger approached, news of the fall of Constantinople had been followed by a revolt of all the Albanians settled in the peninsula. Many Greeks joined the rebels; and Venice gave them surreptitious support. In despair the brothers called on the Sultan to help them. The old general Turahan Bey crossed the Isthmus of Corinth and restored order. He left telling the brothers to live together in peace. But they soon quarrelled again with each other and with their vassals and omitted to send the Sultan the tribute due to him. In the spring of 1458 the Sultan himself brought an army across the isthmus. Corinth itself held out against him till August and a few other fortresses bravely resisted him, but in vain. When Corinth had fallen and the peninsula been ravaged, the Despots went to make their peace with their overlord. They were punished with the loss of half the Despotate, including Corinth, Patras, the Argolid, and Thomas's own capital, Karytena; and they had to pay a heavy indemnity. On his return northward Mehmet paused to visit Athens, a city of whose great past he was well acquainted and to which he wished to pay his respects.

Hardly had he left before the Despots quarrelled again. Demetrius held that the only salvation for the country and himself lay in submission to the Turks. Thomas had hopes from the newly elected Pope, Pius II, who had promised him aid at the Council of Mantua, held in the autumn of 1458. The aid when it arrived in the Morea next summer consisted of three hundred mercenaries, two hundred paid for by Pius and a hundred by Bianca Maria, Duchess of Milan. They soon quarrelled with Thomas and amongst themselves and returned to Italy. Meanwhile Demetrius called in the Turks. But the tribute due to the Sultan was forgotten again. Mehmet, shocked by the chaos in the Despotate and alarmed by the Pope's intervention there, decided to suppress it.

Early in May 1460, Mehmet appeared at Corinth at the head of a great army. After a little hesitation Demetrius surrendered himself and his capital, Mistra. Thomas cowered for a while in Messenia, then fled by sea to Corfu. Deserted by their rulers the Peloponnesians submitted, though a few fortresses, inspired by a proud and hopeless heroism, resisted and were reduced one by one. Whether they were taken by storm or starved into surrender, their populations were massacred. By the autumn the whole peninsula was occupied, with the exception of the castle of Salmenikon, whose commander Graitzas Palaeologus held out till the next summer, the Venetian ports of Modon and Croton which saved themselves by welcoming the Sultan with lavish gifts and honours, and the sea-girt city of Monemvasia, which had acknowledged Thomas as its lord and on his flight had given the lordship first to a Catalan pirate and then to the Pope, who handed it over in 1464 to Venice.[1]

Next came the turn of the Empire of Trebizond. John IV, the Grand Comnenus whom Phrantzes had rebuked for rejoicing at the death of Murad II, and who had purchased immunity in 1453 by promising the Sultan a handsome tribute, had died in 1458, leaving two married daughters and a son, Alexius, aged only four. A long regency would clearly be disastrous; so the Trapezuntines appointed as Emperor John's younger brother, David. David calculated that the Sultan was too busy in Europe to trouble himself about Eastern Anatolia. He was in touch with the Republics of Venice and Genoa and with the Papacy, all of whom promised him help; and he placed especial reliance upon his family's friendship with the greatest of the local Turcoman chieftains, Uzun Hasan, lord of the White Sheep tribe. Uzun Hasan was a formidable prince who had made himself the leader of eastern Anatolia in opposition to the Ottomans. The emirs of Sinope and of Karamania were his allies, as was the King of Georgia, the Emperor David's son-in-law, and the Georgian kings of Mingrelia and Abkhazia. His own blood was mainly Christian. His paternal grandmother had been a Princess of Trebizond and his mother a Christian lady from northern Syria; and he himself had married a Trapezuntine princess, the Emperor John's daughter Theodora, of whom a Venetian traveller wrote that 'it was common knowledge that no woman of greater beauty was living at that time.' With Uzun Hasan as his friend the Emperor of Trebizond believed that he was safe.

Sultan Mehmet could not have afforded to ignore such an alliance; but it was David who provoked the war. He demanded from Mehmet a remission of the tribute that his brother had paid, and he made his demand through the ambassadors of Uzun Hasan who were in Constantinople making still more arrogant demands on behalf of their master. In the summer of 1461 Mehmet prepared an army and a fleet to punish these impertinences. When the fleet, under the admiral Kasim Pasha, had sailed out along the Black Sea coast of Anatolia, the Sultan joined his army at Brusa. At the sight of such force the grand alliance began to crumble. While the army marched in June towards Sinope the fleet paused to overwhelm the Genoese port of Amastris. About the end of the month the fleet and army met before Sinope. The emir Ismail, who was Mehmet's brother-in-law, vainly sent his son Hasan, Mehmet's nephew, to try to avert the danger. Mehmet insisted on the surrender of Sinope. In return he offered Ismail a fief to be composed of Philippopolis and the neighbouring villages. Ismail unwillingly accepted his terms. Sinope was entered without opposition; and the Sultan's army pushed on into Uzun Hasan's territory, storming his frontier fortress of Koylu Hisar. The Karamanians made no move to come to their ally's assistance. Uzun Hasan retired eastward, sending his mother, Sara Khatun, with costly gifts to the Sultan's camp. Mehmet received the Princess graciously. He did not wish as yet to match himself against the White Sheep. He consented to make peace, on condition that he retained Koylu Hisar. But Sara's attempts to save her daughter-in-law's homeland failed. 'Why tire yourself, my son', she asked her host, 'for nothing better than Trebizond?' He replied that the Sword of Islam was in his hand; he would be ashamed not to tire himself for the Faith.

Early in July the Turkish fleet reached Trebizond, and the sailors landed to ravage the suburbs. They could make no headway against the great walls of the city. Early in August the vanguard of the army arrived before the walls, under the Grand Vizier Mahmud. Mahmud, like most of the Sultan's new ministers, was a renegade, the son of a Serbian prince and a lady from Trebizond. He had a cousin living in the city, the scholar George Amiroutzes, a Trapezuntine by birth. Amiroutzes had been one of the advocates of union at Florence; and the Emperor David esteemed him highly, not only for his learning but because his connections with Rome had been useful in negotiations with the West. Mahmud sent into the city his Greek secretary, Thomas Katabolenou, officially to summon the Emperor to surrender and secretly to make contact with Amiroutzes. David at first was obstinate. His Empress, Helena, of the great Byzantine family of the Cantacuzenes, had just gone to Georgia to beg help from her son-in-law. But when Amiroutzes, well primed and well bribed by Mahmud, told him that Hasan had made peace and the news was confirmed in letters from Sara Khatun, and when Amiroutzes further reported that Mahmud guaranteed that the Sultan would provide the Imperial family with estates elsewhere, the Emperor wavered. He sent to Mehmet, who was now approaching with his main force, offering to hand over the city if he were given lands of equal size and value wherever the Sultan might choose, and to send his younger daughter Anna to be the Sultan's bride. Mehmet, who had been angered by the Empress's flight to the Georgians, replied by demanding unconditional surrender. With Amiroutzes continually reminding him that resistance was useless and with Sara writing to give her personal word that he and his family would be honourably treated, David gave way. It is hard to blame him. Uzun Hasan and his Turkish allies had failed him. No Western power could reach him with aid; and the Georgians would not intervene alone. Trebizond with its strong fortifications might have held out for several weeks; but no one was coming to its rescue.[1]

On 15 August 1461 the last capital of the Greeks was entered by the Turkish Sultan. It was two hundred years to the day since Michael Palaeologus had recaptured Constantinople from the Latins and a new dawn had seemed to be breaking for the Greek world. Sara Khatun's promises were honoured. The Emperor and his children and his young nephew Alexius were graciously received by the Sultan and sent on a special ship to Constantinople, together with the officials of the Court and all their personal possessions, except for a pile of jewels which were given to Sara to reward her for her kindly mediation. Not all the Imperial family was allowed liberty. David's sister-in-law Maria Gattilusi, who had married his exiled brother Alexander in Constantinople some twenty years before and had retired as a widow with her young son to Trebizond, was taken into the Sultan's harem. She was still a lady of striking beauty; and Mehmet seems to have grown fond of her, while her son became notorious as one of his favourite pages.[1]

The rest of the population was treated harshly. The leading families were deprived of their property and sent in a body to Constantinople, where the Sultan provided them with new houses and enough money to start a new life. Every remaining male citizen and many of the women and children were enslaved and divided between the Sultan and his ministers. Other women were shipped to Constantinople; and eight hundred boys were picked for the Janissary corps.[2]

The outlying portions of the Empire were quickly overrun. The city of Kerasount held out for a time and surrendered on honourable terms which left the Greek population there in peace. A few mountain villages resisted. The castle of Kordyle was defended for many weeks by a peasant girl, who was long to be celebrated in the old Pontic ballads. But no castle could hold out for long against the might of the Turkish army. By October Sultan Mehmet was back in Constantinople, with the dominions of the Grand Comnenus wholly in his possession.[3]

It was the end of the free Greek world. 'Romania has passed away; Romania is conquered', mourned the ballad makers.[4] There were still a few Greeks living under Christian rule, in Cyprus, in the islands of the Aegean and Ionian Seas and in the sea-ports on the Greek mainland that Venice as yet maintained; but they were living under lords of an alien race and an alien form of Christianity. Only among the wild villages of the Maina, in the south-eastern Peloponnese, into whose rugged mountains no Turk ventured to penetrate, was there left any semblance of liberty.

Soon the whole Orthodox world of the Balkans was in Turkish

hands. So long as Scanderbeg lived the Albanians preserved a precarious independence; but after his death in January 1468 his country was quickly overrun; and Venice before long had lost her ports on the Albanian littoral. Further north, in the district known as Zeta, a few mountaineers held out, to form the principality known later as Montenegro, which might at times admit a Turkish or a Venetian suzerainty but never lost its autonomy. Serbia and Bosnia were enslaved. Across the Danube the Princes of Wallachia had admitted Turkish suzerainty in 1391, to repudiate it whenever a Hungarian army drew near. From 1456 to 1462 Prince Vlad, known as the Impaler from his method of dealing with those who disagreed with him, defied the Sultan and even impaled his emissaries; but on his fall the Sultan's overlordship was firmly re-established. In Moldavia Prince Peter III had accepted this overlordship in 1456. His son, Stephen IV, repudiated it and successfully held the Turks at bay throughout his long reign, from 1457 to 1504; but nine years after his death his son Prince Bogdan submitted to Sultan Selim I.[1]

There was, however, one Orthodox power into whose lands the Sultan's armies never entered. While Byzantium had been falling more and more completely under Turkish sway the Russians had been driving back their Tartar overlords and recovering their independence. The conversion of Russia had been one of the glories of the Byzantine Church. But now the daughter country was growing mightier than the mother. The Russians were fully conscious of this. Already in about 1390 the Patriarch Anthony of Constantinople had been obliged to write to the chief ruler of the Russians, the Grand Prince Basil I of Muscovy, to remind him that in spite of everything the Emperor at Constantinople was still the one true emperor, the Orthodox viceroy of God upon earth. But now Constantinople had fallen and the Emperor had been slain. There was no Orthodox emperor. Constantinople had fallen, moreover, so the Russians thought, as a punishment for its sins, for its apostasy in agreeing to religious union with the West. The Russians had angrily rejected the Union of Florence and had banished the Unionist archbishop Isidore, whom the Greeks had foisted upon them. Now, with their record of Orthodoxy unblemished, they possessed the only potentate to survive in the Orthodox world, a potentate whose power was steadily growing. Had he not surely inherited the Orthodox Empire? The Conquering Sultan might reign in Constantinople and claim the privileges of the Byzantine Emperor. But the true Christian Empire had moved to Moscow. 'Constantinople has fallen', wrote the Metropolitan of Moscow in 1458, 'because it has deserted the true Orthodox faith. But in Russia the faith still lives, the Faith of the Seven Councils as Constantinople gave it to the Great Prince Vladimir. There exists only one true Church on earth, the Church of Russia.' It was to be Russia's mission now to preserve Christianity. 'The Christian Empires have fallen', wrote the monk Philotheus in 1512, addressing his master, the Grand Prince or Tsar Basil III; 'in their stead stands only the Empire of our ruler. . . . Two Romes have fallen, but the third stands and a fourth there will not be. . . . Thou art the only Christian sovereign in the world, the lord of all faithful Christians'. Basil III's father had given some legitimacy to the claim by marrying into the house of the Palaeologi. But to the mystical believers in the Third Rome the marriage was irrelevant. If dynastic claims were needed they preferred to go back to the marriage of their first Christian prince, Vladimir, with the Porphyrogennete princess Anna, five centuries before, a marriage which in fact had been childless. But Moscow's inheritance had nothing to do with earthly diplomacy; it had been clearly ordered by God.

Thus alone among the Orthodox the Russians reaped some benefit from the fall of Constantinople; and to the Orthodox of the old Byzantine world, groaning in servitude, the knowledge that there was still a great if distant Orthodox ruler brought consolation and the hope that he would offer them protection and that some day, perhaps, he would come to their rescue and restore them their liberty. The conquering Sultan barely noted the existence of Russia. His successors in centuries to come would not be able to imitate his disdain.[1]

Russia indeed was far away. Sultan Mehmet had other concerns nearer at hand. The conquest of Constantinople had established him irremovably as one of the great powers of Europe; and he had his part to play in European power politics. The Christians were all his enemies, he knew; he had to see that they did not unite against him.

That was not such a difficult task. The failure of the Christian powers to come to the rescue of Constantinople had showed how unwilling they were to fight for their faith unless their immediate interests were involved. Only the Papacy and a few scholars and romanticists scattered about the West had been genuinely shocked at the thought of the great historic Christian city passing into the hands of the infidel. Of the Italians who joined in the defence of the city some, like Giustiniani and the Bocchiardi brothers may have been moved by Christian sentiment; but their governments were making nice commercial calculations. It would be disastrous to their trade to let Constantinople fall to the Turks, but it would be equally disastrous to offend the Turks with whom they were already trading profitably. The Western monarchs were uninterested. Even the King of Aragon, with his dreams of a Levantine empire, had not been ready to translate his dreams into action. The Turkish government was soon fully aware of all this. Turkey has never lacked good diplomats. The Sultan might have to fight Venice and Hungary and perhaps the few allies that the Papacy could muster; but he would fight them one by one. No one came to the aid of Hungary at the fatal field of Mohacs. No one sent reinforcements to the Knights of Saint John at Rhodes. No one cared when Cyprus was lost to the Venetians. Venice and the Habsburgs were indeed to come together for the naval campaign that triumphed at Lepanto; but little good resulted. The

Habsburg princes had already been obliged to defend Vienna alone. In Germany or in Italy men might shudder for many decades to think that the Turks were so near; but it did not distract them from their civil wars. And when the Most Christian King of France, betraying the part that his country had played in the great days of the Crusades, chose to ally himself with the infidel Sultan against the Holy Roman Emperor, then it was clear for all to see that the crusading spirit was finished.

CHAPTER XIII

THE SURVIVORS

The conscience of Western Europe had been touched but not roused. The Greek Cardinals, Isidore and Bessarion, might preach and plead, and Pope Pius II, with his love of Greek culture, scrape together resources for the rescue of the East. But all that they could usefully achieve was to lighten the lot of the pathetic refugees who had fled before the Turk.

There were not very many of them. The poorer folk had to remain in the East and suffer whatever might befall. Of the greater figures that had played a part in the drama a few accepted voluntarily life under the Sultan. Many more were detained by imprisonment or were put to death. The rest sought refuge in Italy.

The two old Imperial dynasties were soon reduced to virtual extinction. Of the Emperor Constantine's surviving brothers the Despot Demetrius was at first treated kindly by the Sultan. He was given an appanage out of the lands that had belonged to the Gattilusi, the town of Enos and the islands of Lemnos and Imbros and parts of Thasos and Samothrace. They brought him an annual income of six hundred thousand pieces of silver, half from the islands and half from Imbros. In addition, a hundred thousand pieces were sent him annually from the Sultan's mint. For seven years he lived quietly at Enos with his wife Zoe and her brother, Matthew Asen, who in the old days had been his governor at Corinth and now was in charge of the local salt monopoly. He spent his days in enjoying the pleasures of the hunt and of the table and in giving much of his wealth to the Church. In 1467 his appanage was suddenly taken from him. According to the story which Phrantzes believed, Matthew's underlings had tampered with the revenue due to the Sultan from the salt-pans, and Matthew and Demetrius held responsible. Matthew's fate is unrecorded. Demetrius was deprived of his revenues and sent to live in poverty at Didymoticum. There one day the Sultan who was passing by noticed him and felt pity for him. He was made an annual allowance of fifty thousand silver pieces, to be paid out of the Imperial corn monopoly. It was not for long. He and his wife both soon took monastic vows. He died in a monastery in Adrianople in 1470 and she survived him only for a few months. Their one child, Helena, had been officially taken into the Sultan's harem; but it seems that she preserved her virginity and lived in her own residence at Adrianople. She died a few years before her parents, leaving her jewels and her robes to the Patriarchate.[1]

The Despot Thomas had fled with his wife and children to Corfu, taking with them the head of the Apostle, Saint Andrew, which had been kept at Patras. At the end of 1460 he crossed with the relic to Italy, and on 7 March 1461 he made a ceremonial entry into Rome. A week later the Pope, to whom he presented the relic, bestowed on him the order of the Golden Rose. He remained in Italy, hoping some day to return to the Morea. The Pope gave him a pension of three hundred gold ducats a month, to which the Cardinals later added another five hundred out of their revenues. His dignity and his good looks, which he preserved into old age, impressed the Italians; and he pleased them by publicly adopting the Catholic faith. His wife, Catherine Zaccaria, whom he had left in Corfu, died there in August 1462. In 1465 he summoned his children to Rome. A few days after their arrival he died, on 12 May, aged fifty-six.[2]

Thomas had four children. The eldest, Helena, had been married as a child to Lazar III Brankovitch, by whom she had three daughters. In 1459, soon after her husband's death, she had married the eldest, Maria, to King Stephen of Bosnia. When the Turks overran Bosnia the young Queen was taken into the harem of a Turkish general, while Helena and her two younger daughters fled to Leucas. One of the girls, Militza, married the lord of Cephallonia and Leucas, Leonardo III Tocco, but died childless a few months later. The other, Irene, married John Castriota, son of Scanderbeg, and after her father-in-law's death retired with him to Italy. Helena stayed on at the court of her son-in-law in Leucas, eventually entering a convent and dying there in 1474.[1]

Helena's brothers and sisters were very much younger. Andrew had been born in 1453, Manuel in 1455 and Zoe probably in 1456. The orphans were adopted by the Papacy. In June 1466 Zoe was married to a Roman noble of the house of Caracciolo but was soon left a child-widow. In 1472 Pope Sixtus IV achieved, so he thought, a diplomatic triumph by arranging for her marriage with the Tsar of Russia, Ivan III. The marriage took place in the Vatican, the Tsar being represented by proxy. A dowry of six thousand golden ducats was presented by the Pope to the bride. But when she arrived in Russia Zoe, now rechristened Sophia, forgot her Catholicism and plunged ardently into the politics of the Orthodox Church. Her daughter Helena returned to the Catholic fold on marrying the King of Poland, Alexander Jagellon; but her son Basil III and his successors remained champions of Orthodoxy. Queen Helena of Poland died childless. Basil III's line died out a century later, with his great-grand-daughter, Anastasia Feodorovna, and her uncle the Tsarevitch Dmitri.

Thomas's sons had less reputable careers. The younger, Manuel, spent his youth in Italy, on a Papal pension of fifty ducats a month. About the year 1477 he suddenly went to Constantinople and threw himself upon the mercy of the Sultan. Mehmet received him graciously and gave him an estate and a pension. He married there; but the name of his wife is unknown, as is the date of his death. Of his two sons the elder, John, died young; the younger, Andrew, was converted to Islam and ended his days as a Court official with the name of Mehmet Pasha. He seems to have left no descendants. Thomas's elder son Andrew preferred to remain in Italy living on a similar meagre pension of fifty ducats a month. He was treated as heir to the Imperial throne and would sign himself 'Deo gratia fidelis Imperator Constantinopolitanus'. But his behaviour was hardly imperial. In 1480 he married a lady from the streets of Rome, called Caterina; and he fell heavily into debt. He persuaded Pope Sixtus IV to give him two million golden ducats to finance an expedition to the Morea and used the money for other purposes. But neither that nor his readiness to sell titles and privileges to socially ambitious foreigners saved his finances. A journey made in about 1490 to his sister's court in Russia was monetarily unproductive; he was not encouraged to remain there. At last he found a friend in King Charles VIII of France, whom he visited in 1491 and by whom some of his debts were paid. He welcomed Charles' invasion of Italy in 1493 and hastened north to join him. On 16 September 1494 he signed a treaty with Charles, generously allotting to him all his rights to the thrones of Constantinople, Trebizond and Serbia, retaining for himself only the Despotate of the Morea. When Charles was established in Naples the following May he promised Andrew an annual pension of twelve hundred golden ducats. It is doubtful whether the pension was paid once Charles had left Italy; and it certainly came to an end when the king died in 1498. Andrew soon was back in debt. Early in 1502 he signed a new deed giving all his rights to the Spanish monarchs, Ferdinand and Isabella; but he received no money from them. When he died in June that year his widow had to beg the Pope for the sum of a hundred and four ducats to pay for his funeral expenses. He left one son, called Constantine, a handsome but worthless boy who for a time commanded the Papal Guard. The date of Constantine's death is unknown.[1]

With Thomas's two grandsons, Mehmet Pasha in Constantinople and the feckless Constantine in Rome, the Imperial line of the Palaeologi came to an end.[2] The cadet branch, descended from Andronicus II, that had ruled in Montferrat since early in the fourteenth century died out in the male line in 1536, its possessions passing through female inheritance to the Marquesses of Mantua. The Despot Theodore's child, Helena Palaeologaena, Queen of Cyprus, had died in 1458, and her one child, Queen Charlotte, exiled and childless in Rome in 1487.[1] The only descendants of the Emperor Manuel Palaeologus living today are to be found in southern Italy, in families stemming from John Castriota, son of Scanderbeg.[2]

The lot of the Imperial house of Trebizond was more immediately tragic. The Emperor David enjoyed a comfortable pension for two years. But in 1463 his false friend, George Amiroutzes, reported to the Turkish authorities that the ex-Emperor had received a letter from his niece, Uzun Hasan's wife, in which she suggested that her brother Alexius or one of his own sons should come and visit her. The Sultan chose to regard this as treason. David was thrown into a prison at Adrianople on 26 March 1463, and on 1 November he, six of his seven sons and his nephew Alexius were all executed at Constantinople. Their corpses were forbidden burial; and when the Empress Helena dug graves for them with her own hands and committed them there, she was sentenced to a fine of fifteen thousand ducats, to be paid within three days, or she too would be slain. Devoted friends and retainers raised the money; but she retired to spend the short remainder of her life clad in sackcloth in a hovel of straw. Her youngest son, George, a child of three, was brought up as a Moslem. Later he was allowed to visit Uzun Hasan, from whose court he fled to his sister in Georgia. He reverted to Christianity and married a Georgian princess, by whom he seems to have had issue; but the further history of the family is unknown. His other sister, Anna, was sent into the Sultan's harem and was later given, but only for a time, to Zaganos Pasha, governor of Macedonia. She too had been forcibly converted to Islam; but in later life she managed to retire to the countryside near her native Trebizond. She founded a village called Kyranna after her and endowed a church there. The dowager Maria Gattilusi lived on quietly in the Imperial harem; and her son, another Alexius, continued to enjoy the Sultan's affections. His ultimate fate is unknown. According to tradition he was allotted lands just outside the walls of Pera and was known locally as the Son of the Bey. It is to him that the present district of Beyoglu owes its name.[1]

Little is known of the fate of those of the Emperor Constantine's ministers who survived the fall of the Empire, or of their families. If they recovered their freedom they were content to live in obscurity. Once order was restored the Sultan was prepared to permit the redemption of captives. On the receipt of a letter of fulsome flattery from the scholar Filelfo he released Filelfo's mother-in-law, Manfredina Doria, the widow of John Chrysoloras, and sent her to Italy to join her son-in-law, with whom she was said to have been scandalously intimate in the past.[2] Constantine's faithful secretary and friend Phrantzes managed after several years to redeem himself and his wife. They retired to Corfu, where he maintained his interest in his compatriots and his affection for his master's family. He went to Leucas on the invitation of Thomas's daughter, the Serbian Dowager, to visit her son-in-law, Leonardo Tocco, whose sister had been his emperor's first wife; and in 1466 he journeyed to Rome, to attend the wedding of Princess Zoe to her Caracciolo husband. Soon afterwards both he and his wife took monastic vows. In his monastery he completed the writing of his memoirs, and at the end of the work he inserted his declaration of faith. In it, despite his friendship with the Unionist party in his Church, he could not bring himself to subscribe to the doctrine of the Dual Procession of the Holy Spirit. His historical notes extend to the year 1477. He seems to have died in 1478.[3]

Some refugees retired to Venice, to join the daughter of Phrantzes's old enemy, Lucas Notaras. Anna Notaras lived there for many years, devoting what money she had to the relief of her compatriots.[4]

The two Greek Cardinals lived on in Italy. In 1459, on the

death of Gregory Mammas, the Pope elevated Isidore to be Patriarch of Constantinople, in defiance of all the traditions of the
Byzantine Church. He died in 1463 and was succeeded in the
empty title by Bessarion. Bessarion lived on till 1472, spending
his revenues in building up a fine library of Greek texts, which he
bequeathed to the city of Venice, and in giving help to Greek
refugees. Archbishop Leonard returned to his see in Lesbos and
was there when the Turks conquered the island in 1462. Once
again he visited Constantinople, but this time as a prisoner. He
was soon ransomed and went to Italy, where he died in 1482.[1]

George Amiroutzes, who soon after the fall of Constantinople
had written a begging letter to Bessarion to ask for money to
redeem his younger son, Basil, had wormed his way into Turkish
favour by his intrigues at Trebizond. His cousin, Mahmud Pasha,
remained his staunch friend and brought him to the Sultan's
notice; and his position improved when his elder son, Alexander,
turned Moslem. Sultan Mehmet was impressed by his erudition
and commissioned him to make an up-to-date edition of Ptolemy's
Geography, for which Alexander, now a good Arabic scholar,
provided the Arabic names and then a full Arabic translation.
Later on, in 1463, George fell in love with the widow of the last
Duke of Athens, who was living on a pension in Constantinople,
and wished to marry her though his wife was still alive. The
Patriarch Dionysius refused to sanction the bigamous union.
George therefore intrigued to have the Patriarch deposed and
himself turned Moslem. He died suddenly a few weeks later,
while playing dice. It was a divine judgement on him.[2]

Alone of the scholars who had illumined the last years of
Byzantine freedom, George Scholarius Gemistus was called upon
to play a constructive part in ordering the new world, in uniting
the Church of his people and giving them a court in which the old
dramas of Imperial etiquette could still be maintained through the
darkness until the dawn should come and Byzantium like a
phoenix be reborn.[3]

This dawn never came. The old oecumenical Empire of Byzantium was gone for ever.

It is easy to maintain that in the broad sweep of history the year 1453 stands for very little. The Byzantine Empire was already doomed. Diminished, underpopulated and impoverished, it was bound to perish whenever the Turks chose to move in to make the kill. The notion of Byzantine scholars hurrying to Italy because of the fall of their city is untenable. Italy had for more than a generation been full of Byzantine professors; and of the two great intellectual figures amongst the Greeks living in 1453 the one, Bessarion, was already in Italy and the other, Gennadius, remained on at Constantinople. If the trade of the Italian merchant-sea-ports was to wither away, that was due more to the discovery of the ocean routes than to the Turkish control of the Straits. Genoa, indeed, declined rapidly after 1453; but that was largely because of her precarious position in Italy. Venice kept up a lively Levantine trade for many years to come. If the Russians came forward now as the champions of Orthodoxy, with Moscow raised to be the Third Rome, this was not a revolutionary idea. Russian thought had already been moving towards it, with Russian armies driving the infidel Tartars back across the Steppes, while Constantinople sank further into poverty and made an unholy bargain with the West. All these seeds had been sown already. The fall of Constantinople merely hastened the harvest. If Sultan Mehmet had been less determined or Halil Pasha more persuasive, or if the Venetian armada had set sail a fortnight earlier, or, at the last crisis, had Giustiniani not been wounded at the walls and the postern gate of the Kerkoporta not been left ajar, little would have been changed in the long run. Byzantium might have lingered on for another decade and the Turkish advance into Europe been delayed. But the West would not have profited by the respite. Instead, it would have regarded the preservation of Constantinople as a sign that the danger was not so pressing after all. It would have turned away with relief to its own affairs; and after a few years the Turks would have come again to the assault.

Nevertheless the date of 29 May 1453 marks a turning-point in history. It marks the end of an old story, the story of Byzantine civilization. For eleven hundred years there had stood on the Bosphorus a city where the intellect was admired and the learning and letters of the Classical past were studied and preserved. Without the help of Byzantine commentators and scribes there is little that we would know today about the literature of ancient Greece. It was, too, a city whose rulers down the centuries had inspired and encouraged a school of art unparalleled in human history, an art that arose from an ever varying blend of the cool cerebral Greek sense of the fitness of things and a deep religious sense that saw in works of art the incarnation of the Divine and the sanctification of matter. It was, too, a great cosmopolitan city, where along with merchandise ideas were freely exchanged and whose citizens saw themselves not as a racial unit but as the heirs of Greece and Rome, hallowed by the Christian Faith. All this was now ended. The new master-race discouraged learning among its Christian subjects. Without the patronage of a free government Byzantine art began to decay. The new Constantinople was a splendid city, rich and populous and cosmopolitan, and full of handsome edifices. But its beauty expressed the worldly imperial might of the Sultans, not the Kingdom of the Christian God on earth; and its inhabitants were divided in religion. Constantinople was reborn, to be the cynosure of visitors for many centuries; but it was Istanbul, not Byzantium.

Was nothing, then, achieved by the gallantry of the last days of Byzantium? It impressed the Sultan, as his savagery after the capture of the city made clear. He would take no risk with the Greeks. He had always admired Greek learning; he found now that the heroic Greek spirit was not entirely dead. It may well be that when calm was restored his admiration encouraged him to offer fairer treatment to his Greek subjects. The terms that the

Patriarch Gennadius obtained from him reunited the Greek Church and the majority of the Greek people under one autonomous government. The future was not to be easy for the Greeks. They were given the promise of peace and justice and opportunities for enrichment. But they were second-class citizens. Bondage inevitably brings demoralization; and the Greeks could not escape from its effects. Moreover, they depended ultimately upon the good-will of their suzerain. So long as the Conquering Sultan lived their lot was not too bad. But there arose Sultans who had never known of the civilization of Byzantium and who were proud to be the Emperors of Islam, Caliphs and Commanders of the Faithful. And soon the great structure of the Ottoman administration fell into decay. The Greeks had to answer corruption by deceit, injustice by disloyalty and intrigue by counter-intrigue. The story of the Greeks under Turkish rule is unedifying and melancholy. Yet, in spite of its faults and weaknesses, the Church survived; and so long as the Church survived Hellenism would not die.

Western Europe, with ancestral memories of jealousy of Byzantine civilization, with its spiritual advisers denouncing the Orthodox as sinful schismatics, and with a haunting sense of guilt that it had failed the city at the end, chose to forget about Byzantium. It could not forget the debt that it owed to the Greeks; but it saw the debt as being owed only to the Classical age. The Philhellenes who came to take part in the War of Independence spoke of Themistocles and Pericles but never of Constantine. Many intellectual Greeks copied their example, led astray by the evil genius of Korais, the pupil of Voltaire and of Gibbon, to whom Byzantium was an ugly interlude of superstition, best ignored. Thus it was that the War of Independence never resulted in the liberation of the Greek people but only in the creation of a little Kingdom of Greece. In the villages men knew better. There they remembered the threnes that had been composed when news came that the city had fallen, punished by God for its luxury, its pride and its apostasy, but fighting a heroic battle to the end. They remembered that dreadful Tuesday, a day that all true Greeks still know to be of ill omen; but their spirits tingled and their courage rose as they told of the last Christian Emperor standing in the breach, abandoned by his Western allies, holding the infidel at bay till their numbers overpowered him and he died, with the Empire as his winding-sheet.

PRINCIPAL SOURCES FOR A HISTORY OF THE FALL OF CONSTANTINOPLE

The historian of the fall of Constantinople is fortunate in possessing a considerable number of contemporary accounts of the drama, some written by professional historians, others journals or hastily composed reports written by men who were present at the siege. It is remarkable how consistently they bear each other out, so long as allowance is made for the race and religion of the writer. I give here a short account of the more important of them.

1. *Greek.* Of the Greek contemporary historians only one was present in Constantinople during the siege. This was George PHRANTZES, who almost certainly called himself Sphrantzes, though the family may have originally been called Phrantzes (the Frank? or Francis?) and later reverted to that form of the name. He was of Peloponnesian origin and was born soon after 1400. As a very young man he joined the secretariat of the Emperor Manuel II and after Manuel's death attached himself to Manuel's son Constantine, in whose service he remained for the remainder of Constantine's life. He married a distant cousin of the Imperial family, and he became Constantine's most intimate friend and adviser. He himself did not favour the union of the churches but was prepared loyally to support his master's policy. He had his prejudices. He disliked his master's brothers Theodore and Demetrius and he was particularly jealous of the Megadux Lucas Notaras, whom he regarded as a rival at Court and about whom he was consistently unfair. He had the fussy self-importance of a court official, but he did in fact play an important part there. It is easy to make allowances for his dislikes. Apart from them his

narrative is honest, and convincing. His work now exists in two forms, a *chronicum minus* which deals with the period from 1413 to 1477, that is to say, the period covered by his own life, and a *chronicum majus*, giving the whole history of the Palaeologan dynasty and adding material to the *chronicum minus*. Modern research has shown that almost certainly the *majus* was compiled in the following century by a certain Macarius Melissenus. The account of the siege is, however, contained in the original version. Phrantzes presumably lost his original notes at the time of his capture by the Turks but rewrote them while his memory was still fresh. He is a little vague about detailed dates, though he set great store on chronological accuracy, and he never abandoned his prejudices. In all other respects his narrative is honest, vivid and convincing. He wrote good Greek in an easy unpretentious style.[1]

DUCAS, whose first name was probably Michael, was a more obscure personage of whose life we know little. He apparently spent most of it in the service of the Genoese and was probably living at Chios at the time of the siege. He was a passionate advocate of church union and tended to see everything through the eyes of his Latin friends. He begins his work with a brief survey of world history up till 1341, then gives a little more detail and fuller detail still after 1389. It ends at 1462. It is all written in a lively journalistic vernacular. Modern historians rate his reliability highly, more highly, I think, than it merits. For events at Mehmet II's court his account is invaluable; he presumably obtained his information from Genoese agents and merchants resident there. But he was not present in Constantinople and makes a number of slips about events there; and he is grossly unfair about any Greek who did not share his views on church union.[2]

The Athenian Laonicus CHALCOCONDYLAS wrote his history some time after 1480, when he was a very old man. He had been a pupil of Plethon at Mistra and spent most of his life in the Peloponnese. His work, like Ducas's, begins with a short account of world history; but its main theme is the rise of the Ottoman dynasty; the Turks rather than the Byzantines are his theme. He had made an intimate study of Herodotus and Thucydides and wrote in a deliberately archaic Classical style. His chronology is sometimes a little muddled and he does not give many details about the actual siege of Constantinople; but he had a historian's grasp of the general sweep of events. His book has the advantages and the disadvantages of being a conscious work of art.[1]

The fourth contemporary Greek historian, CRITOBULUS, was living as an official at Imbros at the time of the siege. He belonged to the party among the Greeks who saw the Turkish conquest as inevitable though tragic, and he wished to reconcile his compatriots to the new state of affairs. His history stretches from 1451 to 1467. Its hero is the Sultan. Critobulus was moved and impressed by the heroism of the Greeks and makes no attempt to palliate their sufferings, though he is inclined disingenuously to overlook or excuse the savageries committed by Mehmet himself. His account of the siege is of supreme importance as he obtained his information from Turks as well as from Greeks who were present; and, except when he is sheltering the Sultan's reputation, it is honest, unprejudiced and convincing.[2]

The 'synoptic' group of chronicles associated with the names of Dorotheus of Monemvasia and Manuel Malaxos and the *Ecthesis Chronicon* add nothing to our knowledge of the siege of Constantinople but provide useful information about events immediately after the Turkish conquest. For the sake of convenience I have referred to the *Ecthesis Chronicon* and to the two chronicles published in the Bonn corpus under the names of the *Historia Politica* and the *Historia Patriarchica*.[3] The fuller account given in the Χρονικὸν περὶ τῶν Τούρκων Σουλτάνων (Barberini Codex Graecus 111) is remarkable in that for the siege it copies almost word for word the very anti-Greek report of Leonard of Chios.[4]

The various threnes or laments on the fall of Constantinople are of greater interest as folk-poetry than as historical evidence, except in so far as they illustrate the popular traditions and point of view.[1]

Of the Greek correspondence that has survived the most important is that of George Scholarius Gennadius, for the light that it throws on events and personalities in the years immediately preceding 1453. In particular it enables us to appreciate the policy of Lucas Notaras, about whom Phrantzes, Ducas and the Latin sources are consistently unfair.[2]

2. *Slavonic*. There are two important Slavonic sources for the siege. One is usually and incorrectly known as the Diary of the Polish Janissary. The author was a certain Serb, Michael Constantinovic of Ostrovica, who served in the contingent that the Despot of Serbia sent to help the Sultan and who later retired to Poland. He was never a Janissary. He wrote his account in a curious mixture of Polish and Serbian. It gives few details but is of interest as showing the point of view of the Sultan's involuntary Christian allies.

The second appears under various forms, as the *Slavic Chronicle* in an old Slavonic dialect which seems to be Balkan rather than Russian, of which several versions exist, and in a Russian, a Roumanian and a Bulgarian version.[3] It is clearly based on the account of someone who was present in Constantinople and kept some sort of a diary, but has been considerably altered. The dates have been changed and muddled; an imaginary Patriarch and an imaginary Empress have been added. But every now and then episodes are so vividly reported that they bear the stamp of truth. The Russian version is attributed to a certain Nestor-Iskander. Possibly that was the name of the original author?

3. *Western*. By far the most useful of the Western sources is the diary of the siege kept by Nicolo Barbaro. He was a Venetian of good family who studied medicine and came to Constantinople as a ship's doctor in one of the great Venetian galleys

shortly before the siege began. He was in touch with the Venetian commanders and was himself observant and intelligent. He made daily entries into his diary. At some date he went through the text and inserted one or two cross-references, and he must have altered the date of the eclipse of the moon, which is two days out. As a good Venetian he detested the Genoese and delighted to report anything to their discredit; but he was less hostile to the Greeks than most Westerners. It is thanks to him that we know the chronological sequence of events.[1]

Next in importance is the report written by LEONARD OF CHIOS, Archbishop of Lesbos, which he wrote in Chios some six weeks after the fall of the city. His memory was still fresh; and his account is vivid and convincing, so long as we remember his hatred of all Greeks. He even considered the Emperor to be too easy-going and hinted that his superior, Cardinal Isidore, was a little too weak. At the same time he was not uncritical of his fellow-Genoese and was inclined to blame Giustiniani for having deserted his post. He was a harsh, self-righteous man, but a good reporter.[2]

Cardinal ISIDORE's letters to the Pope and to All the Faithful are brief and tell us little, but are written with authority.[3]

The report that Angelo Giovanni LOMELLINO, Podestà of Pera, wrote a few days after the fall of the city to send to the Genoese government is valuable not only for his account of the fate of his own town but also for his views on the fate of the city. He declares that the Genoese of Pera went in large numbers to fight at the walls, knowing that if Constantinople fell Pera could not survive.[4]

A brief account by the Superior of the Franciscans in the city tells little except about the pillage.

Other Westerners who were present at the siege and wrote their accounts were the Florentine soldier TETALDI, the Genoese MONTALDO, Cristoforo RICCHERIO and the Brescian scholar Ubertino PUSCULUS. Of these Tetaldi's account is the most useful. It was written to be sent to the Cardinal of Avignon, Alain de Coëtivy, and gives several details not found elsewhere. He dealt fairly with both the Venetians and the Genoese and admitted that the Greeks fought well. Montaldo also provides a few additional details, as does Riccherio in his lively account. Pusculus, who wrote his story in ponderous verse many years later, is a little inaccurate about the actual fighting, in which he perhaps did not personally take part, and is more interesting about events before the siege began. He loathed the Greeks.

Useful information can be obtained from the Florentine Andrea CAMBINI. For his work on Ottoman history, written towards the end of the fifteenth century, he seems to have consulted survivors from the siege. Zorzo DOLFIN, whose short work is based upon Leonard of Chios's report, also obtained additional information from survivors. The Turkish history written by the Greek refugee Cantacuzino SPANDUGINO reproduces eye-witness accounts of the sack of the city.[1]

4. *Turkish.* The Turkish sources for the siege and fall of Constantinople are peculiarly disappointing. One would have expected this most notable achievement of the greatest of Ottoman Sultans to have been fully recorded by Ottoman historians and chroniclers. As it is, they all tell of the construction of the castle at Rumeli Hisar; but of the siege operations only the land-journey of the Turkish fleet and the final assault interest them. On the other hand they are deeply interested in the intrigues and politics of the Sultan's court. ASHIKPASHAZADE, who wrote just after the end of Mehmet II's reign is violently hostile to Halil Pasha, as was his contemporaries TURSUN BEY and NESHRI; and in their praise of the reigning Sultan, Bayezit II, they are apt slightly to denigrate Mehmet II in favour of his advisers such as Mahmud. Nevertheless their accounts are valuable for giving the political climate amongst the Turks. The first Turkish historian who gives the impression of being interested in the story of the siege and

fall of Constantinople is SA'AD ED-DIN, writing at the end of the sixteenth century, but, as is usual with Moslem historians, reproducing, even copying, the accounts of earlier historians. His account of the siege tallies with that of the Greek historians.[1]

By the early seventeenth century fantasy has begun to come into the story. EVLIYA CHELEBI, who recounts it at length, claiming to have been informed all about it by his great-grandfather, gives a number of fanciful details, including a long saga about a Princess of France who was destined to be Constantine's bride but was captured by the Sultan. Possibly he obtained that detail from Greek acquaintances who were telling him of the fall of the city in 1204 and the princess was really the Empress Agnes, daughter of Louis VII of France and widow of Alexius II and Andronicus I. In any case he seems to have relied on gossip and hearsay, not on earlier written sources.[2]

Later Turkish sources merely reproduce their forerunner's works.

THE CHURCHES OF CONSTANTINOPLE
AFTER THE CONQUEST

By a well established Moslem tradition the inhabitants of a conquered Christian city which had refused to surrender forfeited both their personal liberty and their places of worship, and the conquering soldiers were allowed three days of unrestricted looting. All the historians of the fall of Constantinople tell of the sack of the churches in the city. Undoubtedly many churches and monasteries were pillaged. But in actual fact we only know from contemporary literary sources of the sack of four churches, the Holy Wisdom (Saint Sophia), Saint John in Petra and the Church of the Chora, close to the breach in the land-walls, and Saint Theodosia, close to the Golden Horn.[1] Archaeological evidence shows that the triple church of the Pantocrator was sacked; and that is borne out by the fact that Gennadius who was a monk at the monastery attached to it was taken prisoner. Saint Sophia was at once turned into a mosque; the others were left for a time empty and half ruined and converted later on. There are also a number of other churches which we know were in use in the years before the fall of the city but of which we have no subsequent record. We can assume that they were sacked and abandoned. These include the churches in the old Imperial Palace area and round the citadel, such as the Nea Basilica of Basil I or Saint George of the Mangana.[2] But the history of the following years shows that a number of churches remained in Christian hands and were apparently untouched. The great church of the Holy Apostles, second only in size and repute to Saint Sophia, was handed over by the Sultan to the Patriarch Gennadius for his use, with its relics intact; for he was able to take them with him when he voluntarily gave up the building a few months later. The church of the Pammacaristos, to which he then moved, was functioning as a convent church, the nunnery having been undisturbed; and when he took it over he was able to move the nuns with their holy relics to the nearby church and monastery of Saint John in Trullo.[1] Not far off, on the edge of the Blachernae quarter, the church of Saint Demetrius Kanavou was untouched. In another part of the city the church of the Peribleptos in Psamathia remained a Greek church till the mid-seventeenth century, when Sultan Ibrahim gave it to the Armenians to please his Armenian favourite, a large lady known as Şekerparçe, or 'Lump of sugar'. Saint George of the Cypresses, nearby, was untouched. The churches of Lips, of Saint John in Studion and of Saint Andrew in Krisei seem to have remained in Christian use till they were converted into mosques in later reigns. The convent church of the Myrelaeon seems still to have been a church till the end of the fifteenth century.[2] About the same time a church dedicated to Saint John the Evangelist was disaffected because it was considered to be too close to a newly erected mosque.[3]

How was it that these churches were able to survive? The question was soon to puzzle the Turks. In 1490 Sultan Bayezit II demanded the surrender of the Patriarchal church, the Pammacaristos. The Patriarch, Dionysius I was able to prove that Mehmet II had definitely bestowed the church on the Patriarchate. The Sultan gave way, after ordering the cross on top of the dome to be removed; and he refused to forbid his officials to annex other churches.[4]

Some thirty years later Sultan Selim I, who disliked Christianity, suggested to his horrified vizier that all Christians should be forcibly converted to Islam. When he was told that this was hardly practicable he ordered that at least all their churches should be confiscated. The vizier warned the Patriarch, Theoleptus I, who, thanks to a clever lawyer called Xenakis, was able to bring into the Sultan's presence three janissaries, each aged nearly 100.

Theoleptus admitted that he had no written *firman* protecting the churches; it has been burnt in a fire at the Patriarchate. But the tottering janissaries swore on the Koran that they had been in the Conquering Sultan's bodyguard when he was waiting to enter the city in triumph, and they had seen a number of notables from various parts of the city come to him bearing the keys of their quarters as a sign of surrender. Mehmet had therefore allowed them to keep their churches. Sultan Selim accepted this evidence and even allowed the Christians to re-open two or three churches (their names are not given) which his officials had closed.[1]

The question arose again in 1537, under Suleiman the Magnificent. The Patriarch Jeremias I then referred the Sultan to Selim's decision. Suleiman consulted the Sheikh ul-Islam, as the highest Moslem legal authority; and the sheikh pronounced that: 'as far as is known the city was taken by force. But the fact that the Christians have been left with their churches proves that it surrendered by capitulation.' Suleiman, who was a good lawyer himself, accepted this ruling; and once more the churches were left in peace.[2]

Later Sultans were less indulgent. In 1586 Murad III annexed the Pammacaristos; and by the eighteenth century only three pre-conquest churches were left in Christian hands, Saint George of the Cypresses and Saint Demetrius Kanavou, the first to be soon destroyed by earthquake and the second soon by fire,[3] and Saint Mary of the Mongols, which may have been annexed at the time of the conquest but was given by the Conquering Sultan to his Greek architect, Christodulus, who handed it on to the Church authorities. When in Ahmet III's time the Turks tried to annex it, the Patriarch's lawyer, Demetrius Cantemir, was able to show to the Vizier, Ali Koprülü, the *firman* bestowing it upon Christodulus.[4] It remains a church, though it was damaged in the anti-Greek riots in 1955.

How far can the evidence of the Patriarch's aged janissaries in Selim's reign be regarded as authentic? Demetrius Cantemir, a

Greek with Tartar blood and a man of immense learning, wrote at the end of the seventeenth century a History of the Ottoman Empire, which is a work of great importance, as he used mainly Turkish sources, though he seldom actually names them. In this book he puts forward a theory that Constantinople did actually capitulate; but when the Emperor's envoys were escorting the Sultan's into the city, the Christians misunderstood the position and fired on them; and the enraged Turks therefore assaulted the walls. For that reason the Sultan ruled that as the city had half capitulated, the Christians could keep their churches in half of the city, the half extending westward from Akserai (the Forum of the Bull) to the walls. The story is obviously an invention. Cantemir declares that he obtained it from a Turkish source, from the historian Ali; but actually it was already given in the *Historia Patriarchica*, written a century earlier, but the author seems doubtful about its truth. Presumably it represents the attempt of some Turk to explain why the Christians had retained some churches. The story appears in the works of a certain Hussein Hezarfenn, a slightly older contemporary of Cantemir's; but whether he invented it or took it from some source known to both of them cannot be known.[1]

Though this story may be absurd, its absurdity does not invalidate the story of the ancient janissaries. It is necessary to remember the condition of Constantinople at the time. It was not like a city of today, a solid conglomeration of houses. Even in its most prosperous Byzantine days the various quarters had been separated by parks and orchards. By 1453, with its population less than a tenth of what it had been in the twelfth century, the city was now a collection of villages, many of which must have been at some distance from their neighbours. Each was probably surrounded by its own stockade. The quarter of Petrion had long since been surrounded by a definite wall. It would have been perfectly possible for the headmen of some of these villages, when the news spread that the walls had been breached, to surrender at once to the local Turkish assailants. All was lost and there was no point in further resistance. The local Turkish commander would then have sent the headmen under safe escort to the Sultan to announce the surrender to the Sultan as he waited by the walls. Mehmet had kept back some of his trusted troops to act as military police; and he doubtless sent some of them to protect the surrendered villages from pillage. What the janissaries reported was in fact true.

There is evidence to support this. In the early seventeenth century Evliya Chelebi noted that certain fishermen of Petrion were 'descended from the Greeks who opened the gate of Petrion to Mehmet II' and 'are even now free from all kind of duties, and give no tithe to the Inspector of Fisheries.'[1] In the eighteenth century the English traveller James Dallaway noted a tradition that 'whilst the brave Constantine was defending the gate of Saint Romanos as a forlorn hope, others of the besieged, either from cowardice or despair made terms with the conquerors, and opened the gate of the Phenàr for their admission. From that circumstance they obtained from Mohammed II the neighbouring quarter, with certain immunities.'[2] If we note which were the churches that survived the fall of the city we find that they were all (with one exception) situated either in the quarters of Petrion and the Phanàr or in Psamathia, along the south-western slopes of the city. It is therefore fair to assume that these quarters did in fact surrender just in time and so preserved their places of worship. Whether the inhabitants also kept their houses and their personal liberty is less certain. Critobulus's description of the city after the sack suggests that it was all devastated and the whole surviving population enslaved. But it covered a large area; the immunity of certain out-of-the-way districts might have been unnoticed. Certainly there seem to have been citizens left in the city who were able to redeem some of the captives.

The Sultan had no wish to inherit an entirely ruined city, and, as he was to show, he was anxious to appear as Emperor of the

Greeks as well as Sultan of the Turks. It would suit him to reserve certain quarters for his future Greek subjects and to let them keep their churches there. The timely surrender of a few villages within the walls would have been convenient. This perhaps also explains the fate of the church of the Holy Apostles. That great building stood beside the main street running from the section of the walls through which the Turks first entered the city to Saint Sophia and the hippodrome and the old palace area. Vast numbers of the triumphant soldiers must have passed in front of it; and it seems incredible that they should not have entered it and sacked it, unless they were forcibly prevented. Mehmet must therefore have sent special guards to preserve it. One can only suppose that he had already decided that while Saint Sophia, as the official cathedral of the Empire, must be converted into a mosque to show that the Turks were now the Imperial power, the Greeks, as the second people in his Empire, could keep the second great church. It was apparently without hesitation that he allotted it to the Patriarch within a few days of the fall of the city. The fact that the Patriarch later abandoned it at his own wish is irrelevant.[1]

Thus, though Cantemir's story of the surrender of Constantinople is clearly fictional, Sultan Suleiman's lawyers were not being ridiculous when they ruled that the city had both been taken by storm and had surrendered.

NOTES

Abbreviations

B.Z.   *Byzantinische Zeitschrift*, Leipzig, 1892—(in progress).
C.S.H.B.   *Corpus Scriptorum Historiae Byzantinae*, Bonn, 1828–1897.
M.P.G.   Migne, *Patrologia Graeco-Latina*, Paris, 1859–1866.
Muratori, *R.I.Ss.*   Muratori, *Rerum Italicarum Scriptores*, Milan, 1723–1751.

PAGE 1

1 Adam of Usk, *Chronicon* (ed. Thompson), p. 57; *Chronique du Réligieux de Saint-Denis* (ed. Bellaguet), p. 756. The best account of Manuel's journey is given in Vasiliev, 'The Journey of the Byzantine Emperor Manuel II Palaeologus in Western Europe' (in Russian), *Journal of the Ministry of Public Instruction*, N.S., xxxix, pp. 41–78, 260–304. *See also* Andreeva, 'Zur Reise Manuels II Palaiologos nach West-Europa', *B.Z.*, xxxiv, pp. 37–47. Halečki, 'Rome et Byzance en temps du grand Schisme d'Occident', *Collectio Theologica*, xviii, pp. 514 ff., maintains that Manuel had an interview with Pope Boniface IX in 1402. The evidence seems insufficient; but Manuel did send envoys to the Pope in 1404; Adam of Usk, *op. cit.* pp. 96–7.

PAGE 4

1 The modern usage which distinguishes Galata, the lower town, from Pera up the hill was unknown in the middle ages. Both names were used indiscriminately, Pera usually being regarded as the official name.

2 For the general situation at the time see Ostrogorsky, *History of the Byzantine State* (trans. Hussey), pp. 425 ff.

3 Ostrogorsky, *op. cit.* pp. 476–84.

PAGE 5

1 Nicephorus Gregoras, *Romaïke Historia*, C.S.H.B., ii, pp. 797–8; Johannes Cantacuzenus, *Historiae*, C.S.H.B., iii, pp. 49–53; Bartholomaeus della Pugliola, *Historia Miscella* (Muratori, *R.I.Ss.*, xviii, p. 409), saying that two-thirds of the population of Constantinople perished; *Chronicon Estense* (Muratori, *R.I.Ss.*, xv), estimating the deaths as eight-ninths of the population. For the extent of the Empire in the fifteenth century see Bakalopulos, 'Les limites de l'Empire byzantin', *B.Z.*, lv, 2, pp. 56–65.

2 For Palaeologan art see Beckwith, *The Art of Constantinople*, pp. 134 ff.

3 Gregoras, *op. cit.* ii, pp. 788–9.

4 For Metochites and the intellectual life of his time see Beck, *Theodoros Metochites*, *passim*.

PAGE 6

1 See Meyendorff, *Introduction à l'étude de Grégoire Palamas*, also Beck, 'Humanismus und Palamismus', XIIe. Congrès International des Études Byzantines, *Rapports*, III.

PAGE 7

1 Halečki, *Un Empereur de Byzance à Rome*, esp. p. 205; Charanis, 'The strife among the Palaeologi and the Ottoman Turks', *Byzantion*, XVI, I, pp. 287–293.

PAGE 8

1 For a brief résumé of the theological differences see Runciman, 'The Schism between the Eastern and Western Churches', *Anglican Theological Review*, XLIV, 4, pp. 337–50.

PAGE 9

1 For Cydones and his influence see Beck, *Kirche und theologische Literatur im Byzantinischen Reich*, pp. 732–6.

2 Schneider, 'Die Bevölkerung Konstantinopels im XV Jahrhundert', *Nachrichten der Akademie der Wissenschaften in Göttingen*', Phil.-Hist. Klasse, 1949, pp. 233–44.

PAGE 11

1 Ibn Battuta, *Voyages*, ed. Defremery & Sanguinetti, II, pp. 431–2; Gonzales de Clavijo, *Diary*, trans. Le Strange, pp. 88–90; Bertrandon de la Broquière, *Voyage d'Outremer*, ed. Schéfer, p. 153; Pero Tafur, *Travels*, trans. Letts, pp. 142–6. Gennadius, himself a Constantinopolitan, calls the city poverty-stricken and for the most part uninhabited: *Œuvres Complètes de Gennade Scholarios*, ed. Petit and others, I, p. 287, and IV, p. 405.

PAGE 12

1 Tafrali, *Thessalonique au quatorzième Siècle*, pp. 273–88; Zakythinos, *Le Despotat Grec de Morée*, II, pp. 169–72.

PAGE 13

1 No proper life of Manuel II has been published since Berger de Xivrey, *Mémoire sur la vie et les ouvrages de l'Empereur Manuel Paléologue*, published in 1851. See Ostrogorsky, *op. cit.* pp. 482–98. For Boucicault's expedition see Delaville Le Roulx, *La France en Orient au XIVe. siècle: Expéditions du Maréchal Boucicault*.

PAGE 14

1 Heyd, *Histoire du Commerce du Levant* (1936 edition), II, pp. 266–8, with references. See below, p. 42, n. 1.

2 Fuchs, *Die höheren Schulen von Konstantinopel im Mittelalter*, pp. 73–4; Beck, *op. cit.* pp. 749–50; Pius II, *Opera Omnia*, p. 681.

PAGE 15

1 For Plethon see Masai, *Plethon et le Platonisme de Mistra*.

2 Runciman, 'Byzantine and Hellene in the fourteenth Century', Τόμος Κωνσταντίνου Ἀρμενοπούλου, pp. 27–31.

PAGE 16

1 Ostrogorsky, *op. cit.* pp. 497–8; Tafrali, *op. cit.* pp. 287–8.

PAGE 18

1 See Gill, *The Council of Florence*, an admirable and fair-minded account, though it does not always, I think, quite appreciate the Greek point of view. For the taunt about the Patriarch's grammar, *Œuvres Complètes de Gennade Scholarios*, III, p. 142.

PAGE 19

1 Gill, *op. cit.* pp. 349 ff. The Empress-Mother seems later to have modified her opposition. See John Eugenicos, *letters*, in Lambros, Παλαιολόγεια καὶ Πελοποννησιακά, I, pp. 59, 125.

2 See p. 46, n. 1.

3 See Diehl, 'De quelques croyances byzantines sur la fin de Constantinople', *B.Z.*, XXX; Vasiliev, 'Medieval Ideas of the end of the World', *Byzantion* XVI, 2, pp. 462–502. Gill, *op. cit.* p. 378, believes that Gennadius and his friends considered the end of the world to be coming. I think that he takes too literally their genuine fatalistic conviction that the reign of anti-Christ, by which they meant the Sultan, was inevitable.

PAGE 20

1 'Terre hodierne Graecorum et dominia secularia et spiritualia ipsorum', ed. Lambros, *Neos Hellenomnemon*, VII, pp. 360 ff.

PAGE 21

1 Ducas, *Historia Turco-Byzantina*, ed. Grecu, XXXVII, p. 329; Zoras, Περὶ τὴν ἅλωσιν τῆς Κωνσταντινουπόλεως, pp. 9–70. See below, p. 71.

2 See p. 51 for John's death. For his repairs to the walls see pp. 91–2 and van Millingen, *Byzantine Constantinople: The Walls of the City*. (John is called

John VII by van Millingen.) Some of the repairs were carried out with money provided by George Brankovitch, Despot of Serbia.

PAGE 23

1 For the Akritic life see the brief summary, with references, in Vasiliev, *History of the Byzantine Empire*, pp. 369–71.

2 See Laurent, *Byzance et les Turcs Seldjoucides*, pp. 27–44.

PAGE 24

1 See Houtsma, article 'Tughrilbeg', *Encyclopaedia of Islam*, IV, pp. 828–9.

PAGE 25

1 Laurent, *op. cit.* pp. 45–59; Cahen, 'La Campagne de Mantzikert d'après les sources Mussulmanes', *Byzantion*, IX, pp. 613–642.

PAGE 26

1 Laurent, *op. cit.* pp. 61–101; Cahen, 'The Turkish Invasion: The Selchükids', in *A History of the Crusades*, ed. Setton, I, pp. 135–76.

2 Wittek, *The Rise of the Ottoman Empire*, pp. 18–20; Köprülü, *Les Origines de l'Empire Ottoman*, pp. 101–7; Cahen, *op. cit.* pp. 138–9.

PAGE 27

1 Cahen, 'The Selchükid State of Rum', in *A History of the Crusades*, ed. Setton, II, pp. 675–90.

PAGE 28

1 Cahen, 'The Mongols and the Near East', *ibid.* II, pp. 690–2, 725–32.

2 Wittek, *op. cit.* pp. 25–32, and *Das Fürstentum Mentesche*, pp. 1–14.

PAGE 29

1 Wittek, *op. cit.* pp. 34–7, and *Das Fürstentum Mentesche*, pp. 15–23; Lemerle, *L'Emirat d'Aydin, Byzance et l'Occident*, pp. 1–39.

PAGE 30

1 Wittek, *op. cit.* pp. 4–15; Köprülü, *op. cit.* pp. 82–8.

2 It is not as fantastic as Köprülü suggests that the Ottoman dynasty should have had this Comnenian-Seljuk ancestry; but if it is correct it probably came in later, through Bayezit I's marriage to a Germiyan princess.

PAGE 31

1 Wittek, *op. cit.*, pp. 14–15.

PAGE 33

1 Wittek, *op. cit.* pp. 37-43; Kramers, article 'Othman I', *Encyclopaedia o Islam*, III, pp. 1005-7.

2 Babinger, article 'Orkhan', *Encyclopaedia of Islam*, III, pp. 999-1001.

PAGE 34

1 For the civil war in Byzantium see Ostrogorsky, *op. cit.* pp. 444-75.

2 Babinger, *loc. cit.*; Köprülü, *op. cit.* pp. 125-6. The date of Orhan's death is uncertain. Uzunçarşîlî, *Osmanlî Tarihi*, I, p. 62, gives 1360. Wittek, *op. cit.* pp. 44, 54, gives 1362, relying on the evidence of the Βραχέα Χρονικά.

PAGE 35

1 Wittek, *op. cit.* pp. 42-3, 50.

PAGE 36

1 Köprülü, *op. cit.* pp. 131-2; Pears, 'The Ottoman Turks to the Fall of Constantinople', *Cambridge Medieval History*, IV, pp. 664-5.

2 Uzunçarşîlî, *op. cit.* I, pp. 61 ff.; Wittek, *op. cit.* pp. 44-5; Ostrogorsky, *op. cit.* pp. 478-9.

PAGE 37

1 Charanis, 'The strife among the Palaeologi and the Ottoman Turks', *Byzantion*, XVI, I, pp. 288-300.

2 Köprülü, *op. cit.* pp. 129-130: Jireček, *Geschichte der Serben*, II, pp. 87 ff.

PAGE 38

1 Tafrali, *Thessalonique au quatorzieme Siècle*, pp. 283-5; Charanis, *op. cit.* p. 301; Jireček, *op. cit.* II, pp. 99 ff.; Ostrogorsky, *op cit.* p. 485; Babinger, *Beiträge zur Frühgeschichte der Turkenherrschaft in Rumelien*, pp. 65 ff.

PAGE 39

1 Babinger, *op cit.* pp. I, 24; Jireček, *op. cit.* II, pp. 119 ff. The actual date of the battle of Kossovo is disputed, but 15 June seems to be correct. See Atiya, *The Crusade of Nicopolis*, p. 5, and Ostrogorsky, *op. cit.* p. 486, n. 1, for references.

PAGE 40

1 The whole Nicopolis campaign is fully described in Atiya, *op. cit.* See also Inalcîk, article 'Bayazîd I', *Encyclopaedia of Islam*, new edition, I, pp. 117-9.

2 See above, p. 12.

3 Ducas, *op. cit.* XV, p. 89.

PAGE 42

3 For Timur see Grousset, *L'Empire des Steppes*, pp. 486 ff.

PAGE 43

1 Ducas, *op. cit.* XXIII, pp. 177–9. See above, p. 13.

2 The best account of this period is in Jorga, *Geschichte des Osmanischen Reiches*, I, pp. 325 ff. See also Kramers, article 'Muhammad I', *Encyclopaedia of Islam*, III, pp. 657–8.

PAGE 44

1 Ducas, *op. cit.* XIX–XXII, pp. 129–69.

2 Ducas, *op. cit.* XXXIII, p. 285; Bertrandon de la Broquière, *Voyage d'Outremer*, pp. 181–2, 'They told me that he dislikes war, and it seems to me to be true'; Laonicus Chalcocondylas, *De Rebus Turcicis, C.S.H.B.*, pp. 351–2, saying that Murad vowed to join a religious order at the crisis of the battle of Varna. The statement is unsupported; but Murad's dealings with the Janissaries (see below, p. 47, n. 3), suggest that he was sympathetic with the Bektashis.

3 Ducas, *op. cit.* XXVIII, pp. 229–37; Chalcocondylas, pp. 231–5; George Phrantzes, *Chronicon, C.S.H.B.*, pp. 116–17; Jorga, *op. cit.* I., pp. 378 ff. A contemporary account of the siege, with miraculous details added, is given by John Cananus, published in the *C.H.S.B.* volume of Phrantzes, pp. 457–479.

PAGE 45

1 Ducas, *op. cit.* XXIX–XXXI, pp. 245–270; Chalcocondylas, pp. 236–248; Jorga, *op. cit.* I, pp. 236 ff.; Jireček, *op. cit.* pp. 174 ff. A contemporary account of the capture of Thessalonica, followed by a Monodia, was written by John Anagnostes, published in the *C.H.S.B.* volume of Phrantzes, pp. 483–534.

2 For Scanderberg's career see Radonić, *Djuradj Kastriot Skenderbeg i Albanija u XV veku*, and Gegaj, *L'Albanie et l'Invasion Turque au XVe Siècle*.

PAGE 46

1 Babinger, *Mehmed der Eroberer und seine Zeit*, pp. 19–33. The usefulness of this important book is damaged by the complete absence of source references. The fullest modern account of the Varna campaign, Halecki, *The Crusade of Varna*, makes several very controversial statements. See Pall, 'Autour de la Croisade de Varna', *Bulletin Historique de l'Academie Roumaine*, XXII, pp. 144 ff., and Babinger, 'Von Amurath zu Amurath. Vor- und Nachspiel der Schlacht bei Varna', *Oriens*, III, pp. 229 ff.

PAGE 47

1 Babinger, *Mehmed der Eroberer*, pp. 51–5.

2 *Ibid.* pp. 42–3.

3 Mortmann, article 'Dewshirme', and Huart, article 'Janissaries', in *Encyclopaedia of Islam*, I, pp. 952–3, and II, pp. 572–4. See Birge, *The Bektashi Order of Dervishes*, pp. 45–8, for stories connecting the foundation of the corps with the Bektashi Order. Bartholomaeus de Jano, *Epistola de Crudelitate Turcarum*, M.P.G., CLVIII, coll. 1065–6, says that Murad had reconstituted the corps in 1438.

4 Ducas, *op. cit.* XXXIII, p. 285; Chalcocondylas, *op. cit.* p. 375; Phrantzes, *op. cit.* pp. 92, 211.

PAGE 48

1 Phrantzes, *op. cit.* pp. 121–2, 134.

2 Zakythinos, *Le Despotat Grec de Morée*, I, pp. 165–74.

PAGE 49

1 Zakythinos, *op. cit.* I, pp. 165–225, 299–302, and II, pp. 322–34. Phrantzes, who provides most of our information about Theodore, disliked him as a rival to his hero Constantine, and is consistently unfair to him.

2 For Queen Helena see Hill, *History of Cyprus*, III, pp. 527–544.

3 For Demetrius's part at the Council of Florence see Gill, *op. cit.* pp. 108–9, 252, 262 ff. For his marriage, Phrantzes, pp. 193–4. He had previously been married to Zoe Paraspondyles, who died while he was in Italy. *Ibid.* pp. 161, 191–2.

4 For Thomas's early career see Zakythinos, *op. cit.* I, esp. pp. 241 ff.

PAGE 51

1 Zakythinos, *op. cit.* I, pp. 204–40.

2 Phrantzes, *op. cit.* p. 203 and pp. 324–5, where he suggests that Constantine's failure to marry the Doge's daughter damaged his relations with Venice. The story is not confirmed by any Venetian source. See also Lambros, "Ὁ Κωνσταντῖνος Παλαιολόγος ὡς σύζυγος', *Neos Hellenomnemon*, IV, pp. 433–6.

3 Phrantzes, *op. cit.* p. 202; Chalcocondylas, *op. cit.* p. 342; Krekic, *Dubrovnik (Raguse) et le Levant au Moyen Age*, Regestes no. 1110, p. 349.

PAGE 52

1 Phrantzes, *op. cit.* pp. 204–6; Chalcocondylas, *op. cit.* pp. 373–4.

2 Ducas, *op. cit.* XXXIV, p. 293, says that Constantine, though called Emperor, had never been crowned. See Voyatzidis, 'Τὸ ζήτημα τῆς στέψεως Κωνσταντίνου τοῦ Παλαιολόγου', *Λαογραφία*, VII, pp. 449–56.

PAGE 53

1 Phrantzes, *loc. cit.*; Chalcocondylas, *loc. cit.*

2 All the contemporary writers, Latin and Slav as well as Greek, speak of Constantine with respect. No authentic contemporary portrait of him exists: see Lambros, 'Αἱ εἰκόνες Κωνσταντίνου τοῦ Παλαιολόγου', *Neos Helleno-mnemon*, III, pp. 229-42 and IV, pp. 238-40.

PAGE 54

1 For Constantine's advisers see Phrantzes, pp. 229 ff. It must be remembered that he was prejudiced by his personal dislike of Lucas Notaras.

2 Phrantzes, *op. cit.* p. 217. See Gill, *op. cit.* p. 376, n. 3.

PAGE 55

1 Phrantzes, *op. cit.* pp. 206 ff.

2 Phrantzes, *op. cit.* pp. 211-3.

PAGE 56

1 Babinger, *Mehmed der Eroberer*, pp. 1-12, 22-3.

2 *Ibid.* pp. 34-7.

PAGE 57

1 *Ibid.* pp. 45-7.

2 For the identity of this lady, whose name was Hadije, see Alderson, *The Structure of the Ottoman Dynasty*, p. 94 and tables XXV, XXVI and LIV. Ducas, *op. cit.* XXXIII, p. 287, calls her the daughter of Spentiar (Isfendyar), lord of Sinope.

3 Babinger, *op. cit.* p. 53.

4 *Ibid.* pp. 60 ff. For the correct date see Inalcîk, 'Mehmed the Conqueror (1432-1481) and his time', *Speculum* XXXV, p. 411.

5 Babinger, *op. cit.* pp. 62-4.

PAGE 58

1 Ducas, *op. cit.* XXXIII, pp. 281-3, 287-9, a vivid and convincing account. Ashikpashazade (Derwish Ahmed, genannt 'Aşik-Paşa-Sohn), *Denkwürdig-keiten und Zeitläufte des Hauses Osman*, ed. and trans. Kreutel, pp. 195-7.

PAGE 59

1 The medal in the Cabinet de Medailles of the Bibliothèque Nationale in Paris (Plate IIb) shows Mehmet as a young man. It was probably struck soon after 1453. The medallion by Gentile Bellini in the British Museum and the medallion by Costanzo de Ferrara at Paris, date from 1480 and 1481, at the end of his life.

PAGE 61

1 Ducas, *op. cit.* XXXIII, pp. 289–291; Chalcocondylas, *op. cit.* pp. 375–6; Thiriet, *Regestes des Délibérations du Sénat de Venise concernant la Romanie*, III, no. 2862, pp. 167–8; Babinger, *Mehmed der Eroberer*, pp. 69–70; Hasluck, *Athos and its Monasteries*, p. 50.

2 See Inalcîk, *Fatih Devri üzerinde Tetikler ve Vesikalar*, pp. 110–11.

PAGE 62

1 For a brief summary of the international situation see Gill, *op. cit.* pp. 382–3.

2 Filelfo's letter is given in Jorga, *Notes et Extraits pour servir à l'Histoire des Croisades*, IV.

PAGE 63

1 Gill, *op. cit.* p. 187.

PAGE 64

1 Gill, *op. cit.* pp. 377–380, with references.

2 An admirable, detailed and fully referenced account of Platris's mission is given by Paulová, 'L'Empire byzantin et les Tcheques avant la chute de Constantinople', *Byzantinoslavica*, XIV, pp. 158–225, esp. 203–224. The one contemporary western writer to record the episode is the Brescian Ubertino Pusculus, who was living in Constantinople at the time: Pusculus, *Constantinopoleos*, in Ellissen, *Analekten der mittel- und neugriechischen Literatur*, pp. 36–7.

PAGE 65

1 Ducas, *op. cit.* XXXIV, pp. 291–3; Chalcocondylas, *op. cit.* pp. 376–9.

2 Ducas, *op. cit.* XXXIV, pp. 293–5.

PAGE 66

1 Ducas, *op. cit.* XXXIV, pp. 295–7; Chalcocondylas, *op. cit.* pp. 380–1; Critobulus (Kritovoulos), *History of Mehmed the Conqueror*, trans. Briggs, pp. 15–20.

2 Ducas, *op. cit.* XXXIV, pp. 301–3; Chalcocondylas, *op. cit.* pp. 380–1; Critobulus, *op. cit.* pp. 20–2; Phrantzes, *op. cit.* pp. 233–4. See Inalcîk, *op. cit.* pp. 121–2.

PAGE 67

1 Ducas, *op. cit.* XXXV, p. 309; Nicolo Barbaro, *Giornale dell' Assedio di Constantinopoli*, ed. Cornet, pp. 1–5.

2 Thiriet, *Regestes*, III, nos. 2881, 2896, 2897, pp. 173, 177–8; Heyd, *Histoire du Commerce du Levant*, II, pp. 302–5; Thiriet, *La Romanie Vénitienne au Moyen Age*, pp. 380–1.

PAGE 68

1 Documents cited in Jorga, *Notes et Extraits*, II, pp. 271–3; Heyd, *op. cit.* II, pp. 285–6; Argenti, *Occupation of Chios by the Genoese*, I, pp. 201–2.

2 Krekić, *Dubrovnik (Raguse) et le Levant*, pp. 59–62.

PAGE 69

1 Gill, *op. cit.* pp. 378–9; Marinescu, 'Le Pape Nicolas V et son attitude envers l'Empire Byzantin', *Bulletin de l'Institut Archéoligique Bulgare*, X, pp. 333–4, and 'Notes sur quelques ambassadeurs byzantins en Occident à la veille de la chute de Constantinople', *Annuaire de l'Institut de Philologie et d'Histoire Orientales et Slaves*, X, pp. 419–428; Guilland, 'Les appels de Constantin XI Paléologue à Rome et à Venise pour sauver Constantinople', *Byzantinoslavica*, XIV, pp. 226–244.

PAGE 72

1 Gill, *op. cit.* pp. 382–7, with full references. But see also Paulová, *op. cit.* pp. 192–203, for a more penetrating understanding of Gennadius's psychology. Gill seems to me to simplify the issue by assuming that everyone in Constantinople realized that Western help would not be forthcoming unless the union was implemented. Gennadius's method of checking the delight of the populace at the sight of Western soldiers, which certainly alarmed him, was to remind everyone emphatically that Western help did involve union and that the issue could not be shelved by good-will and economy, as Notaras seems to have believed. Gill rightly stresses the moderating influence of Notaras, who was most unfairly treated by Ducas (whose information was mainly derived from Genoese sources; see below, p. 193), and by the occidental writers, especially Leonard of Chios and by Pusculus (who calls Notaras a hater of fine arts and the grandson of a fishmonger, curious accusations against a man of high lineage who, though personally austere, inhabited a notoriously beautiful palace). The chief original sources for the negotiations are *Œuvres Complètes de Gennade Scholarios*, III, pp. 165–93; Ducas, XXXVI, pp. 315–9; Phrantzes, p. 325; Leonard of Chios, *Historia Constantinopolitanae Urbis Captae*, M.P.G., CLIX, coll. 929–930; Isidore of Russia, letter to the Pope, Jorga, *Notes et Extraits*, II, pp. 522–4; Pusculus, *op. cit.* pp. 21, 23.

PAGE 73

1 See above, p. 58, n. 1.

PAGE 74

1 Ducas, *op. cit.* XXXV, pp. 311–13.

2 Critobulus, *op. cit.* pp. 23–33, a long oration written up by the author, who makes the Sultan retrace the whole of Ottoman history to date; Taci Bey zade Cafer Celebi, *Mahrusa-i Istanbul Fetihnamesi*, ed. 1331 A.H., pp. 6–8, a shorter version, equally written up by the author but recognizably on the same base; see Inalcîk, *op. cit.* pp. 125–6.

3 Ducas, *op. cit.* XXXVII, p. 321; Pusculus, *op. cit.* p. 49, saying incorrectly that Mesembria was one of the towns which resisted the Turks.

PAGE 75

1 Phrantzes, *op. cit.* pp. 234–6; Chalcocondylas, *op. cit.* pp. 381–2.

2 For the warships of the time see Yule, *Travels of Marco Polo*, ed. Cordier, I, pp. 31–41; Pears, *The Destruction of the Greek Empire*, pp. 232–5; Sottas, *Les Messageries Maritimes de Venise*, pp. 52–102.

PAGE 76

1 Barbaro, *op. cit.* pp. 21–2, giving 12 galleys and 70 to 80 long boats; Jacobo Tetaldi, *Informations*, Martene and Durand, *Thesaurus Novus Anecdotorum*, I, coll. 1820–1, 16 to 18 galleys and 60 to 80 long boats; Leonard of Chios, col. 930, 6 triremes and 10 biremes and a total of 250 ships; Phrantzes, *op. cit.* p. 237, 30 large and 330 small ships, but pp. 239–240, a total of 480 ships; Ducas, *op cit.* XXXVIII, p. 333, a total of 300; Chalcocondylas, *op. cit.* p. 384, 30 triremes and 200 smaller ships; Critobulus, *op. cit.* pp. 37–8, a total of 350 excluding transports. Critobulus emphasizes Mehmet's personal interest in the fleet.

2 Critobulus, *op. cit.* p. 38.

PAGE 77

1 For the organization of the Turkish army see Pears, *op. cit.* pp. 222–231; Babinger, *Mehmed der Eroberer*, pp. 91–2. Of the Christian sources Ducas, *op. cit.* XXXVIII, p. 333, gives the total number of Turkish troops as more than 400,000; Chalcocondylas, *op. cit.* p. 383, as 400,000; Critobulus, *op. cit.* p. 38, as 300,000, exclusive of camp-followers; Phrantzes *op. cit.* p. 240, as 262,000; Leonard of Chios, col. 927, as 300,000, including 15,000 Janissaries; Tetaldi, col. 1820, as 200,000, including 60,000 camp-followers; Barbaro, *op. cit.* p. 18, as 160,000. Turkish authorities give about 80,000; see Khairullah Effendi, *Tarikh*, pp. 61–3. See Mordtmann, *Belagerung und Eroberung Konstantinopels*, p. 39. Babinger points out that, for demographic reasons, the Ottoman empire would not have been able to put more than about 80,000 men into the field at the time.

2 Oman, *History of the Art of War in the Middle Ages*, II, pp. 205 ff.

3 Babinger, *op. cit.* p. 88.

PAGE 78

1 Ducas, *op. cit.* XXXV, pp. 305–7; Phrantzes, *op. cit.* pp. 236–8; Chalcocondylas, *op. cit.* p. 385; Critobulus, *op. cit.* pp. 43–6; Barbaro, *op. cit.* p. 21; Leonard of Chios, col. 927. See Babinger, *op. cit.* pp. 86, 88.

PAGE 79

1 Mordtmann, article 'Constantinople', *Encyclopaedia of Islam*, I, p. 867; Hammer, *Geschichte des Osmanischen Reiches*, I, pp. 397–8.

2 Ducas, *op. cit.* XXXVII, p. 327; Barbaro, *op. cit.* p. 18; Zorzo Dolfin, *Assedio i Presa de Constantinopoli*, ed. Thomas, pp. 12–13; Phrantzes, *op. cit.* p. 237, gives the date of the arrival of the Turks as 2 April, when the vanguard probably arrived; Leonard of Chios, col. 927, giving the date as 9 April, when reinforcements seem to have arrived.

3 Critobulus, *op. cit.* p. 35.

PAGE 80

1 Critobulus, *op. cit.* pp. 34–5. Leonard of Chios, col. 934, accuses the Greeks of hoarding their money. Several of the Threnes lamenting the fall of the city give avarice as one of the sins of the Greeks that were punished by the disaster, but the accusation is made rhetorically, without details.

2 See Marinescu, 'Notes sur quelques ambassades', pp. 426–7.

3 Thiriet, *Regestes*, III, no. 2905, p. 130.

4 Marinescu, *op. cit.* pp. 424–5, and 'Le Pope Nicolas V', pp. 336–7.

PAGE 81

1 Thiriet, *op. cit.* nos. 2909–2912, 2917, 2919, pp. 182–4.

2 See p. 100.

PAGE 82

1 Csuday, *Die Geschichten der Ungarn*, I. pp. 422–6. Phrantzes, *op. cit.* pp. 323–8, says that the Hungarians sent an embassy to the Sultan to point out that an attack on Constantinople would damage their good relations with him, but that Hunyadi demanded from the Emperor either Selymbria or Mesembria as the price of his help. He adds that Alfonso of Aragon similarly demanded Lemnos.

Ostrogorsky, *op. cit.* p. 492.

Jorga, *Histoire des Roumains*, IV, pp. 124 ff.

4 Phrantzes, *op. cit.* pp. 325–6. 'The Polish Janissary' describes the indignation of the Serbian troops when they heard that they were to join the Turkish forces. *Pamietniki Janczara Polaka Napisane*, ed. Galezowski, *Zbior Pisarzow Polskich*, v, pp. 123 ff.

5 See Miller, *The Latins in the Levant*, pp. 407 ff.

PAGE 83

1 Barbaro, *op. cit.* pp. 14–18.

PAGE 84

1 Phrantzes, *op. cit.* p. 241; Ducas, *op. cit.* xxxviii, p. 331; Critobulus, *op. cit.* pp. 39–40; Barbaro, *op. cit.* pp. 13–15; Leonard of Chios, col. 928; Dolfin, *op. cit.* p. 14; Tetaldi, col. 1821; Montaldo, *Constantinopolitanum Excidium*; *Slavic Chronicle of the Siege of Constantinople*, ed. Desimoni, *Atti della Società Ligure di Storia*, x, p. 334, ed. Jorga, 'Une source negligée de la prise de Constantinople', *Bulletin Historique de l'Académie Roumaine*, xii, pp. 91–2 (Russian version), and p. 78 (Roumanian version); *Historia Politica Constantinopoleos*, *C.S.H.B.*, pp. 18–19, providing Giustiniani with an elegant speech for the occasion. See below, p. 196, for the men from Pera.

2 Phrantzes, *op. cit.* pp. 252–3.

3 Phrantzes, *op. cit.* p. 256. Francisco claimed descent from Alexius I Comnenus. I have not been able to trace this descent.

4 Phrantzes, *op. cit.* p. 244, calling him Johannes the German; Leonard of Chios, col. 928, gives him the surname of Grande; Dolfin, p. 14, copies it as Grando.

5 Barbaro, *op. cit.* p. 19.

6 Barbaro, *op. cit.* pp. 13–14; Phrantzes, *op. cit.* p. 241, says that a number of Greek families of all classes had left the city earlier to avoid the siege.

PAGE 85

1 Barbaro, *op. cit.* p. 20; Phrantzes, *op. cit.* p. 238; Dolfin, p. 20. Their figures more or less coincide, Barbaro giving most details.

2 Phrantzes, *op. cit.* p. 241. Tetaldi, col. 1820, gives the number as 6,000 to 7,000 adding, according to one MS., 'and not more'; Leonard of Chios, col. 933, followed by Dolfin, p. 22, gives 6,000 Greeks and 3,000 Italians, probably including in the latter the fighting men immobilized in Pera. Tetaldi gives the whole population of the city as 30,000 men; it is uncertain whether he wishes to exclude women. Making allowances for women, old men and children and clergy, a figure of 5,000 men capable of bearing arms would fit with a total population of 40,000 to 50,000; though some monks

were enrolled later, they were probably not included in Phrantzes's lists. Critobulus, *op. cit.* p. 76, says that nearly 4,000 inhabitants were killed at the fall of the city and the rest, just over 50,000 were captured. His figures, as with most medieval writers, are almost always excessive.

PAGE 86

1 Critobulus, *op. cit.* p. 40. Some of the moats seem to have been filled with water. Callistus, *Monodia, M.P.G.,* CLXI, col. 1124.

2 Barbaro, *op. cit.* pp. 15–16; Leonard of Chios, col. 930; Phrantzes, *op. cit.* p. 238; Ducas, XXXVIII, p. 333.

PAGE 87

1 Barbaro, *op. cit.* pp. 18–20.

PAGE 91

1 The fullest and best description of the walls of the city is still that of van Millingen, *Byzantine Constantinople: the Walls of the City.* But I accept unhesitatingly Pears's view that the Romanus Gate mentioned in the accounts of the siege must generally be identified as the Fifth Military Gate. As he points out, the old name 'Pempton' never occurs after the seventh century, nor does the later name of the Gate of Saint Kyriake appear in accounts of the siege. Yet it is the only gate in the Lycus valley, in the section of the walls where the fiercest fighting took place. It seems clear that it was known at the time as the Military Gate of St. Romanus and that when contemporary writers refer to the Romanus Gate they usually mean it rather than the Civil Gate of St. Romanus, the present Top Kapu, up the hill to the south. Pears, *Destruction of the Greek Empire,* pp. 429–435.

PAGE 92

1 Leonard of Chios, col. 936; Chalcocondylas, *op. cit.* p. 384. For repairs to the walls since 1422, including the repairs with inscriptions mentioning Iagrus, see van Millingen, *op. cit.* pp. 104–8, 126. Phrantzes, *op. cit.* p. 225, mentions Neophytus with great respect, though he was highly critical of anyone whom he suspected of disloyalty.

PAGE 94

1 Barbaro, *op. cit.* pp. 16–19; Leonard of Chios, coll. 934–5; Phrantzes, *op. cit.* pp. 252–6, all agreeing in general about the various stations, though Leonard avoids mentioning Greeks as much as possible and Phrantzes alone mentions Manuel the Genoese at the Golden Gate. Phrantzes also places Notaras at Petrion and puts Cantacuzenus, together with Nicephorus Palaeologus, in

command of the mobile reserve. Perhaps Manuel was replaced later by Cantacuzenus; and Notaras's area may have included both Petrion and Petra. Only Barbaro mentions where Orhan was stationed. Pusculus, pp. 64–5, and Dolfin, pp. 23–4, give slightly different dispositions; but the former was writing from memory many years later and the latter was not present at the siege.

2 See Pears, *op. cit.* pp. 250–2.

PAGE 95

1 Critobulus, *op. cit.* pp. 41–2; Tetaldi, col. 1822. No Turkish source gives any details about the disposition of the Ottoman army, except for the highly fanciful account written by Evliya Chelebi two centuries later: of which relevant extracts are given by Turková, 'Le Siège de Constantinople d'après le Seyāhatnāme d'Evliyā Çelebî', *Byzantinoslavica*, XIV, pp. 1–13, esp. pp. 7–9.

2 Critobulus, *op. cit.* p. 42; Phrantzes, *op. cit.* p. 240; Barbaro, *op. cit.* p. 21. The Double Columns (Diplokion) are depicted on Buondelmonte's plan of Constantinople (1422) just across the stream that used to run down the valley between Taksim and Maçka, roughly where the south-western wing of the present palace of Dolma Bahçe now stands.

3 Barbaro, *op. cit.* pp. 19–20.

PAGE 96

1 Critobulus, *op. cit.* pp. 40–1.

2 Barbaro, *op. cit.* pp. 18–20.

PAGE 97

1 Critobulus, *op. cit.* pp. 47–8.

PAGE 98

1 Barbaro, *op. cit.* p. 21; Critobulus, *op. cit.* pp. 48–9; Phrantzes, *op. cit.* pp. 238–9; Ducas, *op. cit.* XXXVIII, p. 339; Chalcocondylas, *op. cit.* pp. 386–7.

2 Barbaro, *op. cit.* pp. 21–2; Critobulus, *op. cit.* pp. 50–1, dating the encounter after the first assault on the walls. The actual date is however clearly given by Barbaro. Critobulus seems to have confused this attack on the boom with the slighter attack made by Baltoghlu on 18 April.

PAGE 99

1 Barbaro, *op. cit.* p. 23; Critobulus, *op. cit.* pp. 49–50.

PAGE 103

1 Phrantzes, *op. cit.* pp. 247–250; Critobulus, *op. cit.* pp. 52–5; Ducas, *op. cit.* XXXVIII, p. 335; Chalcocondylas, *op. cit.* pp. 389–390; Barbaro, *op. cit.* pp. 23–6; Leonard of Chios, coll. 930–1; Dolfin, *op. cit.* pp. 17–18; Pusculus, *op. cit.* pp. 68–9. Ducas says that there were four Genoese ships and one Imperial, and Chalcocondylas one Genoese and one Imperial; but the eyewitness accounts all agree on three Genoese and one Imperial. Barbaro says that the Genoese came tempted by an offer made by the Emperor that the Genoese could import provisions duty-free. Leonard says that they brought soldiers, arms and coin for the defence, and Critobulus says that they were sent by the Pope.

PAGE 104

1 For the Sheikh's letter and the general Turkish reaction see Inalcîk, 'Mehmed the Conqueror', *Speculum*, XXXV, pp. 411–2 and *Fateh Devri*, p. 217.

2 Barbaro, *op. cit.* p. 26; Critobulus, *op. cit.* p. 55; Ducas, *op. cit.* XXXVIII, p. 336.

3 Barbaro, *op. cit.* p. 26; Phrantzes, *op. cit.* pp. 246–7; Leonard of Chios, col. 931.

PAGE 106

1 Barbaro, *op. cit.* pp. 27–8; Phrantzes, *op. cit.* pp. 250–2; Critobulus, *op. cit.* pp. 55–6; Leonard of Chios, col. 930, blaming a Venetian for having given the idea to the Sultan; Tetaldi, coll. 1820–1; Pusculus, *op. cit.* pp. 69–70; Dolfin, *op. cit.* p. 16; 'The Polish Janissary', chap. XXIV; Ashikpashazade, p. 198; Saad ed-Din, *The Capture of Constantinople*, trans. Gibb, pp. 20–1. Ashikpashazade says that 70 ships were transported, though Saad ed-Din's sources suggest a much smaller number; Evliya Chelebi says 50 galleys and 50 small boats (in Turkova, 'Le Siège de Constantinople', pp. 5–6). The Polish Janissary speaks of 30 boats. Christian contemporary sources vary between 67 boats (Critobulus) and 80 (Tetaldi). I follow Pears, *The Destruction of the Greek Empire*, pp. 443–6, in believing that the boats were brought up the steep but short valley behind Tophane rather than up the wider valley to Şişli, a much longer but very little easier route.

PAGE 110

1 Barbaro, *op. cit.* pp. 28–33; Phrantzes, *op. cit.* pp. 257–8; Critobulus, *op. cit.* pp. 56–7; Leonard of Chios, coll. 932–3; Tetaldi, col. 1821; Pusculus, *op. cit.* pp. 72–5; Ducas, *op. cit.* XXXVIII, pp. 347–8. Critobulus, whose evidence probably came from Turkish sources, and Ducas, whose evidence largely came from Genoese sources, both say that the Sultan received a message from Pera warning him. Barbaro, whose hatred of the Genoese makes him suspect,

says that the Podestà of Pera himself sent a message to the Sultan. Leonard of Chios, himself a Genoese, hints that the Genoese were to blame.

2 For the Sultan's relations with Pera see below, p. 116.

PAGE 111

1 Phrantzes, *op. cit.* p. 252; Critobulus, *op. cit.* p. 57; Barbaro, *op. cit.* pp. 43–4; Leonard of Chios, col. 931; Ducas, *op. cit.* XXXVIII, p. 349; Chalcocondylas, *op. cit.* p. 388; Kodja Effendi, MS. p. 170, quoted in Lebeau, *Histoire du Bas Empire* XXI, p. 265. The plaque erected in 1953 to mark the spot where the bridge reached the Istanbul shore must be in the wrong place, as the bridge would obviously not have led to a narrow foreshore dominated by the powerful fortifications of Blachernae, cut off by Diedo's canal from the rest of the Turkish army, but to a spot beyond the range of engines on the walls, as is shown in the contemporary illustration used as the frontispiece of this book. Barbaro, however, who gives the fullest description as well as the date of its completion, says that it ended close under the 'palisade', by which he apparently means the Blachernae wall.

PAGE 112

1 Phrantzes, *op. cit.* p. 256; Barbaro, *op. cit.* pp. 33–4; Leonard of Chios, col. 935.

PAGE 114

1 Barbaro, *op. cit.* p. 35; Thiriet, *Regestes*, nos. 2919–2923, pp. 185–6.

2 *Ibid.* no. 2927, pp. 186–7.

PAGE 115

1 Barbaro, *loc. cit.*; *Slavic Chronicle*, p. 114 (Russian version, p. 95, Roumanian version, p. 79), saying that the Emperor sent for help from Morea, from the other islands and from the lands of the Franks.

2 Phrantzes, *op. cit.* p. 258; Leonard of Chios, coll. 932–3.

PAGE 116

1 This episode is only reported in the Slavic Chronicle; but the chronicler's report bears the stamp of authenticity. *Slavic Chronicle*, p. 118 (Russian version, p. 95, Roumanian version, pp. 79–80).

2 Phrantzes, *op. cit.* pp. 259–260; Barbaro, *op. cit.* pp. 35–6; Ducas, *op. cit.* XXXVIII, p. 347.

PAGE 117

1 Barbaro, *op. cit.* pp. 36–7; *Slavic Chronicle*, pp. 118–9 (Russian version, pp. 95–6, Roumanian version, pp. 80–1), mentioning Rhangabe's heroism.

2 Barbaro, *op. cit.* pp. 37–9.

3 Barbaro, *op. cit.* p. 39; *Slavic Chronicle*, pp. 119–20 (Russian version, pp. 96–7, Roumanian version, p. 81), giving an exaggerated and unconvincing story in which the Emperor was holding a council in the porch of Saint Sophia when he heard that the Turks had actually entered the city. He then rode out and drove them back.

4 Barbaro, *op. cit.* pp. 39–40.

PAGE 118

1 Barbaro, *op. cit.* pp. 40–2, 44–5.

PAGE 119

1 Barbaro, *op. cit.* pp. 42–3; Phrantzes, *op. cit.* pp. 243–5; Leonard of Chios col. 936.

2 Barbaro, *loc. cit.*; Phrantzes, *op. cit.* p. 245; Tetaldi, col. 1821; Leonard of Chios, col. 936; Chalcocondylas, *op. cit.* pp. 388–9.

PAGE 120

1 Barbaro, *op. cit.* pp. 46–7.

2 Barbaro, *op. cit.* p. 47. He refers to it in detail on pp. 33–4, when he tells of the ship's departure, thus showing that he must have gone through his original diary to put in the cross-reference.

PAGE 122

1 Barbaro, *op. cit.* p. 46, dating the eclipse 22 May. But the full moon and the eclipse occurred on the 24 May. Here again, he must have altered his original diary. The other portents are given by Phrantzes, *op. cit.* pp. 264–5, by Pusculus, *op. cit.* p. 79, by Critobulus, *op. cit.* pp. 58–9, by Barbaro again, p. 48, and in a highly exaggerated form in the *Slavic Chronicle*, p. 122.

2 This story is only given in the *Slavic Chronicle*, pp. 122–3 (Russian version, p. 98, Roumanian version, p. 82). Shorn of such imaginary details as the presence of a Patriarch, it is probably true.

PAGE 123

1 Critobulus, *op. cit.* p. 60.

2 Phrantzes, *op. cit.* pp. 263–4, 327; Ducas, *op. cit.* XXXVIII, pp. 341–3. The Hungarian ambassador had given the Sultan useful advice about the employment of artillery.

PAGE 124

1 Chalcocondylas, *op. cit.* pp. 390–2, giving the full story of Ismail's negotiations; Ducas, *op. cit.* XXXVIII, pp. 345, 349; Saad ed-Din, p. 20.

PAGE 126

1 Phrantzes, *op. cit.* pp. 265–70; Leonard of Chios, coll. 937–8; Tetaldi, coll. 1821–2.

2 Tetaldi, *loc. cit.*

3 Barbaro, *op. cit.* pp. 48–9; *Slavic Chronicle,* p. 124 (Russian version, p. 100, Roumanian version, p. 84). Only the Slavic source mentions Giustiniani's wound.

4 Phrantzes, *op. cit.* p. 270; Leonard of Chios, col. 938.

PAGE 127

1 Barbaro, *op. cit.* pp. 48–9.

2 Barbaro, *op. cit.* pp. 49–51; Critobulus, *op. cit.* p. 60; Ducas, *op. cit.* XXXIX, pp. 351–3; Leonard of Chios, col. 938; Dolfin, p. 20, alone mentioning the Sultan's visit to Pera.

PAGE 128

1 Critobulus, *op. cit.* pp. 60–5, gives at length the speech that he thought that the Sultan ought to have made on this occasion. He no doubt received his information from his friend Hamza Bey, who was present on the occasion; so we may assume that the Sultan said something along the lines that he indicates. Phrantzes, pp. 269–70, gives a short speech.

PAGE 129

1 Barbaro, *op. cit.* p. 50; Phrantzes, *op. cit.* pp. 262–3; Leonard of Chios, col. 937.

PAGE 131

1 Phrantzes, *op. cit.* pp. 271–9; Leonard of Chios, coll. 938–9.

2 Phrantzes, *op. cit.* p. 279. Critobulus, Chalcocondylas and the Slavic Chronicle refer to the all-night service when telling of the sack of the city. See below, p. 147.

3 Phrantzes, *op. cit.* p. 280; Andrea Cambini, *Libro della Origine de Turchi* (1529 edition), pp. 8–10.

PAGE 132

1 Phrantzes, *op. cit.* p. 280. The Emperor's mare with the white feet appears in Greek popular poetry, e.g. Ὁ Θάνατος τοῦ Κωνσταντίνου Δράγαζη in Legrand, *Recueil de chansons populaires grecques,* p. 74.

PAGE 133

1 Critobulus, *op. cit.* pp. 66–7.

1 I have derived this narrative from the various sources: first, the eye-witnesses, Phrantzes, *op. cit.* pp. 280–7; Barbaro, *op. cit.* pp. 51–7; Leonard of Chios, coll. 940–1; Tetaldi, coll. 1822–3; Pusculus, *op. cit.* pp. 80–1; Montaldo, *op. cit.* pp. 335–8; Riccherio, *La Presa di Constantinopoli*, in Sansovino, *Dell' Historia Universale*, II, pp. 64–6; 'The Polish Janissary', pp. 132–4. The accounts by Critobulus, *op. cit.* pp. 67–71 and Ducas, *op. cit.* XXXIX, pp. 351–61, were certainly derived immediately afterwards from eye-witnesses. The Turkish sources give brief accounts, reproduced in Saad ed-Din, pp. 21–8. Chalcocondylas, *op. cit.* pp. 354–5, gives a brief account that adds nothing. The *Slavic Chronicle*, pp. 124–5, gives a confused account of the fighting. Only Ducas gives any detail of the entry through the Kerkoporta, but his story is confirmed briefly by Saad ed-Din. For the exact position of the Kerkoporta, see van Millingen, *Byzantine Constantinople*, pp. 89–94. The sources disagree about Giustiniani's wound. Phrantzes says that he was wounded in the foot and Chalcocondylas in the hand, but Leonard by an arrow in the armpit and Critobulus by a ball that pierced his breastplate. It was probably a serious wound somewhere in his body. Barbaro, in his dislike of all Genoese, never mentions the wound at all, merely saying that he deserted his post. Otherwise, there is remarkable agreement between all the sources.

2 Phrantzes, *op. cit.* pp. 287–8; Barbaro, *op. cit.* pp. 57–8. Phrantzes mentions Paolo and Troilo as having escaped and makes no mention of Antonio, but the Podestà of Pera, in his letter to the Genoese government, ed. de Sacy, *Notices et extraits des Manuscripts de la Bibliothèque du Roi*, XI, 1, p. 77, says that Paolo attempted to hide but was captured and perished. Phrantzes probably therefore mentioned Paolo by mistake for Antonio.

3 Saad ed-Din, p. 23. See Ahmed Muktar Pasha, *The Conquest of Constantinople*, p. 228. For the fishermen of Petrion see below, appendix II, p. 203.

1 Barbaro, *op. cit.* pp. 59, 61; Phrantzes, *op. cit.* p. 293.

2 See below, appendix II, p. 203.

3 Critobulus, *op. cit.* pp. 74–5; Ducas, *op. cit.* XXXIX, p. 379; Chalcocondylas, *op. cit.* p. 398.

4 Leonard of Chios, col. 943; Podestà of Pera, p. 77.

5 Riccherio, *op. cit.* p. 66; 'Rapporto del Superiore dei Franciscani', quoted in *Cronica de Bologna* (Muratori, R.I.Ss., XVIII, pp. 701–2); Chalcocondylas, *op. cit.* p. 399. Three letters sent from Rome to the Cardinal of Ferrara, given in

Jorga, *Notes et Extraits*, II, pp. 518–20, give the story in detail. Tetaldi when he wrote his report believed the Cardinal to have perished, col. 1823.

PAGE 142

1 Barbaro, *op. cit.* pp. 57–8; Podestà of Pera, p. 75; Ducas, *op. cit.* XXXIX, pp. 371–3, saying that only five Genoese ships escaped.

PAGE 143

1 Barbaro, *op. cit.* pp. 58–9; Ducas, *op. cit.* XXXIX, p. 373.

2 Phrantzes, *op. cit.* pp. 387–8. See below, p. 148.

3 Tradition says that the Turkish flag shows the sickle moon with a star in its arc because the Sultan entered the city beneath such a moon: which explains why the sickle is of a waning not of a crescent moon. The moon would actually have been in its third quarter.

4 Ducas, *loc. cit.* See below, appendix II, p. 201. The Podestà of Pera does not make it quite clear that he went in person, as Ducas says (Podestà of Pera, p. 76).

PAGE 144

1 Phrantzes, *op. cit.* pp. 290–1; Ducas, *op. cit.* XL, p. 377; Chalcocondylas, *op. cit.* p. 399; *Historia Politica*, p. 23; Barbaro, *op. cit.* p. 53; Tetaldi, col. 1823; Pusculus, *op. cit.* p. 81; Montaldo, p. 338; Saad ed-Din, p. 31; *Slavic Chronicle*, p. 126 (Russian version, p. 102, Roumanian version, p. 87), says that the head was buried under the altar of Saint Sophia and the body buried at Pera. The 'Polish Janissary', p. 133, says that the head was recognized by a peasant called Andrew. The so-called tomb of the Emperor that used to be shown at Vefa Meidan in Istanbul has no historical basis.

PAGE 145

1 Barbaro, *op. cit.* p. 55; Phrantzes, *op. cit.* pp. 288–9; Critobulus, *op. cit.* pp. 71–3. The Church of Saint Mary of the Mongols is traditionally known by the Turks as Kan Kilisse, the Church of Blood, because of the blood that streamed down the street past it from the heights of Petra.

PAGE 146

1 Ducas, *op. cit.* XXXIX, p. 363.

2 Ducas, *op. cit.* XXXIX, p. 369.

3 Archaeological evidence shows that the Pantocrator was sacked and then used as a bivouac. Gennadius who was a monk there was captured presumably in his cell. Gennadius seems first to have retired to the Charsianites monastery (see Beck, *Kirche und theologische Literatur*, p. 760 but during the winter of 1452–3 he was in the Pantocrator (Ducas, *op. cit.* p. 315).

PAGE 147

1 Ducas, *op. cit.* XXXIX, p. 365; Critobulus, *op. cit.* p. 75.

2 Phrantzes, *op. cit.* p. 290; Critobulus, *op. cit.* pp. 75–6; Leonard of Chios, coll. 941–2.

PAGE 148

1 Barbaro, *op. cit.* p. 57; Critobulus, *loc. cit.*; Ducas, *loc. cit.*; Franciscan report, coll. 701–2.

2 Critobulus, *op. cit.* p. 76, mentioning 4,000 slain and 50,000 prisoners. Leonard of Chios, col. 942, gives 60,000 prisoners. Both these figures of prisoners must be exaggerated, as the whole population of the city was probably under 50,000. The Franciscan report, *loc. cit.* estimates the slain at 3,000.

PAGE 149

1 The Slavic Chronicle, p. 127 (Russian version, p. 105, Roumanian version, pp. 86–7), gives the details, which seem to be derived from an eye-witness account, though the imaginary Patriarch features in it; Ducas, *op. cit.* XXXIX, p. 375, giving the account of the Turkish soldier hacking up the pavement but dating the Sultan's visit to the 30th (by which time the pavement would certainly have been hacked up); Phrantzes, *loc. cit.* Ashikpashazade, p. 199, merely says that a Moslem service was held in the building the following Friday.

2 Cantemir, *History of the Othman Empire*, trans. Tindal, p. 102, giving the quotation in Persian but not its source.

3 Phrantzes, *op. cit.* pp. 291–2; Leonard of Chios, col. 942; Critobulus, *op. cit.* p. 82.

PAGE 151

1 Barbaro, *op. cit.* pp. 57–61; Podestà of Pera, p. 77; Leonard of Chios, col. 943. Franciscan report, col. 702. For references for Isidore's adventures, see above, p. 141, n. 5.

2 Matthew Camariotes, *De Constantinopoli Capta Narratio Lamentabilis*, *M.P.G.*, CLX, coll. 1068–9.

PAGE 152

1 Ducas, *op. cit.* XL, p. 381, and Chalcocondylas, *op. cit.* pp. 402–3, whose story I have followed. Ducas had no liking for Notaras; his account is therefore all the more convincing. Critobulus, *op. cit.* pp. 83–4, omits the story of the Sultan's lust, out of anxiety to protect the Sultan's reputation. Leonard of Chios, while mentioning the Sultan's lust, gives a version in which Notaras,

whom he hated, tried to throw the blame on everyone else (col. 943). Phrantzes, *op. cit.* pp. 291–3, gives a different story, very hostile to Notaras. Montaldo, *op. cit* p. 339, accuses Notaras of treachery but mentions the story of his son.

2 Ducas, *op. cit.* XLII, p. 395. The identity of Notaras's wife is uncertain. In letters to him, such as those from Gennadius (e.g. *M.P.G.* CLX, col. 747), he is called the 'son-in-law of the Emperor'—'γαμβρὸς τοῦ Βασιλέως'. If his wife had been a daughter of Manuel II and the Empress Helena, it is impossible that Phrantzes, who gives all the details of the family, would not have mentioned it. She must have been born after 1400, as her son was in his early teens in 1453. It is improbable that Manuel, who was a devoted husband, had any illegitimate children after his marriage. The Byzantines would not, I believe, have used the term son-in-law to mean vaguely a connection by marriage. She must therefore have been a daughter of Manuel's nephew, the Emperor John VII, who married a Gattilusi princess by whom he certainly had no son; but he may well have had a daughter, legitimate or illegitimate. Papadopoulos, *Versuch einer Geneologie der Palaiologen*, p, 90, makes her the daughter of Demetrius Palaeologus Cantacuzenus, but his reference to Phrantzes says nothing of the sort. I do not know on what evidence Lambros, *Συνθήκη*, pp. 153, 170, bases his genealogy of the Notaras family.

3 See p. 186. Sathas, *Monumenta Historiae Hellenicae*, IX, p. vi, states that Anna was at one time betrothed to the Emperor Constantine. The evidence seems insufficient.

4 Phrantzes, *op. cit.* pp. 309–10, 383, 385.

PAGE 153

1 Critobulus, *op. cit.* pp. 76–7, 85; Ducas, *op. cit.* XLII, p. 395; Franciscan report, col. 702; Podestà of Pera, pp. 76–7, writing on 23 June and saying that the Sultan had left the previous night. Babinger, *Mehmed der Eroberer*, p. 107.

2 See below, appendix II.

PAGE 154

1 See below, appendix II.

PAGE 156

1 Phrantzes, *op. cit.* pp. 304–7; *Historia Politica*, pp. 27–8; *Historia Patriarchica*, C.S.H.B., pp. 79–81; Critobulus, *op. cit.* pp. 94–5; Cantemir, *op. cit.* p. 104. See also the full if slightly confusing account in Papadopoullos, *Studies and Documents relating to the History of the Greek Church and People under Turkish Domination*, pp. 1–85.

PAGE 157

1 See below, appendix II.

PAGE 158

1 Phrantzes, *op. cit.* p. 307; *Historia Politica*, pp. 28–9; *Historia Patriarchica*, pp. 82–3, and giving the text of Gennadius's treaties (pp. 83–93).

PAGE 159

1 Critobulus, *op. cit.* pp. 82–3; Ashikpashazade, *op. cit.* pp. 124–6; Ducas, *op. cit.* XLII, p. 393; *Historia Politica*, p. 25. For the forced migration from Trebizond see p. 176. A letter written in 1454 by refugee bishops in Wallachia talks of 30,000 families having been brought to resettle in Constantinople. Jorga, *Notes et Extraits*, IV, p. 67. 4,000 were forced immigrants, and 4,000 came from the 'mainland', i.e. Thrace.

2 The Spanish traveller Cristobal de Villalon, writing in about 1550, claimed to have seen the municipal lists in Constantinople, which showed that there were 60,000 Turkish households, 40,000 Greek and Armenian, and 10,000 Jewish, 4,000 households in Pera (Greek or Occidental), and 10,000 Greek households in the suburbs. Villalon, *Viaje de Turquia*, II, pp. 255 ff. See Jorga, *Byzance après Byzance*. pp. 45–52.

PAGE 160

1 Annotation to a codex in the monastery of Agarathos quoted in Tomadakis, 'Répercussion immédiate de la prise de Constantinople', *Cinq-centième Anniversaire de la prise de Constantinople*, Athens, 1953.

2 Thiriet, *Regestes*, no. 2928, p. 187. See Pastor, *History of the Popes*, trans. Antrobus, II, pp. 271–4.

PAGE 161

1 Tetaldi, col. 1823, believed that if the fleet had arrived in time the city would not have fallen.

2 Critobulus, *op. cit.* p. 81; Thiriet, *La Romanie Vénitienne*, p. 383.

PAGE 162

1 Thiriet, *Regestes*, nos. 2929–2936, pp. 187–190.

PAGE 163

1 Podestà of Pera, pp. 76–8; Montaldo, *op. cit.* p. 342; Ducas, *op. cit.* XLII, p. 393; Critobulus, *op. cit.* p. 76. For the Podestà's name, Lomellino, see Desimoni's preface to Montaldo, pp. 306–7.

2 Heyd, *Histoire du Commerce du Levant*, II, pp. 382–407. The act ceding Caffa to the Consilio is given in *Notices des Manuscripts de la Bibliothèque du Roi*, XI, I, pp. 81–9.

PAGE 164

1 See Argenti, *The Occupation of Chios by the Genoese*, I, pp. 205–8.

2 Heyd, *op. cit.* II, p. 308 and n. 4. Tetaldi, col. 1823, estimates the Anconitans' losses at more than 20,000 ducats.

3 Heyd, *op. cit.* II, pp. 308, 336–8. Tetaldi, *loc. cit.* estimates the Florentine losses at 20,000 ducats.

4 Heyd, *op. cit.* II, pp. 308, 348.

5 Krekić, *Dubrovnik (Raguse) et le Levant*, p. 62 and Thiriet, *Regestes*, nos. 1279 and 1364, pp. 383, 398.

PAGE 165

1 *Ibid.* nos, 2955–6, 3021, pp. 194–5, 212–3.

2 Raynaldi, *Annales*, X, pp. 2–3.

3 Jorga, *Notes et Extraits*, II, p. 518.

4 *Ibid.* IV, pp. 90–1, 101–2, 111–3.

PAGE 166

1 Pius II, *Opera Omnia*, pp. 716–7.

2 Grunzweig, 'Philippe le Bon et Constantinople'. *Byzantium*, XXIV, pp. 51–2.

PAGE 167

1 Olivier de la Marche, *Mémoires*, ed. Beaune et d'Arbaumont, II, pp. 381–2.

2 Critobulus, *op. cit.* pp. 119–21; Ducas, *op. cit.* XLV, p. 423. See Miller, *Essays on the Latin Orient*, pp. 340–3, with references.

3 See Atiya, *The Crusade in the Later Middle Ages*, pp. 236–40.

4 Olivier de la Marche, *Mémoires*, II, pp. 336–7.

PAGE 168

1 Jorga, *Notes et Extraits*, IV, pp. 126–7.

2 Chalcocondylas, *op. cit.* p. 403.

3 Pius II, *Opera Omnia*, p. 394.

PAGE 169

1 Ducas, *op. cit.* pp. XLII, p. 395; Critobulus, *op. cit.* p. 85; Babinger, *Mehmet der Eroberer*, pp. 108–9.

2 Critobulus, *op. cit.* pp. 86–7; Ducas, *loc. cit.*; Miller, *Essays on the Latin Orient*, pp. 334–5.

PAGE 170

1 Phrantzes, *op. cit.* pp. 293–4; Critobulus, *op. cit.* pp. 87–8; Chalcocondylas, *op. cit.* pp. 403–4; Leonard of Chios, col. 943; Ashikpashazade, *op. cit.* pp. 197–9.

See Inalcîk, *Fatih Devre*, pp. 134-6. Ashikpashazade's account is particularly hostile to Halil, but later Ottoman historians, writing when his family, the Chandarlî, had been rehabilitated, are kinder. See Inalcîk, Fatih Devri, pp.132-6. It is probable that Notaras's disgrace and death should be connected with Halil's. Ashikpashazade says that Notaras sent him bribes—money hidden inside a fish. They were certainly on good terms with each other.

PAGE 171

1 See Jireček, *Geschichte der Serben*, II, pp. 201 ff.; Miller, *Essays on the Latin Orient*, pp. 456-7, and 'The Balkan States', *Cambridge Medieval History*, IV, pp. 575-582; Babinger, *Mehmed der Eroberer*, pp. 112 ff.

2 Critobulus, *op. cit.* pp. 105-111, 138-9; Ducas, *op. cit.* XLIV, p. 419, XLV, pp. 423, 427; Leonard of Chios, *De Lesbo a Turcis Capta*, ed. Hopf, *passim*; Miller, *Essays on the Latin Orient*, pp. 335-352.

3 Miller, *The Latins in the Levant*, pp. 435-441, 456-7.

PAGE 173

1 Critobulus, *op. cit.* pp. 126-37, 149-53; Ducas, *op. cit.* XLV, pp. 423-5; 'Polish Janissary', pp. 155-65; Ashikpashazade, *op. cit.* pp. 210-3. See Zakythinos, *Le Despotat Grec de Morée*, pp. 247-84.

PAGE 175

1 Critobulus, *op. cit.* pp. 163-74; Phrantzes, *op. cit.* p. 413; Ducas, *op. cit.* XLV, pp. 429-431; Chalcocondylas, *op. cit.* pp. 490-7; 'Polish Janissary', pp. 165-73; Ashikpashazade, *op. cit.* pp. 218-27. See Miller, *Trebizond: the Last Greek Empire*, pp. 97-104.

PAGE 176

1 Critobulus, *op. cit.* pp. 175-7; *Historia Politica*, pp. 36-7; Miller, *Trebizond*, pp. 105-8.

2 Phrantzes, *op. cit.* p. 308; Critobulus, *loc. cit.*; Miller, *loc. cit.*

3 Miller, *loc. cit.* The ballad about the maiden of Kordyle is given in Legrand, *Recueil de chansons populaires grecques*, p. 78.

4 Ballad on the fall of Trebizond in Legrand, *Recueil de chansons populaires grecques*, p. 76.

PAGE 177

1 Jorga, *Histoire des Roumains*, IV, pp. 131 ff.

PAGE 179

1 See Medlin, *Moscow and East Rome*, pp. 75–95.

PAGE 182

1 Phrantzes, *op. cit.* pp. 395, 412–3, 427–9, 449; Critobulus, *op. cit.* pp. 58–9; *Historia Politica*, pp. 35–6. Princess Helena's death was lamented by a Monodia, given in Lambros, Παλαιολόγεια καὶ Πελοποννησιακά, IV, pp. 221–9.

2 Phrantzes, *op. cit.* pp. 410–5; Miller, *The Latins in the Levant*, pp. 453–4; Zakythinos, *Le Despotat Grec de Morée*, I, pp. 287–90. Phrantzes says that Thomas's wife died at the age of 70. This must be an error, as Thomas was only 56 when he died three years later, and their youngest child, Zoe, cannot have been born before 1456. Thomas married Catherine in 1430. If she were 15 at the time, she would have been 47 at the time of her death.

PAGE 183

1 Phrantzes, *op. cit.* pp. 202, 413, 450. See Lascaris, *Vizantiske Princeze u Srednjevekovnoj Srbiji*, pp. 97–123.

PAGE 184

1 For the careers of Thomas's sons see the fully referenced account in Zakythinos, *Le Despotat Grec de Morée*, I, pp. 290–7, and Typaldos, Οἱ ἀπόγονοι τῶν Παλαιολόγων μετὰ τὴν ἅλωσιν', Δελτίον τῆς Ἱστορικῆς καὶ Ἐθνολογικῆς Ἑταιρίας τῆς Ἑλλάδος, VIII, pp. 129–154. For the career of Zoe-Sophia see Medlin, *Moscow and East Rome*, pp. 76–7, 79, 86–7. For her first marriage, Phrantzes, *op. cit.* pp. 424–5.

2 For the family of the Palaeologi which was in Cornwall in the seventeenth century and eventually died out in Barbados, see Leigh Fermor, *The Traveller's Tree*, pp. 144–9 and Zoras, Περὶ τὴν ἅλωσιν τῆς Κωνσταντινουπόλεως, pp. 287–95. The family claimed descent from a son of Thomas, called John. If this son had existed it is impossible that Phrantzes, who knew the family well and was deeply interested in it, should not have mentioned him. Nor is he mentioned by Bessarion in his instructions to the tutor of Thomas's two sons. It is possible that Thomas may have had a bastard son called John. More probably the Cornish family descended from some collateral branch of the Palaeologi, of which there were many, though none were of legitimate imperial blood; all the legitimate descendants in the male line of Michael VIII, the first Palaeologan Emperor, are known, and it is highly unlikely that any would be omitted by the authorities. The pathetic double eagles carved on the tomb of Theodore Palaeologus in the church of Landulph in Cornwall have, regrettably, no business to be there.

PAGE 185

1 See Miller, *Essays on the Latin Orient*, pp. 502-7. We are told that Queen Helena mourned deeply at the news of the fall of Constantinople and welcomed refugees. Makhairas, *Chronicle*, I, p. 682.

2 For Scanderbeg's descendants see Gegaj, *L'Albanie et l'Invasion Turque au xve. Siècle*, pp. 161-2.

PAGE 186

1 Phrantzes, *op. cit.* pp. 413-4; Chalcocondylas, *op. cit.* pp. 497-8; *Historia Politica*, p. 38; Miller, *Trebizond*, pp. 108-11.

2 Filelfo's letter is given in Legrand, *Cent-dix Lettres Grecques de Fr. Philelphe*, pp. 62-8.

3 Phrantzes, *op. cit.* pp. 408, 411, 424-5, 429-46, 451-3.

4 Sathas, Μνημεῖα Ἑλληνικῆς Ἱστορίας, IX, pp. vi-xi.

PAGE 187

1 See Brehier, article 'Bessarion' in Baudrillart, *Dictionnaire d'histoire et de géographic ecclésiastique*, VIII, coll. 1185-94; Miller, *Essays on the Latin Orient*, pp. 348-9. Leonard of Chios, *De Lesbo a Turcis Capta*, ed. Hopf, *passim*. Isidore was said to have grown soft in the head in old age. See Pastor, *History of the Popes*, trans. Antrobus, II, p. 323.

2 Critobulus, *op. cit.* p. 117; *Ecthesis Chronica*, ed. Lambros, pp. 26-8, 36; *Historia Politica*, pp. 38-9; *Historia Patriarchica*, pp. 96-101. See Tomadakis, "Ἐτούρκευσεν ὁ Γεώργιος Ἀμιρούτζης;" in Ἐπετηρὶς Ἑταιρείας Βυζαντινῶν Σπουδῶν, XVIII, pp. 99-143, who tries, unsuccessfully, I think, to whitewash Amiroutzes

3 See above, pp. 154-8.

PAGE 193

1 For Phrantzes I have used the text published in the Bonn Corpus, as no new critical edition of the relevant part of his work has yet appeared. For the authorship of the *Chronicon Majus* see Loenertz, 'Autour du Chronicon Maius attribué à Georgios Phrantzes', *Miscellanea Mercati*, III. For his real name see Laurent, 'Sphrantzes et non Phrantzes', *B.Z.*, XLIV.

2 For Ducas I have used the new critical edition published by Grecu (together with a Roumanian translation, which will not be of great use to many Western scholars), in Bucarest in 1958, rather than the old Bonn edition, though the latter has the advantage of containing also the old Italian translation of the work. I cannot myself rate Ducas as highly as a source as does Grecu: see Grecu, 'Pour une meilleure connaissance de l'historien Ducas', *Memorial Louis Petit*.

PAGE 194

1 For Chalcocondylas I have not been able to obtain the edition published by J. Darko in Budapest in 1922 and therefore give references to the Bonn edition. For a brief account of his life see Vasiliev, *A History of the Byzantine Empire*, p. 693.

2 For Critobulus I have used the English translation published at Princeton in 1954. Though it is based not on the original Greek but on Dethier's French translation a comparison with the original as published by Müller in 1883 shows it to be reliable. For a brief account of Critobulus see Pears, *The Destruction of the Greek Empire*, pp. x–xi. His Turcophil views have inclined modern Greek historians to underrate him.

3 For these chronicles see Moravscik, *Byzantinoturcica*, I, pp. 128–9, 159, 246–8. The verse chronicle of Hierax, published by Sathas, Μεσαιωνικὴ Βιβλιοθήκη I, is of small value as an historical source.

4 The Chronicle has been published by G. Zoras, in a critical edition which shows the chronicler's indebtedness to Leonard of Chios for the story of the siege and fall of the city.

PAGE 195

1 For a full account of the various threnes see Zoras, Περὶ τὴν ἅλωσιν τῆς Κωνσταντινουπόλεως, pp. 157–283.

2 These letters have been fully used in Gill, *op. cit.* pp. 366 ff.

3 For the whole question of the Slavic Chronicle see Unbegaun, 'Les relations vieux-russes de la prise de Constantinople', *Revue des Etudes Slaves*, IX, and Jorga, 'Une source négligée de la prise de Constantinople', *Académie Roumaine, Section Historique*, XIII.

PAGE 196

1 For a brief account of Barbaro see Pears, *The Destruction of the Greek Empire*, pp. ix–x.

2 I have used for references the Latin edition of Leonard's report, as given in Migne's *Patrologia*. There is also an Italian version, given in Sansovino's *Historia Universale*, III, which varies in certain minor details from the Latin and which is presumably a little later in date.

3 As with Leonard there are two versions of Isidore's report, a letter in Latin addressed to the Pope, given in Migne's *Patrologia*, and in Italian, addressed to 'all the faithful', given in Sansovino, III. Probably the letter to the Pope was translated with certain alterations for transmission round Italy. For Isidore's writings see Mercati, 'Scritti d'Isidoro il Cardinale Ruteno', *Studi i Testi*, XLVI.

4 The Podestà's name is usually given as Zaccaria, but Desimoni, in his preface to Montaldo's report, pp. 306–7, shows that the Podestà of the time was called Lomellino.

PAGE 197

1 I give in the bibliography, see below, pp. 237–9, the editions that I have used for these various authors.

PAGE 198

1 For the Turkish historians see Babinger, *Die Geschichtsschreiber der Osmanen und ihre Werke,* where those that I mention can be found in alphabetical order amongst other Ottoman writers, and the chapters by H. Inalcîk and V. L. Menage in *Historians of the Middle East,* ed. B. Lewis and P. M. Holt. See also Inalcîk, 'Mehmed the Conqueror', *Speculum,* XXXV, *passim.*

2 In justice to Evliya Chelebi it should be added that his description of Constantinople in his own time is trustworthy and valuable.

PAGE 199

1 See above, p. 146 St John in Petra was eventually presented to Mahmud Pasha's Christian mother and reconsecrated.

2 These churches are mentioned as places of worship by such pilgrims as the Russians Ignatius of Smolensk (c. 1390), Alexander (1393) and the anonymous Russian who visited Constantinople about 1440. De Khitrovo, *Itineraires Russes en Orient,* pp. 138, 162, 233–4.

PAGE 200

1 Phrantzes, *op. cit.* p. 307; *Historia Politica,* pp. 28–9; *Historia Patriarchica,* p. 82.

2 For these churches see van Millingen, *Byzantine Churches in Constantinople,* pp. 49, 113, 128, and Janin, *La Géographie Ecclésiastique de l'Empire Byzantin,* III, I, pp. 33, 75, 95, 224, 228, 319, 365–6, 447.

3 This seems to have been the Church of St. John in Dippion, not far from the Hippodrome, which was used in the mid-sixteenth century to house a menagerie. Janin, *op. cit.* pp. 273–4.

4 Hypsilantes, *Τὰ μετὰ τὴν Ἅλωσιν,* pp. 62, 91.

PAGE 201

1 *Historia Patriarchica,* pp. 158 ff.; Cantemir, *History of the Othman Empire,* pp. 102–5. See following note.

2 *Historia Patriarchica, loc. cit.;* Cantemir, *loc. cit.;* Hypsilantes, *op. cit.* pp. 50–2. The *Historia Patriarchica* combines the two episodes in one; but it is clear that

the Janissaries must have played their part in the episode concerning Theoleptus, as it is unlikely that any could have been found still alive in 1537, 84 years after the fall of the city, who could have been present at it.

3 Janin, *op. cit.* pp. 75, 95.

4 Cantemir, *op. cit.* p. 105.

PAGE 202

1 Cantemir, *op. cit.* pp. 102–5; *Historia Patriarchica, loc. cit.* Historians have been, since Gibbon's day onward, too ready to dismiss the whole story as absurd without trying to see what lay behind it. See an important and unjustly neglected article by J. H. Mordtmann, 'Die Kapitulation von Konstantinopel im Jahre 1453', *B.Z.*, XXI, pp. 129 ff. He discusses and identifies Cantemir's sources.

PAGE 203

1 Evliya Chelebi, *Travels*, trans. Hammer, I, p. 159.

2 Dallaway, *Constantinople Ancient and Modern*, pp. 98–9.

PAGE 204

1 The church of St John mentioned above, p. 200, if it is St. John in Dippion, provides another problem, as it was in an area where no other churches seem to have survived.

BIBLIOGRAPHY

Abbreviations

C.S.H.B.   *Corpus Scriptorum Historiae Byzantinae*, Bonn, 1828–1897.
M.P.G.   Migne, *Patrologia Graeco-Latina*, Paris, 1859–1866.
Muratori, *R.I.Ss.*   Muratori, *Rerum Italicarum Scriptores*, Milan, 1723–1751.

1. COLLECTIONS OF SOURCES

ELLISSEN, A. *Analekten der mittel- und neugriechischen Literatur*, 5 vols. Leipzig, 1855–62.

GIESE, F. *Die altosmanischen anonymen Chroniken*. Breslau, 1922.

JORGA, N. *Notes et extraits pour servir à l'Histoire des Croisades au XVe. siècle*, 6 vols. Paris-Bucarest, 1899–1916.

KHITROWO, B. DE. *Itineraires russes en Orient, Société de l'Orient latin, série géographique 5*. Geneva, 1889.

KREKIC, B. *Regestes des archives de Raguse*, in *Dubrovnik (Raguse) et le Levant au moyen age*. See bibliography III.

LAMBROS (LAMPROS), S. P. Παλαιολόγεια καὶ Πελοποννησιακά, 4 vols. Athens, 1912–30.

LEGRAND, E. *Recueil de chansons populaires grecques*. Paris, 1874.

LEUNCLAVIUS (LÖWENKLAW), J. *Annales Sultanorum Othmanidarum*. Frankfurt, 1588.

LEUNCLAVIUS (LÖWENKLAW), J. *Historiae Musulmanae Turcorum*. Frankfurt, 1591.

MARTENE, E. and DURAND, U. *Thesaurus novus anecdotorum*, 5 vols. Paris, 1717.

MIGNE, J. P. *Patrologiae cursus completus. Series Graeco-Latina*, 167 vols. Paris, 1857–76.

MÜLLER, C. *Fragmenta historicorum Graecorum*, 5 vols. Paris, 1878–85.

MURATORI, L. A. *Rerum Italicarum scriptores*, 25 vols. Milan, 1723–51.

Notices et extraits des manuscripts de la Bibliothèque du Roi (la Bibliothèque Nationale). Paris, 1877 ff.

RAYNALDI, O. *Annales ecclesiastici*, continuation of Baronius, *Annales Ecclesiastici*. 15 vols. Lucca, 1747–56.

SANSOVINO, F. *Historia universale dell' origine et imperio de' Turchi*, 3 vols. Venice, 1646.

SATHAS, K. N. Μεσαιωνικὴ Βιβλιοθήκη, 7 vols. Athens, 1872–94.

THIRIET, F. *Regestes des deliberations du Senat de Venise concernant la Romanie*, 3 vols. Paris-The Hague, 1959–61.

II. Individual Sources

ABRAHAM THE ARMENIAN. *Mélodie Elégiaque sur le prise de Stambol* (trans. M. Brosset, in Lebeau, *Histoire du Bas-Empire*, ed. Saint-Martin, XXI, 1836). See Bibliography III below.

ADAM OF USK. *Chronicon* (ed. E. M. Thompson). London, 1904.

ALEXANDRE, scribe. *Voyage à Constantinople* (1393), in Khitrovo, *Itinéraires russes en Orient*.

ALI. *Künh-ul-Akhbar*, 4 vols. Istanbul, A. H. 1284, 1867. *Ἅλωσις τῆς Κορδύλης*, in Legrand, *Recueil de chansons populaires grecques*, no. 51.
Ἅλωσις τῆς Τραπεζοῦντος, in Legrand, *Recueil de chansons populaires grecques*, no. 49.

ANAGNOSTES, JOANNES. *De Thessalonicensi excidio narratio*. See below, Phrantzes.

'Anonymous Giese'. *Tarih Ali Osman*, in Giese, *Die altosmanischen anonymen Chroniken*.

ASHIKPASHAZADE (Derwisch Ahmed, genannt 'Asik-Pasa-Sohn). *Von Hirtenzelt zur Hohen Pforte*, extracted from *Tarih Ali Osman* (ed. and trans. R. F. Kreutel). Graz, 1959.

BARBARO, N. *Giornale dell' assedio di Constantinopoli* (ed. E. Cornet). Vienna, 1856.

BARTHOLOMAEUS DE JANO. *Epistola de Crudelitate Turcorum*. (*M.P.G.*, CLVIII, 1866.)

BARTHOLOMAEUS DELLA PUGLIOLA, *Historia miscella Bononiensis*. (Muratori, *R.I.Ss.*, XVIII, 1731.)

BESSARION, CARDINAL. Letter to the Doge of Venice, in Jorga, *Notes et Extraits*, II. 1899.

CALLISTUS, ANDRONICUS. *Monodia de Constantinopoli Capta*. (*M.P.G.*, CLXI, 1886.)

CAMARIOTES, MATTHAEUS. *De Constantinopoli capta narratio lamentabilis*. (*M.P.G.*, CLX, 1866.)

CAMBINI, A. *Della origine de' Turchi et Imperio delli Ottomanni*. Florence, 1537.

CANANUS, JOANNES. *De Constantinopoli Oppugnata*. See Phrantzes, below.

CANTACUZENUS, JOANNES. *Historia* (ed. L. Schopen, *C.S.H.B.*, 1828–1832).

CHALCOCONDYLAS, LAONICUS. *De Origine ac rebus gestis Turcorum* (ed. E. Bekker, *C.S.H.B.*, 1843).

Chronica Minora (Βραχέα Χρονικά) (ed. S. Lambros). Athens, 1932.

Chronicon Estense. (Muratori, *R.I.Ss.*, XV, 1729.)

Χρονικὸν περὶ τῶν Τούρκων Σουλτάνων (ed. G. T. Zoras). Athens, 1958.

CLAVIJO, R. GONZALES de. *Diary* (trans. G. Le Strange). London, 1928.

CRITOBULUS. *De rebus gestis Mechemetis*, Müller, *Fragmenta historicorum*, V, 1883; also Kritovoulos, *History of Mehmed the Conqueror* (trans. C. T. Riggs). Princeton, 1954.

Description de Constantinople (1424–53), in Khitrowo, *Itineraires russes en Orient.*

DOLFIN, ZORZI. *Assedio e presa di Constantinopoli nell' anno 1453* (ed. G. M. Thomas). Munich, 1868.

DUCAS, MICHAEL (?). *Historia Turco-Byzantina* (ed. V. Grecu). Bucarest, 1948; *also* (ed. E. Becker, *C.S.H.B.*, 1834).

Ecthesis Chronica (ed. S. Lambros). London, 1902.

EUGENICUS, JOANNES. *Varia*, in Lambros, Παλαιολόγεια καὶ Πελοποννησιακά I, 1912.

EVLIYA CHELEBI. *Seyahatname, Narrative of Travels*, trans. J. von Hammer (2 vols.). London, 1834; *also* extracts in Turkova, 'Le siège de Constantinople'. See Bibliography III, below.

FILELFO (PHILELPHUS), F. *Cent-dix lettres grecques de Francois philelfe* (ed. E. Legrand). Paris, 1892.

FILELFO (PHILELPHUS), F. Letter to the King of France, Jorga, *Notes et Extraits.*

FRANCISCANS, FATHER SUPERIOR OF THE, *Rapporto* (Muratori, *R.I.Ss.*, XVIII, 1731).

FREDERICK III, EMPEROR. Letters to the Sultan, in Jorga, *Notes et Extraits*, II. 1899.

GENNADIUS, GEORGIUS SCHOLARIUS. *Oeuvres complètes de Gennade Scholarios* (ed. L. Petit, X. A. Sidéridès and M. Jugie, 8 vols.). Paris, 1928–1936.

HIERAX. *Chronicon*, in Sathas, Μεσαιωνικὴ Βιβλιοθήκη, I, 1872.

Historia Politica et Patriarchica Constantinopoleos (ed. E. Bekker, *C.S.H.B.*, 1849).

IBN BATTUTA. *Voyages* (ed. C. Defrémery and B. R. Sanguinetti, 4 vols.). Paris, 1893.

ISIDORE OF RUSSIA, CARDINAL. Letter to Pope Nicholas V. (*M.P.G.*, CLIX, 1866); letter to All the Faithful, in Sansovino, *Historia Universale*, III.

LA MARCHE, OLIVIER DE. *Mémoires* (ed. H. Beaune and J. d'Arbaumont, 4 vols.). Paris, 1883–8.

LEONARD OF CHIOS, ARCHBISHOP OF MITYLENE. *Epistola ad Papam Nicolaum V.* (*M.P.G.*, CLIX, 1866.) Italian version in Sansovino, *Historie Universale*, III.

LEONARD OF CHIOS. *De Lesbo a Turcis Capta* (ed. C. Hopf). Regensberg, 1866.

MONTALDO, A. DE. *Della Conquista di Constantinopoli per Maometto II* (ed. C. Desimoni); *Atti della Società Ligure de Storia Patria*, X, Genoa, 1874.

NESTOR ISKANDER. *The Tale of Tsargrad* (in Old Slavonic) (ed. Archimandrite Leonid); *Memoirs of Ancient Literature and Art*, Society of Amateurs of Ancient Literature. St Petersburg, 1886.

NOTARAS, LUCAS. *Epistolae* (*M.P.G.*, CLX.)

Notitiae de Portis Constantinopolitanis (ed. Preger and Benescevic), *B.Z.*, XXI, XXIII. 1921, 1923.

PHRANTZES (SPHRANTZES), GEORGIUS. *Chronicon* (ed. E. Bekker, *C.S.H.B.*, 1838), also containing Anagnostes and Cananus. See above.

Pius II, Pope. *Opera Omnia.* Basle, 1551.

Podestà of Pera. *Epistola de excidio Constantinopolitano* (ed. S. de Sacy). *Notices et Extraits de la Bibliothèque du Roi*, XI. 1827.

'Polish Janissary' (Michael Constantinović of Ostrovića). *Memoirs* (in Old Slavonic), in A. Galezowsky, *Zbior Pisarzow Polskieh*, V, Warsaw, 1929.

Pusculus, Ubertino. *Constantinopoleos libri IV*, in Ellissen, *Analekten der mittel- und neugriechischen Literatur*, III, 1857.

Riccherio, Cristoforo. *La presa di Constantinopoli*, in Sansovino, *Historia Universale*, III.

Sa'ad ed-Din. *The Capture of Constantinople from the Taj ut-Tevarikh* (trans. E. J. W. Gibb). Glasgow, 1879.

Sanudo, M. *Vitae Ducum Venetorum* (Muratori, *R.I.Ss.*, XXII, 1733).

Spandugino Cantacuzino, T. *Discorso dell' origine de Principi Turchi*, in Sansovino, *Historia Universale*, II.

Taci Beyzade (Tāğ Beg-zāde Ğaʿfer Čelebi). *Fethnāme-i Istanbul, Revue Historique publiée par l'Institut d'histoire Ottomane*, IV. Istanbul, 1913.

Tafur, Pero. *Travels* (ed. and trans. M. Letts). London, 1926.

Slavic Chronicle (in Old Slavonic). *Conquest of Tsarigrad* (ed. J. J. Sreznevsky), *Publications of the Academy of Science of St Petersburg, 2nd Division*, I, St Petersburg, 1854; Russian and Roumanian versions in Jorga, 'Une source négligée de la prise de Constantinople'. See Bibliography III below.

'Terre Hodierne Grecorum et dominia secularia et spiritualia ipsorum' (ed. S. Lambros). *Neos Hellenomnemon*, VII. Athens, 1910.

Tetaldi, Jacobo (Edaldy, Jacques). *Informations envoyées tant par Francisco de Franc a Mgr. le Cardinal d'Avignon, que par Jehan Blanchin et Jacques Edaldy, marchant florentin, de la prise de Constantinople, à laquelle le dit Jacques estoit personellement*, in Martène and Durand, *Thesaurus novus anecdotorum*, I, 1717.

Θάνατος τοῦ Κωνσταντίνου Δράγαζη, in Legrand, *Recueil de chansons populaires grecques*, no. 48.

Tursun Bey. *Chronicle* (ed. Mehmet Arif), *Revue Historiqué publiée par l'Institut d'Historie Ottomane*, pts. 26–38. Istanbul, 1914–16.

Villalon, C. de. *Viaje de Turquia* (ed. A. G. Solalinde), 2 vols. Madrid, Barcelona, 1919.

III. Modern Works

Ahmed Muktar Pasha. *The Conquest of Constantinople and the establishment of the Ottomans in Europe.* London, 1902.

Alderson, A. D. *The Structure of the Ottoman Dynasty.* Oxford, 1956.

Amantos, C. 'La prise de Constantinople', *Le Cinq-Centième Anniversaire de la Prise de Constantinople, L'Hellénisme Contemporain, fasciscule hors série.* Athens, 1953.

ANDREEVA, M. 'Zur Reise Manuels II Palaiologos nach West-Europa', *B.Z.*, XXXIV. 1934.

ARGENTI, P. *The Occupation of Chios by the Genoese*, 3 vols. Cambridge, 1958.

ATIYA, A. S. *The Crusade in the later Middle Ages*. London, 1938.

ATIYA, A. S. *The Crusade of Nicopolis*. London, 1934.

BABINGER, F. *Beitrage zur Frühgeschichte der Turkenherrschaft in Rumelien*. Brunn-Munich-Vienna, 1944.

BABINGER, F. *Die Geschichtsschreiber der Osmanen und ihre Werke*. Leipzig, 1927.

BABINGER, F. *Mehmed der Eroberer und seine Zeit*. Munich, 1953.

BABINGER, F. Article 'Orkhan', *Encyclopaedia of Islam*, III.

BABINGER, F. 'Von Amurath zu Amurath. Vor- und Nachspiel der Schlacht bei Varna', *Oriens*, III. Leyden, 1950.

BAKALOPULOS, A. 'Les limites de l'Empire Byzantin depuis la fin du XIVe siècle jusqu'à sa chute', *B.Z.*, LV, 1. 1962.

BAUDRILLART, VOGT and ROUZIES (eds., *Dictionnaire d'histoire et de géographie ecclésiastique*, Paris, 1911) (in progress).

BECK, H. G. 'Humanismus und Palamismus', XII Congrès International des Études Byzantines, *Rapports*, III. Ohrid, 1961.

BECK, H. G. *Kirche und theologische Literatur im byzantinischen Reich*. Munich, 1959.

BECK, H. G. *Theodoros Metochites*. Munich, 1952.

BECKWITH, J. *The Art of Constantinople*. London, 1962.

BERGER DE XIVREY, M. *Mémoire sur la vie et les ouvrages de l'Empereur Manuel Paléologue*. Paris, 1861.

BIRGE, J. K. *The Bektashi Order of Dervishes*. London, 1937.

BRATIANU, G. I. *Études Byzantines d'histoire économique et sociale*. Paris, 1938.

BREHIER, L. Article 'Bessarion', in Baudrillart, *Dictionnaire d'histoire et de géographie ecclésiastique*. See above.

BREHIER, L. *Le Monde Byzantin, I: Vie et mort de Byzance*. Paris, 1947.

CAHEN, C. 'La campagne de Mantzikert d'après les sources mussulmanes', *Byzantion*, IX. Brussels, 1934.

CAHEN, C. 'The Mongols', in *History of the Crusades* (ed. Setton), II. (See below.)

CAHEN, C. 'The Selchukid state of Rum'. in *History of the Crusades* (ed. Setton), I. (See below.)

CAHEN, C. 'The Turkish invasion: the Selchukids', in *History of the Crusades* (ed. Setton), II. (See below.)

Cambridge Medieval History, IV. *The Eastern Roman Empire, 717–1453*. Cambridge, 1923.

CANTEMIR, D. *History of the Othman Empire* (trans. N. Tindal). London, 1734,

CHARANIS, P. 'The strife among the Palaeologi and the Ottoman Turks'. *Byzantion*, XVI, 1. Boston, 1944.

CONCASTY, M. L. 'Les "Informations" de Jacques Tedaldi', *Byzantion*, XXIV. Brussels, 1954.

CSUDAY, F. *Die Geschichten der Ungarn*, Zool. Berlin, 1899.

CUSPINIAN, J. *De Turcarum origine*. Leyden, 1634.

DALLOWAY, J. *Constantinople ancient and modern*. London, 1797.

DELAVILLE LE ROULX, J. *La France en Orient au XIVe Siècle*, 2 vols. Paris, 1886.

DIAMANTOPOULOS, A. N. 'Γεννάδιος ὁ Σχολάριος ὡς ἱστορικὴ πηγὴ τῶν περὶ τὴν ἅλωσιν χρόνων', *Ἑλληνικά*, IX. Athens, 1926.

DIEHL, C. 'De quelques croyances byzantines sur la fin de Constantinople', *B.Z.*, XXX. 1930.

Encyclopaedia of Islam (ed. Houtsma, Arnold and Basset), 4 vols. Leyden–London, 1913–34.

Encyclopaedia of Islam (*new edition*, ed. Lewis, Pellat and Schacht). Leyden–London, 1955 (in progress).

FINLAY, G. *A history of Greece* (ed. H. F. Tozer), III. Oxford, 1877.

FUCHS, F. *Die höheren Schulen von Konstantinopel im Mittelalter*, Byzantinische Archiv, VIII. Leipzig–Berlin, 1926.

GEGAJ, A. *L'Albanie et l'invasion turque au XVe siècle*. Paris, 1937.

GIBBON, E. *Decline and Fall of the Roman Empire* (ed. J. B. Bury), 7 vols. London, 1896–1900.

GILL, J. *The Council of Florence*. Cambridge, 1959.

GRECU, V. 'La chute de Constantinople dans la littérature populaire roumaine', *Byzantinoslavica*, XIV. Prague, 1953.

GRECU, V. 'Pour une meilleure connaissance de l'historien Doukas', *Memorial Louis Petit*. Bucarest, 1948.

GRUNZWEIG, A. 'Philippe le Bon et Constantinople', *Byzantion*, XXIV. Brussels, 1954.

GUILLAND, R. 'Les appels de Constantin XI Paléologue à Rome et à Venise pour sauver Constantinople', *Byzantinoslavica*, XIV. Prague, 1953.

GYLLIUS, P. *De topographia Constantinopoleos*. Lyons, 1561.

HALECKI, O. 'Rome et Byzance au temps du grand schisme d'Occident', *Collectio Theologica*, XVIII. Lwow, 1937.

HALECKI, O. *The Crusade of Varna*. New York, 1943.

HALECKI, O. *Un Empereur de Byzance à Rome*. Warsaw, 1930.

HAMMER-PURGSTALL, J. VON. *Geschichte des Osmanischen Reiches*, 10 vols. Pest, 1827–1835.

HASLUCK, F. W. *Athos and its Monasteries*. London, 1924.

HEYD, W. *Histoire du commerce du Levant au moyen âge* (new edition), 2 vols. Leipzig, 1936.

HILL, G. *A History of Cyprus*, 3 vols. Cambridge, 1940–8.

Historians of the Middle East (ed. B. Lewis and R. M. Holt). London, 1962.

History of the Crusades (ed. K. M. Setton). Philadelphia, 1955 (in progress).

Hopf, C. *Geschichte Griechenlands von Beginn des Mittelaltes bis auf unserer Zeit*, 2 vols. Leipzig, 1870–1.

Houtsma, M. T. Article 'Tughrilbeg', *Encyclopaedia of Islam*, IV.

Huart, C. Article 'Janissaries', *Encyclopaedia of Islam*, II.

Huber, A. *Geschichte Österreichs*, 5 vols. Gotha, 1885–96.

Hypsilantis, A. C. *Tà μετὰ τὴν ἄλωσιν* (ed. A. Germanos). Constantinople, 1870.

Inalcik, H. Article 'Bāyāzēd I', *Encyclopaedia of Islam* (new edition), I.

Inalcik, H. *Fatih Devri üzerinde tetikler ve vesikalar*, I. Ankara, 1954.

Inalcik, H. 'Mehmed the Conqueror (1432–1481) and his time', *Speculum*, XXXV. Cambridge, Mass., 1960.

Inalcik, H. 'Ottoman methods of conquest', *Studia Islamica*, II. Paris, 1954.

Janin, R. *Constantinople Byzantine. La géographie ecclésiastique de l'empire byzantin*, Pt. I, iii, *Les églises et les monastères*. Paris, 1953.

Jireček, K. *Geschichte der Serben*, 2 vols. Gotha, 1911–15.

Jorga, N. *Byzance après Byzance*. Bucarest, 1935.

Jorga, N. *Geschichte des Osmanischen Reiches*, 2 vols. Gotha, 1908–9.

Jorga, N. *Histoire des Roumains*, 4 vols. Bucarest, 1937.

Jorga, N. 'Une source négligée de la prise de Constantinople', *Académie Roumaine, Bulletin de la Section Historique*, XIII. Bucarest, 1927.

Khairullah Effendi. *Ta'rikh*. Istanbul, 1851.

Kolias, G. 'Constantin Paléologue, le dernier defenseur de Constantinople,' *Le Cinq-Centième Anniversaire de la prise de Constantinople, L'Hellénisme Contemporain*, fascicule hors série. Athens, 1953.

Köprülü, M. F. *Les origines de l'empire ottoman*. Paris, 1935.

Kramers, J. H. Article 'Othman I', *Encyclopaedia of Islam*, I.

Kramers, J. H. Article, 'Muhammad I', *Encyclopaedia of Islam*, III.

Krause, J. H. *Die Eroberung von Konstantinopel im 13 und 15 Jahrhunderts durch die Kreuzfahren, durch die nicaeischen Griechen und durch die Turken*. Halle, 1870.

Krekic, B. *Dubrovnik (Raguse) et le Levant au moyen âge*. Paris–The Hague, 1961.

Kyrou, A. *Βησσαρίων ὁ ῞Ελλην*, 2 vols. Athens, 1947.

Lambros, S. '῾Ο Κωνσταντῖνος Παλαιολόγος ὡς σύζυγος', *Neos Hellenomnemon*, IV. Athens, 1907.

Lambros, S. '*Αἱ εἰκόνες Κωνσταντίνου τοῦ Παλαιολόγου*', *Neos Hellenomnemon*, III and IV. Athens, 1906–7.

Lambros, S. *Συνθήκη μεταξὺ Ἰωάννου τοῦ Παλαιολόγου καὶ τοῦ δουκὸς τῆς Βενετίας Φραγκίσκου Φόσκαρη*, in *Neos Hellenomnemon*, I, Athens, 1904.

Lascaris, M. *Vizantiske princeze u srednjevekovnoj Srbiji*. Belgrade, 1926.

Laurent, J. *Byzance et les Turcs Seldjoucides jusqu'en 1081*. Nancy, 1913.

Laurent, V. 'Sphrantzes et non Phrantzes', *B.Z.*, XLIV. 1951.

BIBLIOGRAPHY

LEBEAU, C. *Histoire du Bas-Empire* (ed. J. Saint-Martin), 21 vols. Paris, 1824–1836.

LEIGH FERMOR, P. *The Traveller's Tree*. London, 1950.

LEMERLE, P. *L'Emirat d'Aydin: Byzance et l'Occident*. Paris, 1937.

LOENERTZ, R. J. 'Autour du Chronicon Maius attribué à Georgios Phrantzes', *Miscellanea Mercati*, III, *Studi i Testi Vaticani*, CXXIII. Rome, 1946.

LEONERTZ, R. J. 'Pour la biographie du Cardinal Bessarion', *Orientalia Christiana Periodica*, X. Rome, 1944.

MARINESCU, C. 'Le Pape Callixte III, Alphonse V d'Aragon, roi de Naples, et l'offensive contre les Turcs', *Académie Roumaine, Bulletin de la Section Historique*, XIX. Bucarest, 1935.

MARINESCU, C. 'Le Pape Nicolas V et son attitude envers l'empire byzantin' *Bulletin de l'Institut archéologique Bulgare*, X. Sofia, 1935.

MARINESCU, C. 'Notes sur quelques ambassadeurs byzantins en Occident à la veille de la chute de Constantinople sous les Turcs', *Annuaire de l'Institut de Philologie et de l'Histoire Orientales et Slaves*, X. Brussels, 1950.

MASAI, F. *Plethon et le Platonisme de Mistra*. Paris, 1956.

MASSO TORRENTS, J. '40 Octaves à la porte de Constantinople', Εἰς μνήμην Σ. Λάμπρου. Athens, 1938.

MEDLIN, W. K. *Moscow and East Rome*. Geneva, 1952.

MERCATI, G. 'Scritti d'Isidoro il Cardinale Ruteno', *Studi i Testi*, XLVI. Rome, 1926.

MEYENDORFF, J. *Introduction à l'étude de Grégoire Palamas*. Paris, 1959.

MIJATOVICH, C. *Constantine, last Emperor of the Greeks*. London, 1892.

MILLER, W. *Essays on the Latin Orient*. Cambridge, 1921.

MILLER, W. 'The Balkan States', *Cambridge Medieval History*, IV.

MILLER, W. *The Latins in the Levant*. London, 1908.

MILLER, W. *Trebizond, the last Christian Empire*. London, 1926.

MORAVCSIK, G. *Byzantino-Turcica*, 2 vols. Budapest, 1942–3.

MORDTMANN, A. Article 'Dewshirme', *Encyclopaedia of Islam*, I.

MORDTMANN, A. 'Die letzten Täge von Byzanz', *Mitteilungen des deutschen Exkursions-Klub*. Istanbul, 1893 and 1895.

MORDTMANN, A. *Esquisse topographique de Constantinople*. Lille, 1892.

MORDTMANN, A. D. *Die Belagerung und Eroberung Constantinopels durch die Türken im Jahre 1453*. Stuttgart-Augsburg, 1858.

MOSCHOPOULOS, N. 'La prise de Constantinople selon les sources turques', *Le Cinq-Centième Anniversaire de la prise de Constantinople, L'Hellénisme Contemporain*, fasciscule hors série. Athens, 1953.

NORDEN, W. *Das Papsttum und Byzanz*. Berlin, 1903.

OMAN, C. W. C. *History of the art of war in the Middle Ages*, 2nd edition, 2 vols. London, 1924.

OSTROGORSKY, G. *History of the Byzantine State* (trans. J. Hussey). Oxford, 1955.

PALL, F. 'Autour de la Croisade de Varna', *Académie Roumaine, Bulletin de la Section Historique*, XXII. Bucarest, 1941.

PAPADOPOULOS, A. T. *Versuch einer Genealogie der Palaiologen*, Amsterdam, 1962.

PAPADOPOULLOS, T. H. *Studies and documents relating to the history of Greek church and people under Turkish domination*. Brussels, 1952.

PASPATES, A. G. Πολιορκία καὶ ἅλωσις τῆς Κωνσταντινουπόλεως. Athens, 1890.

PASTOR, L. *History of the Popes from the close of the Middle Ages* (trans. F. I. Antrobus), 5 vols. London, 1891–8.

PAULOVÁ, M. 'L'Empire byzantin et les Tcheques avant la chute de Constantinople', *Byzantinoslavica*, XIV. Prague, 1953.

PEARS, E. *The destruction of the Greek Empire and the story of the capture of Constantinople by the Turks*. London, 1903.

PEARS, E. 'The Ottoman Turks to the fall of Constantinople', *Cambridge Medieval History*, IV.

RADONIC, J. *Djuradj Kastriot Skenderbeg i Albanija*. Belgrade, 1942.

RUNCIMAN, S. 'Byzantine and Hellene in the fourteenth century', Τόμος Κωνσταντίνου 'Αρμενοπούλου. Thessaloniki, 1952.

RUNCIMAN, S. 'The schism between the Eastern and Western Churches', *Anglican Theological Review*, XLIV, 4. Evanston, 1962.

SCHLUMBERGER, G. *Le siège, la prise et le sac de Constantinople en 1453*. Paris, 1926.

SCHNEIDER, A. M. 'Die Bevölkerung Konstantinopels im XV Jahrhundert', *Nachrichten der Akademie der Wissenschaften in Göttingen, Phil.-Hist. Klasse*. Göttingen, 1949.

SOTTAS, J. *Les Messageries Maritimes de Venise au XIVe et XVe siecles*. Paris, 1938.

STASIULEVICH, M. M. 'The siege and capture of Byzantium by the Turks' (in Russian). *Memories of the Imperial Academy of Science, 2nd division*, I St. Petersburg, 1854.

TAFRALI, O. 'Le siège de Constantinople dans les fresques des églises de Bukovine', *Mélanges G. Schlumberger*, II. Paris, 1924.

TAFRALI, O. *Thessalonique au quatorzième siècle*. Paris, 1913.

THIRIET, F. *La Romanie Vénitienne au moyen âge*. Paris, 1959.

TOMADAKIS, N. B. ''Ετούρκευσεν ὁ Γεώργιος 'Αμιρούτζης;' in 'Επετηρὶς 'Εταιρείας Βυζαντινῶν Σπουδῶν, XVIII. Athens, 1948.

TOMADAKIS, N. B. 'Répercussion immédiate de la prise de Constantinople', *Le Cinq-Centième Anniversaire de la prise de Constantinople, L'Hellénisme Contemporain*, fascicule hors série. Athens, 1953.

TYPALDOS, T. E. 'Οἱ ἀπόγονοι τῶν Παλαιολόγων μετὰ τὴν ἅλωσιν', Δελτίον τῆς Ἱστορικῆς καὶ Ἐθνολογικῆς Ἑταιρείας τῆς Ἑλλάδος VIII. Athens, 1922.

ULGEN, ALI SAIM. Constantinople during the era of Mohammed the Conqueror. Ankara, 1939.

UNBEGAUN, B. 'Les relations vieux-russes de la prise de Constantinople', Revue des Etudes Slaves, IX. Paris, 1929.

ÜZÜNÇARSILI, I. H. Osmanlî Tarîhî, 3 vols. Ankara, 1947–51.

VAN MILLINGEN, A. Byzantine Churches in Constantinople. London, 1910.

VAN MILLINGEN, A. Byzantine Constantinople: the walls of the City. London, 1899.

VASILIEV, A. A. A History of the Byzantine Empire, 324–1453. Madison, 1952.

VASILIEV, A. A. 'Medieval ideas of the end of the world', Byzantion, XVI, 2. Boston, 1944.

VASILIEV, A. A. 'The journey of the Byzantine Emperor Manuel II Palaeologus in Western Europe' (in Russian), Journal of the Ministry of Public Instruction, N.S. XXXIX. St. Petersburg, 1912.

VAST, H. Le Cardinal Bessarion (1403–72). Paris, 1878.

VOIGT, G. Enea Silvio Piccolomini als Papst Pius II und sein Zeitalter, 3 vols. Berlin, 1856–63.

VOYATZIDIS, J. 'Τὸ ζήτημα τῆς στέψεως Κωνσταντίνου τοῦ Παλαιολόγου', Λαογραφία VII. Athens, 1923.

WALTER, G. La Ruine de Byzance. Paris, 1958.

WITTEK, P. Das Fürstentum Mentesche: Studien zur Geschichte Westkleinasiens im 13–15 Jahrhundert. Istanbul, 1934.

WITTEK, P. The rise of the Ottoman Empire. London, 1938.

YULE, H. The travels of Marco Polo (ed. H. Cordier), 3 vols. London, 1902–20.

ZAKYTHINOS, D. 'La prise de Constantinople, et la fin du Moyen Age' and 'La prise de Constantinople, tournant dans la politique et l'économie européennes', Cinq-Centième Anniversaire de la prise de Constantinople, L'Hellénisme Contemporain, fascicule hors série. Athens, 1953.

ZAKYTHINOS, D. Le Despotat grec de Morée, 2 vols. Paris, 1932–55.

ZIEGLER, A. 'Isidore de Kiev, apôtre de l'Union florentine', Irenikon, XIII. Chevetogne, 1936.

ZORAS, G. Περὶ τὴν ἅλωσιν τῆς Κωνσταντινουπόλεως. Athens, 1959.

INDEX

NOTE: Names that recur continually in the text, such as Constantinople, Greeks, Byzantines, Turks, Ottoman, Italians, are not listed.

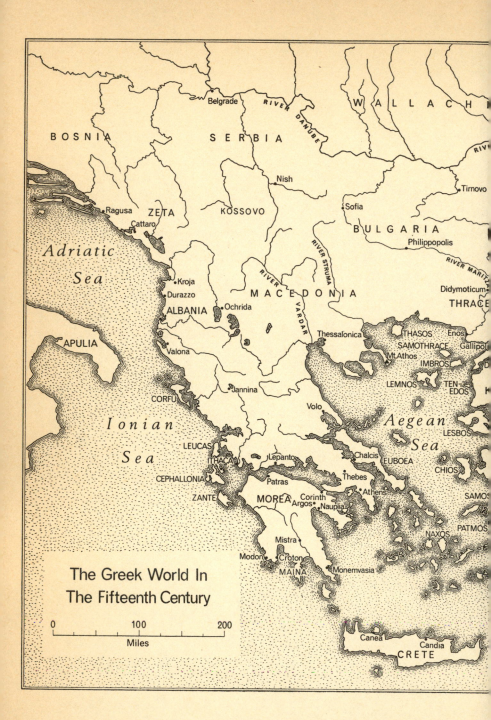

The Greek World In
The Fifteenth Century

0 100 200

Miles

Fig. 4